Maybe I'll Pitch Forever

A great baseball player tells the
hilarious story behind the legend

by LeRoy (Satchel) Paige

As told to David Lipman

Introduction by John B. Holway
Afterword by David Lipman

University of Nebraska Press
Lincoln and London

Introduction and afterword © 1993 by the University of Nebraska Press
Manufactured in the United States of America

First Bison Book printing: 1993
Most recent printing indicated by the last digit below:
10   9   8   7   6   5   4   3

Library of Congress Cataloging-in-Publication Data
Paige, Leroy, 1906–
Maybe I'll pitch forever: a good baseball player tells the hilarious story behind
the legend / by Leroy (Satchel) Paige, as told to David Lipman; introduction by
John B. Holway; afterword by David Lipman.
p.   cm.
Includes bibliographical references and index.
ISBN 0-8032-3702-2.—ISBN 0-8032-8732-1 (pbk.)
1. Paige, Leroy, 1906–   .   2. Baseball players—United States—Biogra-
phy.   I. Lipman, David.   II. Title.
GV865.P3A3   1993
796.357′092—dc20
[B]
92-35221   CIP

Originally published by Doubleday & Company in 1962.
Reprinted by arrangement with David Lipman, represented by McIntosh and
Otis, Inc.

Introduction

by John B. Holway

I first saw Satchel Paige on a muggy May night in 1945. He was pitching for the Kansas City Monarchs against Josh Gibson's Homestead Grays. I was one of thirty-thousand fans packing Washington's old Griffith Stadium to watch the duel, and I remember Satch taking his famous windmill windup for two innings before retiring.

None of us, including Satch or me, even guessed that within six months sixty years of apartheid would be swept away with the revolutionary signing of Jackie Robinson. And, though no one thought of him that way, the Satch who stood in the middle of the diamond that night was a leader of the revolution. For, without Satchel Paige, there just might not have been a Jackie Robinson in Brooklyn.

Satch himself followed Robinson into the major leagues, and in October 1948 I joined eighty-seven thousand fans in Cleveland's Municipal Stadium to see him pitch in the World Series. By then he had entered white history, with all its statistics and records. Before then, he had lived his life as a mythic figure in black legends passed along orally by the *griots* of baseball.

Not only was Paige an amazing athlete, he was one of the great American humorists in the tradition of Mark Twain, Will Rogers, and Yogi Berra.

It is this figure, the most famous black player of his era—and still the most colorful ever—who shines through the pages of this remarkable autobiography, *Maybe I'll Pitch Forever*. He almost did. He pitched his first professional game in 1926 and his last one almost forty years later, in 1965 for the Kansas City Athletics.

Today, more than four decades after his Cleveland Indian debut in 1948, we have added the black records and statistics to fill out the legend. Now the official Macmillan Encyclopedia lists *all* the wins and losses, strikeouts and walks, of Paige's amazing career, the Negro League stats and the American League stats alike. (Of course some Negro League games were not reported and will never be found, but a large body of numbers has been rescued.)

How old was Paige? He gave so many contradictory dates for his birth that a teammate finally asked how old he really was. "As old as [Indians owner] Mr. Veeck wants me to be," Satch replied.

After a year in the black minor league at Chattanooga, Paige pitched his first "big league" game for the Birmingham Black Barons on July 3, 1927, at the presumptive age of twenty-two. The game was played in Detroit, and Satch was knocked out of the box in the second inning. Two weeks later he beat the Memphis Red Sox 12–1, and he "never looked back."

With two older men, Sam Streeter and Harry Salmon, teaching him control, the wild youngster could soon throw a ball over a Coke bottle cap and, in his own words, "nip frosting off a cake." Paige bounced along the early highways of America packed in a roadster, sleeping with his knees up against his chin, and keeping the club loose with tunes on the Jew's harp. He was a great musician and in later years loved to strum the ukelele and lead his teammates in songs or harmonize with the radio favorites, the Mills Brothers.

Satch won eight and lost three in the second half of the year, leading the Barons from fifth to the second-half flag. If they had given out Rookie of the Year Awards then, he'd have surely won it. Twenty-one years later, when he was named American League Rookie of the Year, he asked, "What year?"

The next year, 1928, Satchel won twelve and lost four. (The Negro Leagues played about eighty games a year then, and not all of the games have been found.) He boasted a variety of pitches—the Midnight Creeper, the Four-Day Rider, the Be Ball ("It be where I want it to be")—but, whatever their names, they were all fastballs. "He changed the *size* of the ball," said old-time sports writer Eric "Ric" Roberts. Old-time batters variously described the balls he whizzed by as "white dots" or "white marbles." "That last one sounded a little low, didn't it, ump?" one hitter protested. "He threw *fire*," whistles Hall of Famer Buck Leonard, who says he didn't get a hit off Paige in seventeen years.

Satchel raised his foot up to hide his face before he let go. The batters said he had "FAST BALL" written on the sole, but they still couldn't hit it; they knew what was coming, but not where.

He threw overhand, sidearm, and underhand. He occasionally threw his "Little Tom," or change-up, and later even experimented with a "Wobbly Ball," or knuckler.

When he was inducted into Cooperstown in 1971, Paige declared that "there were many Satchels, there were many Joshes" in the Negro Leagues. He faced some of the best players in America—hitters like Mule Suttles and Turkey Stearnes, and pitchers like Big Bill Foster and Bullet Joe Rogan. The latter, he acknowledged, was the greatest "until I came along."

In 1929 most of the Barons stars left, including his favorite catcher, Bill Perkins. Satchel's won-lost dropped to 11–11, though he did strike out seventeen men in one league game, which was one more than the white major league record at that time. In all, he whiffed 184 men in 196 innings to set a Negro League record that was never broken.

As the Great Depression struck in 1930, the Kansas City Monarchs unveiled a revolutionary portable lighting system, which would save the Negro Leagues in the decade of hard times ahead. Satchel jumped to the Baltimore Black Sox to try to make some extra bucks. There he met the great black-Indian pitcher, Smokey Joe Williams of the New York Lincolns (originally from Lincoln, Nebraska). Joe was either in his forties or fifties and still winning ball games. The arguments over Joe's age probably inspired Satchel's own public relations guessing game after he reached the Indians. He found no gold in the East, however, so he returned to Birmingham. His combined record for the year was 12–5.

In 1931 Satchel jumped again, to the Cleveland Cubs, who played a block away from the Indians' home, League Park, which was closed to him, of course. Then the flamboyant Gus Greenlee signed him for the new Pittsburgh Crawfords, where he would soon be united with Josh Gibson in the greatest battery in baseball history.

That winter Satchel traveled to California. In one game against big leaguers Frank Demaree, Wally Berger, Babe Herman, and others, Paige, after hearing a racial slur, ordered his fielders to sit down, and struck out Demaree and Berger. His catcher, Larry Brown, confirmed the tale. "Satch, you're the biggest fool ever I've seen in my life," Larry chortled. "I never saw anybody but you do that with a one-run lead." They were invited to play in San Diego provided that Satchel "put on a good exhibition." "God damn!" Larry exploded. "That's all Satchel's *got,* is a good exhibition!"

Paige received the honor of opening Greenlee Field in 1932, though he lost the game 1–0 when Gibson's ninth-inning 450-foot smash was caught by the Black Yankees' leaping Clint Thomas at the fence. Satch later got revenge, however, by whipping the Black Yanks on a no-hitter and ended the season with a 14–8 mark.

Some experts call the Crawfords the best black team of all time. They boasted five Hall of Famers—Satch, Josh, Cool Papa Bell, Judy Johnson, and Oscar Charleston. Some experts wonder how they'd have done in a series against Babe Ruth's 1927 Yankees.

Satch had a poor year in 1933. He accrued only 5–7 before he jumped to a white semipro team in Bismarck, North Dakota, and the Craws lost the pennant by a single game.

He was back in 1934, however, and enjoyed perhaps the finest season of his career, with a 13–3 mark, giving up only 1.99 runs per nine innings—those are *total* runs; earned runs were not available.

On July 4 he threw another no-hitter, this one against the Homestead Grays. The last two outs were strikeouts, giving him a total of 17 to tie the new white record just set by Dizzy Dean.

Once again, however, he jumped the team to pitch in the big Denver semipro tournament, and once again the Craws lost the pennant, as a sensational rookie, left-hander Slim Jones of the Philadelphia Stars, trumped Satch with perhaps the best season a black pitcher ever had: 22–3.

The two met in a Yankee Stadium showdown in September. Fans say it was the greatest baseball game they ever saw. Jones pitched a no-hitter for six innings, sensational fielding plays saved both matadors several times, and Paige went into the last of the ninth tied 1–1. An error put a runner on third with one out, as the shadows got darker. Paige whiffed the last two men, for a total of 18, and the umpires called the game.

Two weeks later Jones and Paige returned to settle the issue. When Judy Johnson stopped in a Bronx barber shop and heard the boys bragging that Slim "would close Satchel's big mouth," he duly reported it to Paige. Satch won the game 3–1, strode over to the Stars' dugout, and snapped, "Go over to the barber shop and tell them about this."

Satchel and his new bride jumped the Craws entirely in 1935 to pitch in North Dakota again. While he was gone, Lefty Leroy Matlock stepped into the breach and won twenty straight games to lead the Crawfords to the pennant.

Paige and the veteran catcher, Ted "Double Duty" Radcliffe, traveled with Bismarck to the Denver semi-pro tournament, where they swept the title in seven straight games. "Those are big leaguers," the other teams muttered. "They're niggers, but they're big leaguers."

That winter Paige hooked up against Dizzy Dean, who gladly called him the best pitcher he ever saw—"and I been lookin' in the mirror a long time."

In San Diego, young Ted Williams watched Paige pitch. Satch was so skinny, Ted said, he had trouble holding his pants up. "But he made the ball pop!"

Moving to San Francisco, Paige gave up an infield hit to minor league star Joe DiMaggio. "I know I can make the Yankees now," Joe said.

Greenlee forgave his star and welcomed him back in 1936, when Satch compiled a 10–3 record.

But the next spring agents of the Dominican dictator Rafael Trujillo opened a suitcase full of dollars and lured Satch to that island. Negro Leaguer Chet Brewer beat him there with a no-hitter, but Satchel wound up with an 8–2 record and pitched Trujillo's team to the pennant while armed guards stood menacingly on the sidelines.

In 1938 Satch flirted with the Newark Eagles, or at least with the Eagles' glamorous owner, Effa Manley, who coyly turned away his advances. So he was off again, this time to Mexico, where his golden arm suddenly went dead. His fabulous career was seemingly at an end.

The kindly owner of the Kansas City Monarchs gave him a job playing first base on his "B" team that toured the small towns of the prairies. With trainer "Jewbaby" Johnson massaging the wing, it suddenly came back, and Paige, at the age of thirty-five, charged off on a new career. He learned a curve and toyed with a knuckler, and sailed to Puerto Rico, where he ran up a record of 19–2. The long brown arm was golden again.

At last the white world found out about Satchel Paige as *Time* magazine, *Life,* and *The Saturday Evening Post* all ran feature stories on him. Though the last was filled with outrageous racial stereotypes (it said

Satch spoke "in a Stepinfetchit accent"), the publicity elevated Paige onto a pedestal alongside fighter Joe Louis and Olympic champ Jesse Owens.

From then on, when Satch pitched for the Monarchs, he drew crowds of thirty thousand instead of the usual Depression crowd of three thousand. He was demanding, and getting, 15 percent off the top, and the other players, whose own paychecks were fatter, didn't begrudge it at all. "He made the payroll for a lot of teams," the Monarchs' Buck O'Neill says warmly.

Paige's won-lost record that year was 7–1.

He had a nickname for everyone. O'Neill was Nancy. He got it one night when Paige tiptoed out of one hotel room and rapped softly on the adjoining door, whispering, "Nancy? Nancy?" When the first door flew open and an irate woman demanded, "Who's Nancy?" O'Neill innocently opened a third door and saved the pitcher by asking, "What you want, Satch?"

Brewer was Dooflackem. Assigned to get the tardy Paige to games on time, Brewer hid his eyes as Paige made U-turns across pedestrian islands, zig-zagged through oncoming cars on one-way streets, and led police on 95-mph chases across the landscape. "Now instead of one pitcher being late, you got two pitchers late," a shaken Brewer sputtered to Wilkinson. "You're gonna get me killed!"

The year 1942 opened with UCLA football star Jackie Robinson getting a tryout from the Chicago White Sox, and when Satchel and Dizzy Dean outdrew the White Sox in their Sunday duel in Chicago, people began asking why the doors weren't open to all blacks. There followed a flurry of rumors—that the Pirates, the Phils, the Indians, and other teams would offer tryouts to black stars. "We're fighting a war for democracy," the Communist *Daily Worker* declared, and singer Paul Robeson appealed to the major league owners to "have a heart." There was no response from major league baseball.

Paige's record was 8–5. In fact, he led the league in defeats. But he was at his best that fall against Gibson's Homestead Grays in the black World Series. Josh had boasted that he'd like to face Satch in a big game with the bases loaded, so Satchel obliged. While his manager and owner shouted helplessly at him, he deliberately walked the bases loaded, taunted Josh that he would throw nothing but fastballs, and struck him out with three sidearm fastballs at the knees. Satch boogied off the mound and called it "the best day I ever had."

The Series went six games, and Paige performed the iron-man feat of hurling in all six of them, either as a starter or in relief, something that no white big leaguer has ever done, as the Monarchs crushed the Grays four games to one with one tie.

In 1943 most of the Monarch stars were in the military, and Satchel's record fell to 5–9.

But the wartime boom brought a belated prosperity to the Negro Leagues. In the big East-West, or All Star, game at Chicago's Comiskey Park, with fifty thousand fans on hand, Satch got Josh to join him in a strike. They demanded $50 to appear, and the helpless owners agreed to pay it. The next year the rest of the players pulled their own strike for $150 a man, and they also got it, so Satchel turned out to be almost as good a labor agitator as he was a pitcher.

Paige himself boycotted the 1944 game. He had urged the owners to play it as a benefit for the wounded GIs returning on stretchers from overseas, and when the owners refused, Satch stayed home. He was roundly criticized, but he wouldn't relent.

More and more Paige was pitching every night to draw a crowd, going two or three innings before retiring to do it again the following night. Thus his victory totals were depressed. In 1944 his Total Run Average was 1.25 per nine innings, but his won-lost was only 5–5.

In 1945, the year I saw him, it had dropped to 3–5. That summer a discharged army lieutenant joined the team as a rookie and started hitting the ball hard. His name was Jackie Robinson. By winter the news was out—Jackie had been signed by the Brooklyn Dodgers. It sent both Paige and Gibson into deep depression.

With the war veterans back in 1946, Paige improved to 5–1, and the Monarchs won the pennant, Satch clinching it with a nine-inning victory over the Indianapolis Clowns. He won the first World Series game in relief against Larry Doby and Monte Irvin of the Newark Eagles. He also came in as relief in game two and lost it. He got no decision in game four, and the teams went into the seventh game tied at three wins apiece. Paige of course was slated to hurl for the Monarchs. But he didn't show up, and the Eagles beat his replacement 3–2.

Perhaps Satchel's mind was on the big barnstorming trip he had scheduled with Bob Feller's All stars—Stan Musial, Mickey Vernon, Phil Rizzuto, Bob Lemon, Charlie Keller, Ken Keltner, Spud Chandler, etc.

Against this stellar cast, Satchel's Stars won six of the seven games, and Satchel himself emerged with a 2–1 record. The big leaguers batted a mere .159 against him and averaged only 1.73 *total* runs per nine innings. Best of all, the crowds were so huge that Musial chortled that he made more money on the tour than he had in the World Series against the Red Sox.

When Robinson joined the Dodgers in 1947, the black fans deserted their old teams to see Jackie in every city he played. "We couldn't draw flies," Buck Leonard said. Roy Campanella and Don Newcombe had been signed by the Dodgers. Satchel's own teammates, Willard Brown and Hank Thompson, had joined the St. Louis Browns. Surely, when Bill Veeck signed Doby to the Indians, he would also bring Satchel up. In fact, Satch wrote to Veeck, asking for a job. Have patience, Bill wrote back. "It will happen."

But it was hard to have patience. Gibson, who had waited seventeen years, was dead of a broken heart and a drug overdose, and the down-hearted Paige appeared in only two games.

That fall he took his frustrations out on Feller's stars again. His won-lost was only 1–1 on the tour, but they batted only .144 against him and averaged exactly one run per nine innings. In the final game, the promotors asked Feller and Paige to go a full nine innings against each other. Paige won it with a four-hit shutout while striking out 15. But still there was no offer from the majors. Disconsolate, he sailed to Puerto Rico and lost all three games he pitched.

After 21 years and 123 victories (against 79 defeats) in the Negro Leagues, his career seemed over. Only one man, Bill Foster with 137, had ever won more. And no one had ever struck out more—Satchel had almost twice as many whiffs as his nearest rival, Foster.

Satchel didn't pitch at all in 1948. Nearing forty-four, he sat down at the kitchen table with his wife, Lahoma, and talked about calling it quits. "I was sick of hopping around," he would say later, "My mind was made up."

Then came Veeck's telegram with an offer from the Indians! Suddenly Paige was alive again. For a salary of $6,000, Satchel won six crucial games for the Indians in their tight pennant race. His only loss was on an unearned run. Better yet, in one three-game stretch, he put 150,000 people in the seats. At an average of two dollars per fan, that was a net profit for Veeck of about $294,000.

Eventually, Bill's darling became Veeck's bad boy as Satchel began missing too many games, trains, and automobiles, and manager Lou Boudreau benched him for the critical last month. Lou should have talked to Satchel's old manager on the Monarchs, Buck O'Neill. Paige was easy to handle, O'Neill insists. You couldn't order him to be on time, Buck said. But tell him, "I'll bet you we'll get to Cleveland before you do, I'll bet you a dollar," and Satch would beat the team there every time.

In 1971 Buck Leonard and I drove to Cooperstown to watch Satchel's induction. Only two years earlier, man had walked on the moon; now a Negro Leaguer was in the Hall of Fame. Buck stayed up most of the night thinking of the dizzying succession of miracles. "We never thought it would come," he said.

The last time I saw Paige was in 1981 at Ashland, Ohio, at a reunion of black old-timers. He was suffering from emphysema and breathing through a portable oxygen pack that he carried like a handbag. He was glad to be there, Paige told the others. "At my age, I'm glad to be anywhere."

Looking back, he said he'd enjoyed his seventy-five years. "I've had more fun than Rockefeller," he said.

Willie Mays was one of the guests. "You were the pioneers," he told Satchel and the others. "You made it possible for us."

And Ric Roberts, who had covered most of Satchel's career for the *Pittsburgh Courier*, recalled the white magazines' discovery of Satchel in 1940:

"For the first time a white magazine had burned incense at the foot of a black man outside the prize ring. Satchel brought people back to the ball game. He got blacks in the habit of going to ball games and spending their money, and it caught the eyes of Branch Rickey, who was a money changer from way back. Satchel Paige led us to the promised land. He was the guy that gave black baseball its first real economic solvency. We won't see his like again in our lifetime.''

The reader who wants to get to know this remarkable personality will find him coming vibrantly back to life in the following pages.

Maybe I'll Pitch Forever

Chapter One

MOST OF THE PLAYERS were already in the Cleveland Indians' locker room when I got there for our baseball game with the Chicago White Sox.

Some of the guys were talking and joking, but not real loud. They were all pretty loose. The Indians'd won seven in a row and had three straight shutouts up to this game on Friday night, August 20, 1948. With that kind of luck, any player'd be loose. But Ol' Satchel Paige wasn't. And for a guy who'd thrown better than two thousand professional games, that funny feeling in my stomach was a mighty unusual thing.

But this was a mighty unusual game for me.

First of all, even as early as it was, we already knew there'd be more people out there than ever before at a major league night game. And if I pitched a shutout, it would tie the American League team record of four shutouts in a row.

I'd been working up to this kind of a setup since Bill Veeck signed me about six weeks before. That was the day I celebrated my forty-second birthday. Some liked to say I was forty-two going on forty-nine.

Two days later I got into my first game and became the first Negro ever to pitch in the American League and the fifth ever to play in the major leagues.

Since then, I'd won four and lost only one. In my last game I'd shut out these same Chicago White Sox. But this was my real chance to show all those people who said I was too old to be in the majors, who said I never really had the ability anyway. If I didn't show them now, they'd never believe I was one of the greatest of all times.

Lots of people'd said I was one of the best, but there were some who figured otherwise because I'd done all my pitching in the Negro leagues and barnstorming—a whole lifetime of pitching.

But a shutout would set everybody straight.

All that thinking wasn't helping me any. The miseries were doing more playing in my stomach than most teams did on the field.

I was an old pro, but this wasn't the 1930s when I was in my prime. This was 1948 and I was a rookie again, so I had a right to be nervous, even if I was the oldest rookie that ever walked into the major leagues.

The other players'd started getting dressed. That meant I had to hurry. I pulled off the rest of my clothes and headed for the shower. I needed one to soothe me before the game.

I turned on that water so hot it was almost scalding. There weren't many who could stand it that hot like I could. I let that boiling water run over my right arm.

"What're you doing in there, Satch?"

I looked through the steam. It was Lou Boudreau, my manager.

"Everything all right?" he asked me.

"It's fine."

"Aren't you afraid you'll weaken yourself in there?"

"No, sir, Mr. Lou. This just gets me nice and loose. It gets the juices flowing."

I stepped out of the shower and started rubbing my arm. Lou just shook his head and walked away.

"You ready now, Satch?" one of the guys yelled at me.

"Ol' Satch'll be in there. Them boys are gonna have their troubles. I'm telling you so."

But I didn't feel that sure about it.

○ ○ ○ ○ ○

I knew there were going to be a lot of people out there, but all those filled rows still surprised me. There were people everywhere.

When they finished counting, there were 78,382 there. Ol' Satchel could do at least one thing better than most— set attendance records about everywhere. Counting this game, 201,829 cash customers were on hand for my three starts. Some teams didn't draw many more than that for a whole season.

The miseries started hopping up and down in my stomach again. I grabbed me a baseball. No need for me to be jittery when I had ahold of a baseball. I knew what to do with it.

"You better warm up, Satch," Lou Boudreau called to me.

"Don't worry about Ol' Satch warmin' up," I yelled back. "There ain't any need to hurry and wear myself out. Those White Sox ain't goin' anywhere. They'll wait."

After a little while I started throwing on the sidelines. I kept throwing until the arm was loose, until I wasn't thinking about anything but getting that ball over the plate. Then I stopped and went into the dugout.

A couple of minutes later my teammates took the field. The crowd really whooped it up for them, but it was nothing like what the fans did when I stepped out on the field.

You couldn't hear yourself think.

It was all noise. For a minute I just listened. Then I looked in to Jim Hegan, my catcher.

He was ready.

Ralph Hodgin, Chicago's right fielder, was the first man up. I reared back, kicked that left foot of mine up in the sky, then pivoted and threw my fast one. The crowd oohed. There wasn't many that showed speed like that. And they were calling me the old man. Why, there were guys half my age who were throwing those soft pitches like knucklers and letups. I got Hodgin out of there in no time.

Tony Lupien, the White Sox first baseman, and old Luke Appling, one of the best ever and Chicago's third baseman, followed Hodgin to the plate and back to the bench for outs. The first inning was out of the way.

We didn't score in the last of the first. Nobody scored in the second and third innings either. Lupien led off in the fourth for Chicago. I got cute and walked him. I wasn't worried, even though Luke Appling was up again.

I fired my fast ball at Luke. There was a sharp crack and the ball streaked toward deep center field. Appling raced to first and Lupien headed around second for third. There goes the shutout record, I thought.

Then Larry Doby appeared from nowhere, grabbed that sizzler on the first bounce, and threw to third. The ball beat Lupien and he was tagged out by Ken Keltner. I started breathing again. I got the next two guys out to retire the side, leaving Appling on base.

"Get me some runs," I yelled when we went in for our bats in the last of the fourth.

Lou Boudreau must have been listening. He singled. Then Ken Keltner singled. It was up to Larry Doby, the other Negro on our club.

Larry singled and Boudreau scored. We were ahead, one to nothing.

We didn't get any more runs that inning, but I felt like a kid with that one-run lead.

I cut down the White Sox in the fifth and sixth innings in order. In the seventh I got Appling out quick. That brought up Pat Seerey, Chicago's left fielder. I fired my bee ball. Seerey smacked it. The ball zoomed higher and higher toward the left-center field fence. That's really good-bye shutout, I thought.

Then Doby was there. He pressed up against the fence, reached back over it and caught the ball.

I really blazed my fast one in after that and got Aaron Robinson out.

Listen to them mutter, I thought. Listen to them mutter at the old man's speed.

I still had that one-run lead and that shutout when I walked out there to pitch the ninth. Everybody was standing. Everybody was cheering me. I didn't let them down. I retired the side in order.

We'd won, one to nothing. I'd pitched the shutout and the Indians'd tied that American League record. I'd given up only three hits and had me my fifth win against only one loss.

There'd be no more worrying about the old man now. The pressure had been on, but I'd come through. I felt like yelling, "When I throw, nobody hits." But I didn't. I just laughed and pushed my way toward the locker room.

A dozen baseball writers came after me while I was dressing.

"Looks like you're rookie of the year, Satch," one of them said.

"You may be right, man," I said, "but twenty-two years is a long time to be a rookie."

But those twenty-two years since I first pitched for a professional club didn't seem like anything any more.

"You looked like you were in top shape, Satch," another writer said.

"You should'a seen me five or six years ago. I was twice as good as I am now."

o o o o o

For a guy who'd been around as long as me, making the majors was a big thing. It meant I'd done what death had kept Josh Gibson from doing and what age'd kept a bunch of others from doing, big-name guys like Smokey Joe Williams, Turkey Stearnes, Home Run Johnson, Bullet Joe Rogan, George Seales, Terris MacDuffie, Showboat Thomas, Ted Strong, Frank Duncan, John (Neck) Stanley, Oscar Charleston, Willie Wells, Lefty Williams, Ray Dandridge, Leon Day, Theolic (Fireball) Smith, Hilton Smith, George Perkins, Dave Barnhill, John Henry Lloyd, and Cannonball Dick Redding.

They'd always had to listen to that same old sentence: "If you were only white so you could be in the majors."

If you were only white . . . that had pressed me, too, but it was gone. The guy who couldn't get into the major leagues for twenty-two years because of Jim Crow was in the majors. Now everybody could see how ten years ago I could have won thirty-five or forty games a season in the majors. They could see if I'm kept out of the Hall of Fame it won't be because of lack of ability, but because of organized baseball's color line.

I wasn't the only one who felt something deep. Take Clarence M. Markham, Jr. After the season was over, he wrote in the October-November, 1948 issue of the *Negro Traveler:*

"Not even the signing of Jackie Robinson, Larry Doby or Roy Campanella meant as much to Negroes as a whole as the signing of LeRoy Paige, who had been the baseball hero of Negro America for years.

"They knew he had it and could prove he had it if just given a chance. Don't get me wrong. The Negro race is an appreciative one regardless of what anyone says. No, they have not forgotten that it was Branch Rickey who took the biggest step and made it possible for all that followed. Even when Bill Veeck signed Larry Doby they were very grateful. But when it came to Satchel Paige—well, that was something different. Here was a Negro player who all Negro America knew needed no advance publicity because he had proved his worth down through the years. To Negro America he was no amateur but a star—the biggest they knew—one who knew baseball like an old fox and could play against the finest the white league could find."

o   o   o   o   o

I never figured I'd be some kind of symbol. Well, if I was, I had to admit I was a little rusted up.

You get rusted when you got to come all the way from the slums of Mobile, Alabama, from hiding from truant officers and cops, from reform school.

And while I was coming all that way I guess I'd been a lot of things people said I was—a no-good kid, a guy who left his team when money looked better someplace else, a chaser.

I'd been those things, but I'd also been a fine pitcher— one of the best.

The majors was the peak when it came to that pitching, but it wasn't the end of the line. It'd taken me twenty-two years to get to the majors, but that first season in 1948 was only about the mid-point in my career. There was a lot more to go.

But it sure was a long time from Mobile.

Chapter Two

IT DON'T MATTER what some of those talkers say, I wasn't born six feet, three and a half inches tall, weighing a hundred and eighty pounds and wearing size fourteen shoes.

And there wasn't a baseball in my hand, either.

I was just a baby like any other baby born south of Government Street, down by the bay in Mobile. That was where all the Negroes lived and if it hadn't been for my right arm, I probably would have ended up there.

After I hit the top, every couple of months just about I got my name in the papers when those writers played guessing games about when I was born. I never put a stop to it and my family and my buddies didn't help because they kept giving different dates. You see, nobody paid much attention when us kids by the bay was born. There were so many of us I guess it just didn't matter much.

But the government paid attention and there's a birth certificate in Mobile saying I was born July 7, 1906. Now I know it's made out for a LeRoy Page, but my folks started out by spelling their name "Page" and later stuck in the "i" to make themselves sound more high-tone.

But my Mom didn't put much stock in that certificate. She told a reporter in 1959 that I was fifty-five instead of fifty-three; said she had it down in her Bible. Seems like Mom's Bible would know, but she ain't ever shown me the Bible. Anyway, she was in her nineties when she told the reporter that and sometimes she tended to forget things.

There are all kinds of other dates floating around, too, but I'll go by that birth certificate. It doesn't really make any difference how old I tell people I am. They've been carrying on so long about my age, nobody will believe what I say. Like that old gent I ran into in 1947. He was eighty-three and quit playing in 1910, but he swore he played against me. I just let him talk.

o   o   o   o   o

Our place on South Franklin Street was called a "shotgun" house because the four rooms were one behind the other, just a straight shot from the front door to the back.

I was the seventh of eleven children in that little shack. My Dad, John, was a gardener, but he liked to be called a landscaper. My Mom, Lula, was a washerwoman. She was the real boss of our house, not Dad.

John, Jr., and Wilson were my older brothers and Julia, Ellen, Ruth, and Emma Lee were my older sisters. After I was born, Clarence, Inez, Palestine, and little Lula came along. Ruth, Emma Lee, and Clarence all died before I ever quit pitching. Clarence drowned in a boat accident on the Great Lakes.

My Dad died in that house of ours, when I was about eighteen, I guess, although I don't remember for sure.

I only remember pieces and snatches about him. He wasn't hardly a part of my life. We didn't talk too much, but after I started playing baseball as a kid he used to ask me ever so often, "You want to be a baseball player 'stead of a landscaper?"

"Yes," I'd answer and he'd just nod his head like he was satisfied.

○　○　○　○　○

Those first few years I was no different from any other kid, only in Mobile I was a nigger kid. I went around with the back of my shirt torn, a pair of dirty diapers or raggedy pieces of trousers covering me. Shoes? They was somewhere else.

Us kids played in the dirt, getting it on our faces so the gnats want to come around. We played in the dirt because we didn't have toys. We threw rocks. There wasn't anything else to throw. And we ran and we chased around. Then we raced for the bay and washed the dirt off. Only we didn't just go anywhere on the bay. Just to certain parts.

The white man got all the rest.

Outside of playing like that, there wasn't much else Negro kids could do in Mobile. Mighty few of them had money for anything like a show.

But I didn't play all the time. Everybody got to work when there are thirteen mouths to stuff. By the time I was about six, all my older brothers and sisters had steady jobs, even Wilson, who was only about nine or ten. We all gave our money to Mom so she could get food. She took real pains with what she bought. That was why I can't remember us ever missing a meal.

We didn't always have a belly-busting dishful, but we had something. Mom made sure everybody got their share. She'd stand at the table and ladle out the food, looking real close at each spoonful.

When there wasn't money for store food, we went fishing. There was always plenty of fish around Mobile.

But even with the fish, it was poverty-stricken living before I knew what that meant.

o o o o o

Mom had me in W. H. Council School by the time I was
about six or seven years old, but I didn't go too often. The
first few times I missed, Mom came looking for me. Finally,
she got kind of used to it. Fact was, she didn't put real big
store by book learning. It ended up so she didn't get nearly
as mad when I missed school as she got when I didn't come
home with any money for food from selling empty bottles
I'd found in the alleys and trash bins.

When I was still about seven, Mom decided my bottle
selling wasn't enough and that I had to get me a job somewhere to help out more. You'd have thought I was fifty or
sixty years old the way they worried about my work.

Finally, Mom remembered some of the kids around the
neighborhood worked down at the depot, toting bags and
satchels.

"You're goin' down there tomorrow," Mom said.

I told her playing would be more fun, but she didn't listen
to me.

The next day I was down there, dragging a bag. I got a
dime for it. We weren't going to be eating much better if I
made only a dime at a time so I got me a pole and some
ropes. That let me sling two, three, or four satchels together
and carry them at one time. You always got to be thinking to
make money.

My invention wasn't a smart-looking thing, but it upped
my income.

The other kids all laughed.

"You look like a walking satchel tree," one of them yelled.

They all started yelling it. Soon everybody was calling me
that, you know how it is with kids and nicknames. That's
when LeRoy Paige became no more and Satchel Paige took

over. Nobody called me LeRoy, nobody except my Mom and the government.

A lot of the kids shortened Satchel to Satch. Later, some even called me Satchmo, but not because I blew a mean trumpet like Louie Armstrong. I just blow that fast ball—blow it right by the hitters.

When spring came, I got me some work picking up empty bottles and sweeping up at Eureka Gardens. That was a semi-pro baseball park and the Mobile Tigers played there a lot.

Watching those semi-pro ballplayers got me kind of interested in throwing. Only I couldn't afford a baseball. So I took up rock throwing.

That's when I first found out I had control. It was a natural gift, one that let me put a baseball just about where I wanted it about anytime I wanted to.

I could hit about anything with one of those rocks. Like the day Mom sent me out in the back yard to get us a bird from our chicken coop.

Three chickens came prancing along the path toward me. The one in the middle looked the plumpest. I picked up a rock. The chickens were about thirty feet from me. I took aim and threw. There was a squawking and feathers flew and two chickens went tearing off. The third one, the one in the middle, was knocked dead on the ground.

After that I used to kill me flying birds with rocks, too. Most people need shotguns to do what I did with those rocks.

o   o   o   o   o

It didn't take me long to find out that rocks were good for something besides knocking over birds. They made a real impression on a kid's head or backside. I had plenty of chances to use rocks that way, too. Chester Arnold and Julius Andrews and some of my other buddies all were guys who played hookey a lot, just like me, and they liked trouble even better than me. When we weren't fishing, we were out looking for trouble. And we found it. Then I'd start throwing rocks.

Our biggest fights came on the way home from school. We went right by a white school and a big gang from there was always out waiting for us. When we got close, the rocks started flying. I crippled up a lot of them, and I mean it. It got so bad they had to put a policeman there.

Maybe I got into all those fights because I wasn't real smart and didn't take too good to books. But maybe it was because I found out what it was like to be a Negro in Mobile. Even if you're only seven, eight, or nine, it eats at you when you know you got nothing and can't get a dollar. The blood gets angry. You want to go somewhere, but you're just walking. You don't want to, but you got to walk.

Those fights helped me forget what I didn't have. They made me a big man in the neighborhood instead of just some more trash.

Mom didn't take to my fighting. I once tried to fool her, but I found out you don't fool a church-going woman much.

"You been fighting again?" she yelled after seeing how I was sweaty and messed up.

"No. Just playing."

"I know different," she said.

Smack. She caught me one on the ear. She hit harder than I ever got hit in a fight. I used to think she'd hit me because she didn't know how I felt. She didn't know how it was when they told me I couldn't swim where the white folks did.

Then I realized maybe she did.

She must have been chased away from the white man's swimming places. She must have gotten run off from the white man's stores and stands for just looking hungry at a fish.

She must have heard those men yelling, "Get out of here, you no-good nigger."

She must have heard it. I guess she learned to live with it.

o   o   o   o   o

Chapter Three

SINCE I THREW THOSE ROCKS so straight, I guess it was just natural that I started firing a baseball.

By the time I was ten years old, I was throwing it harder than anybody in the neighborhood. I also was belting it farther. When Wilbur Hines, the coach of the team at W. H. Council School, held baseball tryouts that year, I figured I was ready even if I was just ten.

I made the team. It was easy for me. When I was ten and when I was fifty, there was one thing I could do—play baseball. And you better believe it.

Hines put me in the outfield; sometimes he let me play first base, but I didn't do any pitching. I never gave it much thought.

I kept pounding that ball and playing the outfield until a game about halfway through the season. They'd knocked two of our pitchers out of the box in the first inning so Hines decided to try me.

I was all arms and legs. I must have looked like an ostrich. When I let go of the ball, I almost fell off that mound. But that ball whipped past three straight batters for strikeouts. I kept pumping for eight more innings. When I was done I had struck out sixteen and hadn't given up a hit. We were behind, six to nothing, when I started. When I was done we were ahead, eleven to six.

"That was some throwing, boy," Hines told me after the game.

"You know it. I showed them who was number one around here."

"You sure did," he said. "From now on you're number one with me, too—number one pitcher."

o o o o o

Even though I was a kid, I soon became pretty well known all over the South Side as just about the best school pitcher they ever saw around there.

There weren't too many even up in the high schools who could throw as hard and sure as I did. And when those kids my age came up to the plate and I threw my trouble ball, they just wet their pants or cried. That's how scared they were of my speed.

With all those kids I played with on the baseball team, I guess I should have had a lot of friends. But even when I was a kid, I was pretty much of a loner.

That's how it was then and how it always is.

Maybe I didn't have time for other kids because every day was a busy one for me—I worked at the ball park, I toted bags, I played baseball. That kept me pretty busy, but I always had time for trouble. That is, I had time for trouble until 1918.

I was walking home from a game. My clothes were dirty and stained. It was getting dark.

I walked by this store and stopped. Unless you've gone around with nothing, you don't know how powerful a lure some new, shiny stuff is. I turned and looked in the window. There must have been thirty or forty toys there.

I went in the store. I don't know why. I didn't have any money.

Then I saw all those toy rings, those gold bands, and those blue and red and green and black stones.

I looked around. No one was watching.

I grabbed a handful, stuffed them in my pocket.

"Hey, what're you doing?" someone yelled at me.

I looked around. This big white man was coming down on me. I ran.

He caught me by the front door.

They dragged me down to police headquarters. Then they got my Mom and even talked to the truant officer. They knew all about my playing hookey and being in trouble with those gang fights and rock throwing.

But they let me go home with my Mom. They told us to see the truant officer the next morning.

Mom cried when they got her down to the station. She cried all the way home. I thought she'd never stop. I don't guess she did until after we'd all been in bed half the night.

She hadn't spanked me. After the police quit yelling, no one had yelled at me. I just didn't understand that. No one had hit me. I guessed things couldn't be as bad as they seemed at first.

But in the morning Mom still looked worried. Her eyes were red and she moved real slow.

"We goin' to see that truant officer?" I asked.

"Yes. Get dressed."

We walked to the truant officer's place. The truant officer was the same woman who'd been chasing me for a couple of years. I don't know her name. I just called her Mrs. Meanie.

She talked . . . about the rings . . . about fights . . . about school . . . about playing hookey. I never thought anybody could talk that much. It wasn't a court hearing or anything like that. Just this truant officer, my Mom, and me.

Then she quit talking, but only for a minute. When she started in again it didn't make much sense to me, but it was all written down in a book in the county courthouse in Mobile:

"On this day, the twenty-fourth of July, 1918, LeRoy

Paige is ordered committed to the Industrial School for Negro Children at Mount Meigs, Alabama."

"No!" screamed my Mom. "Not for just that little bit of junk!"

Then I was scared. Real scared. I cried.

I couldn't stop shaking.

o   o   o   o   o

A kid is too scared to think at first when they tear him away from his family and send him to a reformatory. To me it was all like a dream, going to Montgomery and then those ten–twelve miles more out to Mount Meigs.

It seemed like a dream until they closed the door on me. Then I knew it was real.

I was in the industrial school.

But after I was there it didn't seem too bad. Everybody was real kind to me. Those five and a half years there did something for me—they made a man out of me. If I'd been left on the streets of Mobile to wander with those kids I'd been running around with, I'd of ended up as a big bum, a crook. That's what happened to a lot of those other kids.

But Mount Meigs got me away from the bums. It gave me a chance to polish up my baseball game; it gave me some schooling I'd of never taken if I wasn't made to go to classes; it learned me how to pass time without getting into trouble.

I know it may sound funny to talk about a reform school that way, but when you grow up as poor as me, a place like Mount Meigs can be mighty warm and good.

They gave me some clothes and took me to a big room, sort of like a dormitory, right after I got there. There were double beds in the dorm and two kids slept in a bed, just like we did at home.

On the wall were some pegs where we could hang our

clothes, but most of us didn't have anything to hang there outside of what they gave us.

After we got checked in, a couple of men came in and started calling off our names and telling us which beds were ours.

Then they started making a list of what things we liked to do. They were real careful on the Mount to get everybody doing something—woodwork, singing, baseball playing, drawing, anything.

About a week later they let those of us who wanted to go out for baseball.

"What do you play?" one of the coaches asked me.

"I pitch. But I can play outfield and first, too."

"Let's see how you throw," he said.

I went out to the mound and warmed up real quick. I wasn't worried. Then I started throwing. Nobody was hitting me. I just threw easy. No windup. Nothing.

The coach called me over afterwards.

"That arm may do you some good some day," he told me. "Take care of it. You concentrate on baseball and you might make something out of yourself."

I guess from that day on I was aiming at baseball, but it wasn't the only thing I did on the Mount. I went out for the choir and soon I was the choir leader. And I made the drum and bugle corps, banging those drums.

After summer was over, I put in most of my time singing. Of course there was school, too. And I did pretty good in those classes. Not that I liked it better than I did before being sent up, but you don't play hookey on the Mount.

So I went to school.

And I learned a lot of stuff. If they make you go where learning is flying around, some of it is bound to light on you.

By the time I was fifteen or sixteen I'd already grown to

six feet, three and a half inches. But I weighed only about a hundred and forty.

"Look, there goes the crane," some of the guys on the Mount yelled at me whenever I walked across the yard or went into a ball game.

I guess I did look like one. There was a lot of me, but it was all up and down.

But that tall, skinny look helped out. My coach showed me how to kick up my foot so it looked like I'd blacked out the sky. And he showed me how to swing my arm around so it looked like I let go of the ball when my hand was right in the batter's face.

Being all arms and legs sure helps when you do things that way.

My coach also taught me how to watch a batter, how you had to watch him just like a bullfighter watches a bull. You never look at a batter anywhere except at the knees, just like a bullfighter. The bullfighter can tell what a bull is going to do by watching his knees. I learned the same. When a batter swings and I see his knees move, I can tell just what his weaknesses are. Then I just put the ball where I know he can't hit it.

That teaching came in mighty handy later. It came in so handy you might say I traded five years of freedom to learn how to pitch. At least I started my real learning on the Mount.

o   o   o   o   o

I was seventeen and a half when they finally opened the door for me in December of 1923 and let me out of Mount Meigs. It seems so hazy I don't even remember how I got home to Mobile from Montgomery, but I got there.

My brothers and sisters weren't the same. They were all

bigger. But so was I. Fact was, I was bigger and taller than all the rest now.

The old shotgun house wasn't any different, though. When a family lives in a place about thirty years, it begins to look just like them. That's how my house seemed.

Another thing was still the same, too. We still needed money, money to buy food and clothes.

Nobody thought of that when I got home. We celebrated.

But Mom didn't let that celebrating go on too long. She only let me roam around for about a month or so getting used to things again. Then that came to an end.

"It's time you started helping out," Mom finally told me. "We got lots of mouths to feed. You better find you a piece of work."

o   o   o   o   o

Chapter Four

THE NEXT DAY I went looking for work, but those who knew where I'd been turned me down and those who didn't know didn't seem to have any steady work. Or maybe I wasn't really looking.

That afternoon I ended up over at Eureka Gardens, where the semi-pro Mobile Tigers still played, just like they did before I went up. My brother, Wilson, pitched and caught for them.

I sat down in the stands and leaned back to watch. The Tigers were getting ready for the regular 1924 season and were still trying out some guys for the club.

I looked all over but couldn't spot Wilson. He must not have come out that day.

The Tigers worked out about an hour and the longer I watched them the worse that itch to play got. Finally all the players except the catcher and the guy who'd been running the practice session left.

After the field was clear, a kid who'd been sitting down on the first row walked out on the field.

The kid went to the pitcher's mound and threw a few warmup pitches to the catcher. Then the Tigers' manager picked up a bat and stepped into the batting box. The kid started pitching again.

The Tigers' manager cracked those pitches all over the park.

He'd bat two thousand if he could come up against that kid every day, I thought.

One thing I was sure of was if that kid could try out for the Tigers, I sure could.

Then I got excited. Why not?

I looked close at that kid again.

I knew I could throw better than that shuffler.

Down I went, fast.

I waited at the side of the field until the kid walked off. I guess the manager had figured like me. That kid wouldn't cut it.

I walked up to the manager.

"You still looking for a pitcher?" I asked.

He just looked at me. "Go home, boy," he said. "I'm tired."

But when I told him I was Wilson's brother, he decided to let me pitch. He flipped a ball to me.

"Where've you been pitching?" he asked.

"Oh, around," I said.

He just nodded.

I felt good out on the mound. I whistled in a few of my fast ones, not bothering to wind up. They popped against the catcher's glove like they was firecrackers.

They never heard anything like that, I thought.

"I'm ready for you, mistah," I called to the manager.

He stepped into the box.

I threw. Ten times I threw. Ten times he swung. Ten times he missed.

I grinned. I stuck my foot up in his face and then tore the catcher's hand off with my blazer. He didn't have a chance against me.

The manager was grinning too.

"Do you throw that fast consistently?" he asked me.

"No, sir, I do it all the time."

That's the day I learned a new word.

o o o o o

The manager gave me a dollar and told me to come back with Wilson for the next game. I felt like that dollar was a thousand.

That was the point where I gave up kid's baseball—baseball just for fun—and started baseball as a career, started doing what I'd been thinking about doing off and on since my coach at the Mount'd told me about getting somewhere in the world if I concentrated on baseball.

And getting somewhere in the world is what I wanted most. Baseball had to be the way, too. I didn't know anything else.

o o o o o

Wilson, they called him Paddlefoot, and I were real tough for the Tigers. Actually, Wilson could throw about as hard as I could and we would have made one of the best two-man staffs you ever saw if he'd stuck with baseball, but he didn't.

First of all, he didn't want to leave Mobile then, and Wilson didn't love baseball like me. I'd do anything—practice for hours, watch and study for hours—just to get a little better.

While we were with the Tigers, though, we made a lot of people talk about us.

Wilson already was a big man around Eureka Gardens when I joined the team. It only took me a few games to become another hero. All the guys wanted to buy me drinks. All the gals just wanted to be around, squealing and hanging on my arms.

That's a mighty comforting feeling.

It's funny what a few no-hitters do for a body.

But those no-hitters don't make you rich. Not in semi-pro

ball. I'd get about a buck a game when enough fans came out so we made some money after paying for expenses. When there wasn't enough money, they gave me a keg of lemonade.

I got to laugh at that now. Back in 1924, I'd get a keg of lemonade to pitch and just a few years later I was getting as much as $500 for pitching those same nine innings.

I won just about all the games I pitched for the Tigers. We had a pretty good club and one of our best players was my old buddy, Julius Andrews. He played first base.

Sometimes I pitched for other teams. I jumped whenever there was some green waved.

The Tigers didn't like it too much, but my pocketbook did.

And I don't like to be tied down. Never have. I like to fly free.

'Course playing for a semi-pro club ain't a job, so I had to get me some work too. I landed a job over at the Mobile Bears' stadium. That was the white team, a minor-league club. Pretty soon those guys over there started hearing about Ol' Satch.

They heard good.

But all of them weren't buying what they heard. One day about four of them came up to me and told me how they been told I was some pitcher.

"We made a bet you couldn't throw as good as all of them say," one of them told me.

He offered me a dollar to show them.

That's the easiest dollar I ever made.

We went down on the field and one of them grabbed a bat and another a glove to catch me. I threw four or five real easy like, just to warm up. Then the batter headed for the plate.

"No need for you to tote that wood up there," I yelled at him. "It's just weight. You ain't gonna need it 'cause I'm gonna throw you nothin' but my trouble ball."

I threw. Them little muscles all around me tingled. They knew what we were doing. The first guy up there swung and missed three fast ones.

Another tried it. He just caused a breeze.

"We sure could use you," one of them finally told me. "If you were only white . . ."

That was the first time I heard it.

o   o   o   o   o

Chapter Five

FOR AN EIGHTEEN-YEAR-OLD KID, the cheers I got were mighty pleasing. I got plenty of laughs, too. But that was just by luck. I was a serious pitcher.

But when you're as tall and skinny as I am and when you got feet that are feet, maybe you look a little funny. And I like walking slow. Moving that way got them to laughing, too.

Laughing is a pretty sound and soon I was reaching for more laughs. But I never joked when I was pitching. Between pitches, okay. But that ball I threw was thoughtful stuff. It knew just what it had to do.

It did it.

In the 1924 season, I won about thirty games. I lost onoo. That was the start of a long string of winning streaks for me. I don't know which one was the longest. They were all long. I went by the years without losing a game.

By the next year, every team around town wanted me. And the best team was the team I was on.

But I still was a poor man. I still lived in that shotgun house on South Franklin and we still had to struggle to get money for all the food we needed. That don't sit well when you've found out there is dancing and hunting and fishing, with the fine rods and reels and all the equipment.

That was the fishing I wanted.

So you just keep scratching and trying to get a dollar. Sometimes you do and sometimes you don't. Sometimes you forget you got to go hungry. Sometimes you forget how you can't buy clothes. Sometimes you forget, but usually you don't.

I didn't forget and the more times I remembered how poor I was, the more I wanted to have something better. And the only way I knew how to get something better was with pitching.

That meant I had to get a professional ball club interested in me.

I pitched harder. About halfway through the 1926 season I had me a twenty-five game winning streak going. I was going for number twenty-six when suddenly it looked like that winning streak was going to go up in smoke.

I was pitching for the Down the Bay Boys and we were playing some other Mobile semi-pro club. I slid through the first eight innings of the game without any trouble. The first two guys up in the ninth also were easy outs. Then the troubles began. My infield fell apart.

There were three straight errors and the other team had the bases loaded. Since I only had a one to nothing lead, a hit would tie the game or lose it for me.

I was burning. I walked off the mound and kicked the dirt. I was so mad my stomach felt it. Then I heard the crowd. They sounded like someone was twisting their tail. They were booing to beat all getout, not really booing me but just booing.

Hearing that booing made me even madder.

Somebody was going to have to be showed up for that.

I looked around and then I waved in my outfielders. When they got in around me, I said, "Sit down there on the grass right behind me. I'm pitching this last guy without an outfield."

"What?" one of them said.

The other two started screaming, too. You'd have thought I'd declared war on the government.

But finally I talked them into sitting down.

The crowd went crazy. They weren't booing now. They were watching me and only me.

I heard the roar all around. Everybody was yelling. I took my time, then pumped back and forth and threw.

It was strike one, but you couldn't hear the umpire for all the yelling. He just waved his arm.

He waved strike two and you couldn't even hear yourself.

Back I leaned and then I threw. The batter swung but my quickie hopped right over the wood into the catcher's glove.

The crowd really went crazy. You wouldn't think a few hundred could make that much noise. But they did.

My outfielders danced around like they'd sat on hot coals.

My infielders just walked off the field, but not before I wagged my nose at them.

o   o   o   o   o

After that the victories kept piling up for me and the longer my winning streak got, the more attention I got. Finally it paid off.

My old buddy, Alex Herman, offered me a job with a professional club, not a semi-pro outfit.

Alex had left Mobile and gone up to Chattanooga. He was managing the Chattanooga Black Lookouts in the old Negro Southern League.

He was back in Mobile one day in 1926 and came up to me after a ball game. I was in a powerful hurry and tried to brush him off when he said he wanted to talk to me about pitching. I thought it was just another semi-pro job.

"This ain't peanuts," he yelled at me. "This is steady money with a league team."

He slowed me down to a baby amble.

It didn't take him long to convince me that I ought to hop to Chattanooga. Fifty dollars a month was big money to me.

Before Alex would leave with me, he said we had to get Mom's permission.

"I ain't going to get in trouble with the law for taking a kid away from his Mom," he told me.

I wasn't exactly a kid then, but I figured he knew what he was talking about so we went to see Mom.

She was tougher than a no-hitter.

"Your Pa ain't been dead more'n a year and you're going off and leaving," she yelled at us. "You're just a boy. You'll probably even play on Sundays."

"He'll be making good money, Mrs. Paige," Alex told my Mom. "He can even send some home to help out with the bills and for food."

Mom was looking a little more interested.

"I'll send the money myself to make sure you get it," Alex said.

That did it. Mom said I could go, but she gave Alex a list of orders for me that'd take care of an army.

But I had my first full-time, professional job.

It may seem funny, but years later I couldn't remember that 1926 was the year I took that job. When I got in the major leagues in 1948, people were saying they saw me pitch professional back in 1920. Well, I told all the reporters there was no proof or truth to such stories and I was willing to pay five hundred dollars to the first person who showed me a clipping that I was in professional baseball before 1927.

So a guy named Carl Goerz of Cleveland goes to Memphis and gets ahold of his brother-in-law who found him a newspaper clipping dated May 16, 1926, showing I pitched for the Chattanooga Black Lookouts against the Memphis Red Sox.

Alex, who still lives in Mobile, said he was right.

I paid Carl Goerz the five hundred dollars.

"How much did that photostat of that box score cost you?" I asked him when I handed over the check.

"Two dollars," he told me.

"Five hundred for two," I said. "Maybe I ought to quit pitching and start looking for suckers like me. I must have slept a year someplace."

o o o o o

Before we left Mobile, Alex signed up Julius Andrews to play first base for Chattanooga and tried to sign up Wilson but got turned down.

"I'm staying here," is all Wilson would tell us.

So Alex, Julius, and I moved on. We showed up in Chattanooga late in April.

Nobody seemed too happy about seeing me. Later everyone was happy when Ol' Satch showed up, but to the Black Lookouts I was just another rookie.

After I loosened up, Alex hustled me up a catcher. The catcher paced off the pitching distance on the sideline. A bunch of the other players stood around watching. I figured I'd better show them quick who was number one.

"Here, use this for home plate," I told the catcher, giving him a piece of rag I was using for a handkerchief.

"This wouldn't make half a plate," he told me.

"Go ahead and use it anyway. I just need a scrap for a target."

My catcher crouched down. I threw. The catcher didn't even have to move his glove. The ball popped into it, right over the middle of that rag.

Some of those players standing around whistled, they were so surprised.

I kept throwing, throwing until my arm whipped around real loose-like. I didn't miss that rag once.

They all crowded around me. Those players all wanted to talk to me now. I was their meal ticket.

I've been a meal ticket for lots of people since then.

We split up for a practice game, then.

I guess I should have been nervous but I wasn't, even though I was playing against real professionals for the first time and not against some semi-pros.

I just fired my bee ball at them a few times and my team ended up with a three to two win. After the game, my catcher came up to me and handed me a couple of bucks.

"What's this for?" I asked.

"We had a 'leven dollar jackpot for this game," he told me. "Each of us chipped in. You didn't chip in, but you sure earned this."

o   o   o   o   o

Chapter Six

EVERY TIME I THINK of that first professional job, I get the feeling there should have been some drums banged or maybe a trumpet played. But there wasn't. One day I was in Mobile, playing with semi-pro teams like the Tigers, and the next day I was in Chattanooga with a Negro Southern League club.

You can't say I really missed home. There wasn't a whole lot there to miss. And I must have been born to travel.

If you keep moving, Old Age ain't got a chance of catching you. He moves mighty slow.

I got the first room I ever had to myself in Chattanooga. It was in a boarding house and really wasn't much more'n a flop. But it only cost me two dollars a week.

There was a big closet, but I didn't have anything to put in it. I got to Chattanooga with a couple of shirts, an extra pair of socks, and underwear wrapped in an old pair of pants. That was it. I looked more like a guy who was ready to go on the bum than one who was starting out on his first big job.

It was some time before I ever had enough money to start buying clothes. It took about all I got to live. Anyway, baseball and running around were all I thought about. How I had to live didn't seem to matter.

Alex let me get the feel of Chattanooga before pitching me. My first game out with the Black Lookouts was against

New Orleans, who had a guy called Diamond throwing for them.

It don't make much difference who throws when Ol' Satch's in there. We won, one to nothing. I gave up two hits.

Two days later Alex threw me again. I gave up only three hits this time. I struck out fourteen. My fast ball was really working.

"Those guys needed headaches to go with all those aspirins you were throwing," Alex told me after the game. He slipped me an extra five, too.

I took that five and headed for the pool hall. I was a pretty good sticker, but about an hour later I'd found out I was a little out of practice.

The guys who I'd beat—who let me beat them—when we were playing for fun, shot like they owned the table when I put up the five for some action.

"Come back when you got some more dough to give away, kid," one of the sharpies yelled to me when I headed for the door.

I went back, too, but it was about a week later. I'd spent the time at another pool hall, sort of polishing up my game.

The sharpies were all over me when I walked in. They smelled that green and were ready to take it, even before they saw how I was shooting. They should have been patient.

I got the five bucks I'd lost back, plus a little interest.

Pool wasn't the only thing I practiced. I was putting in plenty of hours on the baseball field, before the other players got up in the mornings and after they went home at nights.

I'm still trying to rest up from all that practice.

Alex was the one who pushed me into it. He was always pushing me and I guess he taught me more'n anybody else.

"The way you throw," he said, "you ought to be able to get the ball over the plate every time and I'm gonna make sure you do."

I laughed. I just figured he was joking.

I learned different.

The first thing he had me do was knock over pop bottles he'd line up by home plate. I got pretty good at that. One day some guy in the stands was watching Alex line up about ten bottles.

"You gonna knock those over?" he yelled at me.

"That's right."

"Bet you only get half of them."

"Man, I'll get all of them," I answered.

We bet.

That man bought Alex and me dinner that night.

Alex also had me throwing the ball through a hole in the fence no bigger than the insides of a man's hat. That was easy, too.

It got so I could nip frosting off a cake with my fast ball. Because of that control, I got clear to the top in baseball. If you know where that ball is going, you can do a lot no one else can and you can stay around long after the real good stuff you throw has gone. I know now. I didn't know it then. So I tried ducking practice, but Alex made sure I didn't have too much luck at it.

By the time I'd satisfied Alex with my control, we were ready to leave on our first road trip.

"This how we going?" I asked Alex when I saw the beat-up bus waiting for us.

"That's it."

I didn't like it, but I got on that bus and just about got broken in half bouncing over those big holes in them Tennessee roads.

We got into Memphis about eight or nine o'clock that night. But the bus just kept driving through town and didn't stop until we got to the ball park.

"Everybody out," Alex yelled.

All the other players minded him. I just stayed put. It

was dark as pitch out there. No telling what you'd find outside on a night like that.

"Let's go," Alex yelled at me.

"No, sir," I told him. "I'll just stay here 'til you night birds get through with what you're doing."

"This bus is leaving," he said. "You got to get off."

"Just have that driver take me to the hotel or wherever we're staying."

"Stayin'g?" Alex laughed. "This is where you're staying, Satch. You think we can afford staying in a hotel?"

And that's where we stayed, sleeping on our suitcases in that ball park because we didn't have money for anything else.

I had the miseries in the morning. My back was sore, my arms and legs ached, and my mouth was full of dust. I looked around. The ball park wasn't much better than the way I was feeling.

It was little and splintery and the rocks cut you when you slid.

But we played and we won there, even with those stiff muscles and sore backs and no breakfast except a hot dog and some warm orange we got there.

That's how you lived in the Negro Southern League. That's how it was until I started pulling in crowds that paid good money. Then things got better, but not a whole lot. Even when we got to stay in hotels, they were the Negro hotels. And those down South you don't cheer about.

I hit up Alex about it, but he couldn't do much except let me stay with friends when we were on the road.

But I stopped worrying about where I was staying because my salary was getting big enough to make any place pretty good. By the time the season was a month old, I was pulling down about a hundred a month.

Alex was happy to give it to me. He hadn't even argued.

"You seen all those crowds I've drawn?" I'd asked him

when I'd gone up to him to see about more money. He just nodded. "I figure I should be getting a hundred a month because of them."

"That's what you'll be getting," Alex said. But he still kept some money out to send to my Mom.

When that next payday came around, nobody could have held me down.

For the first time since I could remember, I had me some new clothes. And there was a steak. And I bought a bottle and went looking for a gal. And I got me a shotgun, my first.

Nobody saw me for two days. Alex was at the park when I finally showed up.

"You're just the man I'm looking for," I told Alex when I saw him. "Loan me a couple of dollars for my rent."

"You've blown all that money, already?"

"Now don't go riding me, Alex. I had lots of buying to do. Just take it out of what I make the next month. There's plenty more coming then."

Alex gave me the two bucks. He knew there was plenty more coming, too. It kept coming for a lot of years.

o   o   o   o   o

Chattanooga hadn't been much of a ball club in 1925, but with me tossing them in there in 1926, we won the first-half championship. I didn't lose a ball game that first half. In two years with Chattanooga I only lost two.

They thought of passing a law against me. It would have been the only way they could stop me.

All around Chattanooga they talked about me, about how I was good enough to be in the big time—and not just big-time Negro ball, but big-time major league ball, with New York or Cleveland or Philadelphia or St. Louis.

I thought I should be there too. I got real hotheaded

every time someone told me it was too bad I couldn't play in the major leagues because of my color.

But there were some folks who wanted me to pitch against the whites. One of them was Stran Niglin, who ran the Chattanooga Lookouts in the white Southern Association.

He wanted me so bad he tried everything to get me into a game.

One day he even came up to me and offered me five hundred dollars to pitch against the Atlanta Crackers.

I just had to let him paint me white.

When Alex Herman heard about it, he got as mad as anybody I've ever seen.

I guess I was always causing Alex a bad time.

Alex finally talked me out of it, but I sure hated to pass up that five hundred dollars. And I think I'd have looked good in white-face. But nobody would have been fooled. White, black, green, yellow, orange—it don't make any difference. Only one person can pitch like me.

That's Ol' Satch, himself.

o   o   o   o   o

Near the end of the season, I jumped the Black Lookouts for a few days and hopped over to New Orleans. But this time it wasn't money that got me to jump.

The real reason was that they offered me an old jalopy. The eighty-five dollars they gave me for a month of pitching wasn't anything. I was up to almost two hundred a month with the Black Lookouts by then.

That jalopy was something else. It was my first. But the money ran out pretty quick and I hopped out of New Orleans. Those guys still probably are waiting for me to pitch that last week of ball.

It didn't worry me.

About a week after I got back to Chattanooga, Alex got

over being mad about my leaving. Then I got him all upset again.

"How 'bout learning to throw a curve?" I asked him.

He turned so quick he stirred dust.

"You want to ruin that arm of yours?" he finally asked, sounding like he was going to hit me.

That ended the curve right there. Pretty soon Alex made a believer out of me, too. If you had the real fast ball, that was all you needed. And that was all I needed for a long, long time.

But I finally learned to throw the curve and about ninety other pitches, too. That was years later.

o   o   o   o   o

Alex kept as close tab of me off the field as he did on. With him around all the time, we got to be pretty close buddies.

Dancing was the big thing with us. We'd hunt up a couple of dolls and off we'd go—doing the shuffle, trots, waltzes, anything.

It kept my legs in shape.

But it didn't do much for my sleeping.

Those moonshiners liked us, too. I guess I was living it up pretty high. I'd never had any money to do it before and every payday I feared might be my last.

I acted like it was.

By the time I finished my second year with Chattanooga, I was busting around in a flashy roadster that could really scoot. A big man like me couldn't be seen in that old jalopy I'd picked up in New Orleans.

My roadster was such a beauty I just about rubbed the paint off it polishing it so often. Sometimes I was late for a game getting that car looking good enough to drive.

That car and my two-year record at Chattanooga were all

I had when the Birmingham Black Barons bought me from the Black Lookouts and gave me a contract for two hundred seventy-five dollars a month.

Birmingham looked mighty good.

So did 1928.

o   o   o   o   o

Chapter Seven

BIRMINGHAM SHOWED ME a new world of baseball. I had a manager who polished that good teaching Alex Herman had given me and I got a catcher who was one of the best ballplayers of all time—Negro or white.

My manager was Bill Gatewood. He was from Boonville or Columbia, Missouri, I forget which, and was managing the Black Barons for R. T. Jackson. My catcher was George Perkins, who handled a pitcher like nobody's business.

When I first showed up at the ball park, Gatewood brought George over to meet me. We talked around awhile and then George asked, "What kind'a signs you want to use?"

"There ain't any need for signs, I guess. I don't take to them too good. Anyway, I'm the easiest guy in the world to catch. All you have to do is show me a glove and hold it still. I'll hit it."

I could see George didn't believe me. Neither did any of the other Black Barons standing around, so I had one of them hold a couple of bats about six inches apart. I fired my fast ball right through that space. I did it a couple of more times just to show I wasn't getting by on luck alone.

From then on we went without signs. George held up his glove and I fired my bee ball or my jump ball. I throw both overhand, only the bee ball goes off my fingers on the smooth hide of the ball and rides on the level, and my jump ball I throw with my fingers across the seam and that makes it jump four to six inches.

"That's all I'll use," I told George. "When I'm an old man I'll use a curve. All I need now is that fast ball."

"You sure think a lot of yourself," was all George would say.

I guess I was pretty confident, all right. I even thought of calling in my outfield like Alex and I'd done to build up the crowds. We'd done it a lot, but we always made sure we were way out front before we did. There wasn't any reason to lose a ball game because some fellow got lucky and blooped the ball.

But I gave up on the idea. I didn't think Bill Gatewood would put up with it until he'd seen me around some. But the way all the players were talking, you could see they expected me to put on a show every time out. So in that first ball game with Birmingham, I yelled over to the other team, "I'm gonna strike out the first six guys up against me."

You should have seen those other guys burn.

I repeated what I'd yelled the first time, making sure some of the fans heard this time. It spread through the stands in no time.

The whole place was jumping when the first guy came up against me.

I fired in close to him and he couldn't untangle himself. He struck out quick. The next two batters also struck out.

We didn't score in the last half of the first inning and went out to the field again.

The crowd cheered when they saw me. I pulled off my hat and waved at them. They liked that.

The fourth batter up against me whipped that bat back and forth like he really meant business.

I struck him out.

He did foul off the first pitch, but I came back with two of my jump balls and he fanned. That fifth batter swung three times. He didn't do anything and I had five strikeouts.

One of the guys on the other team's bench pulled out a white towel then and waved it back and forth.

They'd surrendered.

The crowd went wild and I knew I was in around Birmingham.

The sixth batter came up and I grinned at him and threw quick. He popped out.

George Perkins cornered me at the bench.

"You didn't get those six in a row like you said you would," he said.

"They'd already surrendered," I told him. "When Ol' Satch needs a strikeout, he gets it."

o o o o o

With Birmingham I drove that car of mine everywhere I had to throw. And I got there fast. Fact is, I got tickets for speeding in every state I went through and just about every town.

It's not that I wanted to get tickets. I just always seemed to get started late and then had to hurry.

One day I got started so late for a ball game it was the next day. I didn't find out different until I got there.

That first season with Birmingham I traveled North and East and West, too. I got that taste of traveling. I was in my fifties before I ever decided it'd be nice to rest my feet in the same room every night.

One of my first trips was to St. Louis to play the St. Louis Stars down behind the car barn where Mule Suttle Redus, Cool Papa Bell, and Willie Wells used to bash out flocks of "Chinese" homers. They were names most baseball fans probably never heard of, but they were among the best of the old Negro stars.

You take Cool Papa Bell, for example. Why, he was the best fielder you ever saw. He could grab that ball no matter where it was hit. He was just like a suction cup. And he was fast. If schools had known Cool Papa was around and if Cool Papa had known reading real good, he'd have made the best track man you ever saw.

Nowadays when they talk about that first game in St. Louis, some people who saw me then say I was nervous and wild. No such thing.

I hit a few batters that day, but I meant to. Why, I haven't hit more than two batters in my entire life except when I wanted to.

Against the Stars, I put my first pitch right into the side of the lead-off batter. He hurt, but he could walk down to first base. I'd thrown my letup so I wouldn't kill him.

I took a long look at the second batter and saw he still was crowding my plate. I threw and the ball caught his arm even though he was falling out of the way.

The Stars' manager, Candy Jim Taylor, came roaring off the bench. He threatened to take his players off the field if I hit another one.

He didn't scare me.

A buddy of mine named Henry Murray was up, but on the field I ain't got any buddies.

I put that ball right in the small of his back. He out-roared Candy Jim.

And then Murray lit out after me with that baseball bat, screaming, "I'll split that skull of yours."

Henry must have forgot we was buddies. I circled second base, staying away from him until he threw the bat at me.

It missed.

I picked it up and I did the chasing. The last I saw of Henry he was heading through the gate in center field. He didn't come back.

o   o   o   o   o

Our hotel in St. Louis was a dump, like all the hotels we had to stay in.

Out on the field there'd be some white folks in the stands. Some of them'd call you nigger, but most would cheer you. After the game, though, none of them would get near you. They could cheer you, but they couldn't talk to you or be seen with you. And they couldn't let you stay where they did.

Or even stay in places as nice as theirs.

As bad as it was, it still was better than Mobile. I didn't have to sell ice and empty bottles just to buy a baseball glove.

And the baseballs weren't those three-week-old jobs that felt like mush. 'Course, when I'm throwing it don't matter too much what I use. No one is going to hit it.

But I still remember those, "Sorry, we can't serve you here."

I'd get served in a lot of those places now. The world and me both got up a little higher, but we had to scrap to get there. And it meant a lot of pitching for me.

o   o   o   o   o

When I wasn't throwing for Birmingham, Bill Gatewood would rent me to another club so I could pick up a piece of change and get him some.

One of those games about got me in jail. And all I did was hit the ball too good.

It was in Albany, Georgia, and I was pitching for the visiting club against some of the home boys. That whole game started out wrong.

My catcher showed up and he must have been Old Man Moses. He was so old he didn't have to crouch. He was bent naturally. He got behind the plate to catch me during warmup.

"Ain't you gonna put on a protector?" I asked him.

"No," he said.

So I wound up and fired. The ball ripped right past his gloved hand and busted him on the chest. He dropped to his knees like he was praying.

He put on that protector real fast. I finished warming up and we went in for our first bats. The first two batters up for us singled.

I was batting third because this club needed my hitting about as much as my pitching.

I swung on the first pitch but I got around late and the ball zipped out to right field. The right fielder, who'd been over toward center, went legging after it and I cut around first.

I clipped second and headed for third, sliding in safe.

Then I looked back and saw the second baseman running in with the ball. He touched second and that umpire called me out. I blew up.

When I got good and loud, that umpire looked at me and said, "You watch your mouth. I'm the sheriff in this town and I'll throw you in jail if you keep that up."

That did it. I sat down right there in front of him, stuck my feet up in his face.

"How could I miss second base with feet that big," I yelled. "All I got to do is stomp down anywhere near it and I'll hit it."

If there'd been anybody else to pitch, I think he would have thrown me in jail. But I guess he was getting a cut of the gate and didn't want to give the money back to the spectators. So he had them drag me to the bench and I sat until I cooled off.

I didn't cool off enough to ease up. That fast ball of mine was going so quick it sounded like a snake—sort of hissed.

When I was done I had a no-hitter, seventeen strikeouts and that umpire's goat.

I didn't dare go back to Albany until I heard that sheriff had been beaten in an election.

o   o   o   o   o

Chapter Eight

NEAR THE END of the 1929 season, Bill Gatewood asked me to stay after one game.

When the rest of the players cleared out, I went over to him.

"You've been sold to Nashville," he told me.

I felt kind of numb. Then it passed. Tom Wilson's Nashville, Tennessee club was a pretty good one.

I grinned.

"Well, I guess I'm moving up a little, then," I said.

Gatewood nodded.

When I first got back to my room, I felt like someone had given me a hundred dollars. Then I realized Wilson didn't need me until the start of the 1930 season. That meant I had all winter to get through and I didn't even have a job.

No club, no more games, and not a dime on me.

There wasn't any use going back to Mobile. There was no money there for me, just semi-pro jobs again.

It looked pretty bad.

Then I got a pardon.

A guy named Señor Linares from Santa Clara in Cuba called me and said they were getting some teams up down that way and he wanted me to pitch for them. He waved plenty of green in my face and I was packed and down there before he got his hat back on.

Now baseball down in the islands is a little different than

up here. Or it was. They take it mighty serious. You win and lose elections on a ball game.

When I got there they put me in the best hotel I'd ever stayed in.

"Man, this is the life," I told everybody.

No winter, no cold weather, just nice, warm breezes. You don't even have to buy a coat when you hit the islands for the winters.

And that's how it was, everyone treating me like I was the top man in the world. They sure like their baseball players, I thought.

That afternoon I wandered down into the lobby and cornered one of my teammates.

"Let's get someone to mix us up a snort," I told him.

He looked like I'd shot him.

"Don't let them hear you saying that around here," he told me.

That's when I found out these people put even more store by winning than I'd thought. They figured their ballplayers went to bed early, ate good, and never drank, so they could go all out when it came to game time. If there was any snorting to be done, you had to do it behind locked doors in your room.

So I walked easy.

The next day I went out to the field. We had a game starting in about a half hour. There were a bunch of players already there. They all looked like natives.

And remembering what they told me about how they felt about baseball, I was just a little bit shy of them. I edged toward the bench, but they saw me and all of them came toward me, jabbering to beat all hell.

"Speak English, boys," I yelled. "I is with you."

Well, it turned out they weren't going to chop me up. They were just coming over to say hello.

I found out those boys in the islands like you real good

if you can throw that ball. They liked me so well they even wanted me on the coaching lines. But you still have to watch your step. I remember one year down in Venezuela when a bunch of soldiers had to march me out of the park to keep away about a hundred guys with machetes who wanted to carve me up because an error cost me a ball game.

And down in Puerto Rico I once won twenty-three games in a row and then lost one about one to nothing and everybody said I must have been drunk.

Usually things were quiet down in the islands, but sometimes there was political troubles and Sam had to get us out. But most of the time you didn't need Uncle's help. And Puerto Rico was always nice because Sam owned it.

Anyway, the pay was good everywhere down there. Always good.

o   o   o   o   o

After that first year of winter ball in 1929, I played year-round baseball—spring, summer, winter, and fall—until 1958. That's about twenty-nine years worth.

Most players last ten or fifteen years playing six months a year. I heard of a few that made it to twenty-five years, maybe a little more. But they were playing six months at a crack most of the time, too.

But me—I played almost every day, winter and summer, for those twenty-nine years and I didn't quit then; I just cut out winter ball.

Like most people, I won't forget 1929. 'Course most will remember it because that's the year the stock market crashed, but for me 1929 was the year Ol' Satch's stock just started going up and up.

It got so I'd pitch so many games every year I couldn't count them. Tell the truth, I pitched more than twenty-five hundred games, I guess. I even threw 153 in one year. And I guess I've had more than a hundred no-hitters, but I just tell people it's a hundred.

I don't want to sound big-headed.

o   o   o   o   o

After that first swing in the islands, I joined Tom Wilson and his Nashville Elite Giants for the 1930 season.

Before long, Tom moved the club up to Cleveland and we started playing out of there, but we still were known as the Nashville Elite Giants.

I was getting a lot more attention around Cleveland and through the North and East because that's where the major leaguers played and that's where the baseball writers were.

But attention ain't everything. I'd look over at the Cleveland Indians' stadium, called League Park. That was the big money there. I got mad. All season long it burned me, playing there in the shadow of that stadium. It didn't hurt my pitching, but it sure didn't do me any good.

Then I got a chance to soothe that angry feeling inside as well as getting one of the biggest breaks in my career.

"Babe Ruth's getting up a barnstorming team of major leaguers," Tom told me near the end of the season.

"What's that mean to me?" I asked.

"He's gonna play against the Baltimore Black Sox. They want you to pitch for them."

I snapped at the offer. That started my real rise to fame. It wasn't the major leagues but it was the next best thing—playing against big leaguers. That always got headlines and headlines make a reputation.

When you barnstorm, they pay big for reputation.

I joined the Black Sox and we worked out for a couple of days. That's all we needed to get acquainted. We were ready for the Babe Ruth All-Stars and the big man himself.

He was something I was looking forward to. Babe wasn't the only big gun on that club. They had Hack Wilson. He hit over fifty homers and knocked in about a hundred and ninety runs in the 1930 season with the Chicago Cubs. And there was Babe Herman. He batted almost four hundred with Brooklyn.

I was real curious to see those boys. They were just as curious to see me. I'd done pretty well and they'd heard about it. Fact was, a couple of my boys told me those major leaguers were laying for me.

I was laying for them, too.

Babe Ruth wasn't in the line-up the first time the two clubs met.

They could have used him. I beat them Stars easy and struck out Hack Wilson and Babe Herman to boot. Hack came up to me after the game.

"That was some pitching," he said. "It looked like you were winding up with a baseball and throwing a pea."

o o o o o

During the whole tour I never pitched against Babe Ruth. When I was pitching he was bench-managing and when I was getting a day off he was playing.

That was the only chance I ever had at him, but as it turned out I didn't need him to boost up my reputation more than it was.

When we got to the West Coast, I was just breezing along. And I guess that was when I really showed them I could put that fast ball of mine by the best batters there was.

It was a warm night in Los Angeles and I was throwing real easy. The innings rolled by and I was ahead. I was getting a lot of strikeouts, but I didn't pay much attention to them.

In the last half of the ninth, I cut down Babe Ruth's boys quick-like and started off the field.

My manager hopped off the bench and came running at me.

"You know what you did?" he yelled.

"I won."

"You struck out twenty-two of them," he said. "That's way better than the major league record."

By that time everybody in that whole place was mobbing me. I almost lost an arm getting it pumped so many times. Then this old-timer pushed his way through to me.

"Boy," he said, "you seem to have everything. When I was playing I never saw so many fast balls as you pitch."

He turned out to be Sam Agnew, who was a catcher for St. Louis, Boston, and Washington in the American League. What he said about my fast ball was pretty high praise, coming from a guy who first played against and later caught a top strikeout man like Walter Johnson of Washington.

Even with that praise, I never counted those twenty-two strikeouts as my one game record. I always said it was eighteen even though I hit twenty-two in other games, lots of times. But when I talk about records, I'm talking about league games and those twenty-two strikeouts always came in exhibition games. I don't count exhibition games. I know some of the boys ain't in shape when I whiff them in those games.

o   o   o   o   o

After the Baltimore Black Sox called it quits with the big leaguers, I went to the islands again. It was just like the year before, only better because I was a bigger man.

They had a *fiesta* when I got there and this big boy, the town mayor, and all his aides got out and said big things about me. They didn't give me the key to the city, but down there nobody was locking their doors to Ol' Satch anyway.

I won about twenty and lost maybe one or two. I don't know how I lost that many.

The mayor of the town called me into his office after the winter season ended.

He jabbered at me real fast.

I just nodded my head "yes."

He looked like he was going to bust and started jabbering at me again.

"That's fine," I said, and grinned and nodded my head again.

He almost jumped over his desk and one of those guys standing around watching us had to hold him down. They got me out of there quick.

"What was all that about?" I asked one of the fellows with me.

He looked real blank and then asked me, "You don't speak the language?"

"Not so you could tell it."

"The mayor asked you if you had deliberately lost a game because of gamblers. That is what you nodded 'yes' to."

I was glad there'd been some guys to hold the mayor down. I'd hate to think what he'd done if he had gotten across that desk.

Knowing how the mayor felt, those boys got me out of town fast.

When I got back to the States, I bought me a new car and moved on up to Cleveland to join the Elite Giants for the regular 1931 season.

The season didn't last long for the Elite Giants. We hardly got started when the club busted up.

But the bust-up was another break for me.

I ended up on about the best team ever put together in any country—the best team, Negro or white.

That was Gus Greenlee's Pittsburgh Crawfords.

Gus was organizing the team when Tom's club folded. I'd met Gus a little before and when he heard I was free he whistled.

I came running, especially after Gus told me I'd be pulling down two-fifty a month regular from him.

And there'd be plenty on the side to boost that.

Everybody was wanting me since all the papers were writing how I'd won about sixty games a year the last three years and had averaged about fifteen strikeouts a game. Not many did any better, not even the likes of Bullet Joe Rogan, the greatest Negro pitcher anybody ever heard of before I came along.

o   o   o   o   o

Chapter Nine

WHEN I GOT TO PITTSBURGH, the first place I headed was Gus Greenlee's restaurant, the Crawford Grill.

Gus had a real good thing in Pittsburgh in 1931. He had the restaurant and a boxing stable and the ball club and Josh Gibson, the world's greatest catcher and hitter. Josh could have hit home runs around Babe Ruth's home runs if they'd let him play in the majors—that's how good he was.

He was a powerful man, all right.

A couple of my Nashville teammates, Harry Simon and George Perkins, came along to Pittsburgh with me.

As soon as Gus heard I was in, he came busting over.

"We're gonna open against the Homestead Grays," he said. "They're the best there is, Satch. You beat them and you're number one right from the start."

I just nodded.

"Remember, they got Smokey Joe Williams and Lefty Williams—both of 'em," he said.

"They don't worry Ol' Satch none."

My arm was in shape and my control always was good. That all-year playing had me at the top of my game.

Pittsburgh never saw a big crowd like the one that turned out. Gus had done a good job of building up the Crawfords. The Homestead Grays didn't need building up. They were built.

I went out to warm up. This was Pittsburgh's first look

at me, but I didn't feel very nervous. I was young and I could throw like nobody else.

When I kicked up my foot and threw that first one, the crowd screamed.

The ball ripped into Josh, skipped off his mitt, and missed his head only because he leaned to the side. He hadn't expected me to throw that hard either.

I kept kicking that foot up in the sky, twisting like a pretzel, pausing, and throwing.

I beat the Grays without any trouble and struck out sixteen to boot.

We celebrated like no one ever had after that game. Gus just locked the door on the grill and we went to town.

I couldn't get away from anybody there. They mobbed me like money'd rub off if they touched me. All Gus' waitresses pressed around me, smiling those smiles I'd gotten mighty used to.

But one of those waitresses stood off a little. Oh, she was close, but she acted kind of like she was bashful. I didn't see any more of those smiles around me, I just saw her.

I pushed away from the other gals around me and headed over to her.

"'Lo. I'm Satch."

"I know you, all right, Mr. Paige. Everybody knows you now. I'm Janet Howard."

She was all big eyes for me. I could tell that. And I just figured those big eyes was because I was such a fine-looking man and because I'd just beat the champions. What I didn't know was those eyes were so big because they were trying to look at all of me at once, trying to spot a weak point so Janet could hook me.

Right then and there, she was starting to write the end to my bachelor days. I didn't even know it.

I just figured I'd never get tied down because I'd learned you got to be mighty careful of love. Up to meeting Janet,

I'd been wounded so many times by love I had to learn something. I'd learned to be careful.

The way I felt was if you got married it was like walking in front of a firing squad without anybody making you do it. Not that I'd give up women, not on a bet. You don't give up women no more than carp gives up doughballs. They're a mighty powerful lure.

I didn't say much to Janet. I never do around women. A lot of the guys thought I was bashful because of that. They didn't know Ol' Satch, though. I'd found out long before that with women you don't have to talk your head off. You just say a word and let them fill in from there. What they fill in can be mighty interesting.

That's the way with women.

What I didn't know was that if you kept chasing, you were bound to trip sometime. And when I'd chased over after Janet, she was all set to trip me. She did, too, in 1934.

She didn't let on what she was planning during that celebration. She just acted like a school girl who was with the team captain, sort of shy and real proud. Before she got away from me that night, I asked her for another date.

After I took her home, I wandered back to the grill. The celebration still was going strong. I guess it should have been. I'd beaten the champions.

That was something. It meant I wouldn't be looking for any more jobs now for sure. They'd be looking for me. When you're on top everybody wants you. When you ain't, then you got to scratch and take what they drop your way.

When I got inside, Gus Greenlee spotted me.

He yelled and came rushing over to me. "After that game, Satch, anything you want I got."

"Well, I got me a date and I'm a little short. How about a few bucks?" Even with all the money I was making, I was always broke. I just lived a little better.

Gus just looked at me a couple of minutes and then said,

"I'll do better'n that. Tomorrow you go down and buy yourself a couple of suits and hats on me. And you got a bonus —seven hundred bucks a month now instead of two-fifty."

"What?"

"That's right. Seven hundred. That ought to keep you happy enough to stay with me."

"For that kind of money I'd go nowhere else."

That next day I bought five suits, not two, but I only charged two to Gus. And I got some of the fanciest red and green and bright blue and yellow ties you ever saw.

"You look like a walking barber pole," Janet said to me that night when she saw me. Then she laughed and grabbed my arm real tight. "You look fine."

o o o o o

I'd grown up without suits and these I'd bought really were something. They showed I'd made good.

And I kept those suits as stiff and clean as a West Pointer. Why, I even started sending out my folding money to be cleaned and pressed. And I bought me a super-super job that was so long that when I parked it at the curb I had to walk three houses back to see if the tail light was on.

A couple of the boys warned me to go easy.

"That was only one game," they said.

I laughed at them. I knew there'd be more. But not even I knew how many more there'd really be. When they said Satchel Paige years later, there was at least three generations who knew what that meant.

o o o o o

The Crawfords played everywhere, in every ball park you could find. And we won, won like we invented the game.

Every time Gus announced I was going to pitch, they had

to get cops to watch the gates because there were so many trying to crowd their way inside. If the cops hadn't kept them out, the fences would have split right in two.

Gus was so worried about the fans they were turning away that you'd have thought I was losing him money. He went around looking like he lost his best friend until about halfway through the season.

Then he came knocking at my door with nothing but smiles.

"Get ready for a big show in Cleveland," he told me.

"What show?" I asked.

"We're going to play a team there and we're going to play in the Cleveland Indians' stadium. We won't have to turn away those crowds when you pitch."

I just sat there. They'd opened up the major league parks to the Negro leagues, opened them up because the parks we played in wouldn't hold the crowds I pulled.

"That means the money's gonna be rolling in fast now," I said.

Gus grinned. Man, did he grin.

Some of the Negro league owners worried that we wouldn't get enough fans into those major league parks to take care of the bigger expenses. Sometimes we didn't, but most of the time we did.

There always was a mob around when I tossed.

And those fans who were seeing us regularly for the first time now were watching top baseball, baseball like only guys like Josh Gibson could play.

There's never been power like Josh's. He wasn't just a slugger either. He was a high-average man, too. If I had to rate top hitters, I'd put him ahead of Ted Williams of Boston, Joe DiMaggio of New York, and Stan Musial of St. Louis, and right in that order.

But don't you think Josh was the only one. There were lots

of others, guys like Chainey White, who played with the Homestead Grays. He was a close fifth after Josh, Williams, DiMaggio, and Musial.

o   o   o   o   o

Josh and I were such big guns on that 1931 club that Gus Greenlee started advertising us instead of the Crawfords. He sent out a bunch of posters saying, "Josh Gibson and Satchel Paige, greatest battery in baseball—Josh Gibson guaranteed to hit two home runs and Satchel Paige guaranteed to strike out the first nine men."

And old Josh hit those two home runs, and I struck out those first nine men, too. But you got to remember a lot of those pitchers Josh played against wouldn't even get the ball near the plate because they were so afraid of him. There were plenty of those home runs he hit by jumping a foot after the ball.

It was great playing with Josh, but I had more fun playing against him, like the time in Puerto Rico I hit two home runs in one game, knocking in three runs and pitching my team to a three to nothing win over Josh's club.

"How was that, buddy?" I called to Josh after the game.

He didn't answer me.

"What's wrong, Josh?" I asked.

He just glared and kept walking.

He wouldn't say a word. I kept after him, though, and finally he wheeled around.

"Anytime a pitcher outhits me I don't talk to him any more. I ain't talking."

He was a hard loser but I knew how he felt. I was a hard loser, too. Still am. I love baseball but only if I win. I don't like to lose at anything—baseball, cards, trapshooting.

○ ○ ○ ○ ○

Even though he advertised both Josh and me, Gus knew I was pulling in the big crowds.

When I was out there, there'd be a park full watching. But when only Josh was there and somebody else was pitching, there'd be only about half or two-thirds as many.

Gus took good care of me because of that. Toward the end of the 1931 season he started giving me top billing and running Josh second. The others weren't getting hardly any billing. That caused a handful of guys to get jealous, I guess. Anyway, you never heard such a row as started up. Even the reporters got in on it.

One day I picked up the morning paper and right smack in the middle of the sports page was a story about the squabble.

"Satchel is a great pitcher, but he can't be used as an example of colored baseball players," it said. "Satchel was picked up by Gus Greenlee when all the other owners were disgusted with him. Gus exploited Satchel throughout the United States and forgot all about such men as Gibson, Matlock, Bell, Oscar Charleston, Perkins, the men who made the Pittsburgh Crawfords."

I laughed at first. Why, the only owners disgusted with me were the ones who couldn't make that big money because I wasn't pitching for them.

There was one thing for sure. Before I started cutting loose around Pittsburgh in 1931, there was no big money for anybody in the Negro leagues. Guys were making only about a hundred twenty-five a month. Then they started getting nice, fat checks—and those checks were paid by the fans.

I got the fans out and I opened up the major league parks to hold them.

That's why they paid me more. Some guys didn't like it,

but most of my teammates wouldn't say Gus Greenlee had forgotten them and was just taking care of me. Fact is, they were probably glad Gus was taking such good care of me so I wouldn't head someplace else.

With me someplace else, the fans would be someplace else.

No one questioned that years later when they looked back on 1931.

I got clippings to prove it—five suitcases full of them. Take that clipping from the September 6, 1945 issue of the Detroit *Free Press.*

"Paige is one of the phenomenons of the crazy-quilted American sporting scene," Lyall Smith wrote. "He is the Negro counterpart of the greatest names in big league baseball. As a drawing card he has been the magnet that has jammed baseball fans—Negro and white—into parks all over the country for the last twenty-one years."

Those other players ate that lean meat because I pulled like that. If it wasn't for me, they'd have been eating side meat, that's what.

o   o   o   o   o

Chapter Ten

MORE AND MORE PITCHING offers came my way before the end of that first season in Pittsburgh.

They wanted me in every ball park, every park there was.

It seemed funny. A couple of years before, a lot of those owners would have died before they'd let a Negro team play on their fields. Now they just smiled and opened up the gates. They opened them because of all the money we paid them in rent.

Those owners didn't pay much attention to how anybody feels. All they paid attention to is their pocketbooks.

Most of them seem about the same today.

If it hadn't been for Gus, I never could have kept all those offers to pitch straight. He was my agent, booking me around when I didn't have to pitch for the Crawfords. He was a sharp—a real one. He knew just how to book so I'd make plenty. He was so sharp that they must have a school for what he could do and he learned real good at that school.

I pitched in about every town you can think of. And I was getting as much as five hundred a game for some of those jobs.

"You can keep this up for ten years and save some dough and you'll be in great shape," Gus told me.

If Gus'd bet on that, he'd have lost twice. I tripled the years he wanted me to pitch and there wasn't much saving.

You can't tell the guy who's got good gravy all over his

shirt front that the gravy bowl is going to be empty some day.

I didn't realize that until I'd just about sopped up all that gravy.

When Gus didn't have me playing somewhere, I did some fishing and shooting. It was like being a kid again—being a kid for a guy who never really had a chance to be one.

I guess I had me ten or fifteen shotguns. It was mighty nice having those big paychecks so I could buy those beauties.

I also took a shine to boxing and I got friendly with the guys at Gus' gym. His gym was my favorite hangout when I was in Pittsburgh.

The trainers there even let me do a little sparring.

My favorite sparring partner was John Henry Lewis. He was one of Gus' boys and was light-heavyweight champion of the world from about 1935 to 1939, when he quit the division to fight heavyweight.

John Henry and I usually went about three rounds. He'd take it pretty easy, but I kept after him all the time.

We'd just come back from our last road trip of the year when I dropped down to the gym to say good-bye before heading out for the winter season.

"How 'bout a couple of rounds to carry me over to next year?" I asked John Henry.

He grinned and I stripped down.

"Wow, look at them shorts," one of them hangers-on yelled.

It didn't bother me. I thought those red and yellow flowered jobs I had on were pretty nice. I was just as careful about buying my shorts as I was my ties and they were just as flashy too.

I danced up and down in the ring, getting a couple of laughs. Then the bell rang.

I raced across the ring and jumped to the side real quick when John Henry came stomping out. Everybody laughed.

I guess I looked sort of like a moving scarecrow.

I flicked out my left a couple or three times, but John Henry just picked it off. We danced around some. He didn't try too hard to hit me.

I popped him on the body and then the bell rang.

"How's that for a pitcher?" I yelled down to the spectators. They just laughed.

At the bell I whipped across the ring fast. John Henry wasn't looking for that. I threw my right. It cracked him on the jaw. I started to grin. That's all I remember.

When I came to, I was flat on my back, looking up at the light. I still can remember how bright it was. My head ached and my jaw ached.

When Gus found out about that, he had a fit.

"You trying to ruin a gold mine?" he yelled at me. "You're a pitcher, not a boxer."

Gus told me never to show up at the gym again and told the guys in the gym I was banned for good.

That ended my fight career.

And I'd always figured when I got too old to pitch I'd take up boxing.

o   o   o   o   o

Pittsburgh and Janet Howard were home base for me during the 1931 season. No matter where I went, I always ended up back in Pittsburgh.

And that was where Janet was.

She was always glad to see me, but she didn't like my being out of town all those times and my going down to the islands in the winters.

She got upset that first time I was going to leave on a long barnstorming trip after we'd started going strong together.

"It's my job, you know that. It's got to be that way."

"I don't like it."

I kept trying to tell her that without those trips there wouldn't be any money to do the things we did and buy the things I was buying for her.

"I don't like being alone," she said again.

I had to head out anyway, but after that first time, every time I got back and started out again we sort of went through the same thing. We kept it up until I finally told her it had to be that way or no way. Then there wasn't any arguing.

I couldn't really blame her. I was always on the run. I ran from Pittsburgh to Memphis, from Los Angeles to New York. I ran from the States to Puerto Rico, from the Dominican Republic to Hawaii, from Venezuela to Canada, from South America to Panama or Mexico—all over.

That fast ball of mine was popping against town druggists who were playing only on Sundays and against major leaguers who were earning a few more bucks after the regular season was over.

It didn't make any difference who it was. My fast ball was popping into the catcher's glove a lot more times than it did into the outfield.

They got to calling me "Black Matty" for Christy Mathewson, the guy who won more than three hundred games with the old New York Giants in the National League.

They also called me "Black Magic."

In three years with the Crawfords alone I won better than a hundred games and only lost a handful, maybe five or six.

It seems like I remember the games I lost better. I guess that's because there weren't as many to remember.

Take that game against a barnstorming team of major leaguers led by Joe Judge. He was a first baseman for Washington and a pretty fair hand. He had lots of help, too. Guys like Charlie Gehringer, Eric McNair, Red Kress, Heinie Manush, Babe Herman, Bill Dickey, Earl Whitehill, and Lefty Grove—all top major leaguers.

We went into the eighth inning with me leading two to one. I could tell the major leaguers were fit to be tied. They didn't like the idea of losing to a hick team. I could hear them yell, "Get a hit—get a hit," every time a guy went to the plate against me.

In the eighth, Heinie Manush singled. It didn't worry me. Then it looked like the inning was over when Babe Herman hit a lazy fly. My outfielder came running in like crazy. That fool kid misjudged it so bad it sailed over his head for a home run.

I lost, three to two.

Afterwards, though, Joe Judge came up to me and said, "You convinced us you're quite a pitcher."

I just nodded my thanks.

I always figured a man shouldn't talk too much. Let the other fellow bring you some news.

News like Joe Judge brought was mighty pleasing.

But he wasn't really telling me anything I didn't know. My fast ball and control is what did it, especially that control. I was born with it and I'll die with it. Rhythm with me comes natural.

o   o   o   o   o

When the 1932 season opened, I was back with the Crawfords. The whole town was glad to see me. I'd walk down the streets in Pittsburgh and everybody tried to talk to me.

I was out on the streets whenever I could, but Janet kept pretty close watch on me. A gal who got her eye on a man got ways of keeping him so busy he never gets out enough for another gal to get him.

But I was a tough one to hold. I didn't like being pinned down and when I got on the road I cut loose. But in

Pittsburgh, Janet was with me most of the time. And she came out to see a lot of the ball games I pitched. Some of the guys on the team knew I liked to put on a good show when she was there.

They used to tell the other players, "If Satchel's girl is in the stands today it will be just too bad for you boys. When she's there, he really bears down and wheels that ball in there looking no bigger than buckshot."

Usually I tossed a pea.

I was riding that high tide of success, not just the wave because of talk like that. I thought it would last forever and acted like it could. Money was something I just passed along.

Even Gus got worried about it.

"You must know something, the way you spend money," my boss told me one day.

"Know something," I answered. "I don't know anything. I've been trying to know something for a hundred years."

I guess I never learned. Whatever Janet wanted or whatever I had a notion to buy, I bought. And there were plenty of parties, too.

About the only good thing I did with all that money was send some home to Mom each month. I always took care of her.

o   o   o   o   o

By 1933 I'd hit my full stride, which is a pretty long step when you figure the size of my legs.

For the Crawfords that season I pitched in forty-one games, winning thirty-one and losing only four. I had sixteen shutouts in those games, so there wasn't too many guys scoring off me. With me going strong like that, people began saying we could hold our own against the New York Yankees or Chicago Cubs or St. Louis Cardinals or New York Giants or Washington Senators or any of the top major league clubs. I figured we could too.

"You write that I'll take a team from the Negro leagues and we'll play the all-stars from the major leagues," I told some baseball writers in Pittsburgh. "We'll play 'em right across the country, anywhere and anytime. You write that, hear, and you write we'll beat 'em so bad they won't ever play anymore."

Everybody made a big thing out of what I said, but no major league all-star club was got up to play any Negro team. Those club owners didn't want the people all over the country to know there were Negro players better than a lot of the white boys.

That might mean they'd have to take us into the majors.

But even the major league players themselves wouldn't say anything about taking us on. I guess I can't blame them. Who wants to play against guys like Josh Gibson, George Perkins, Cool Papa Bell, Judy Johnson, Poindexter Williams, or a couple of dozen others I could name?

I'd given up on that all-star game by the time the regular 1933 season ended. The only plans I had were to take a couple of weeks off and squire Janet around, then get me some work for the rest of the winter. But I never got those two weeks off. Before I even got started on a vacation, I got me an offer to go out to the West Coast and do some throwing there.

I didn't lose a game that season on the Coast. In fact, I went from 1933 to 1937 without hardly losing there. And my ball clubs won something like a hundred and fifty games and lost maybe twenty-five in that same time. A third of those games was against major leaguers, too—pitchers like Dizzy and Paul Dean, and hitters like Rogers Hornsby and Jimmy Foxx and Charlie Gehringer and Pepper Martin. And I struck out those guys.

I don't know just how long I stayed out West that year,

but when I felt the cold weather touching, I jumped for Venezuela. That was because I didn't have a topcoat.

I wired Janet I'd see her when there was some sun in the sky again.

o o o o o

Chapter Eleven

MY FIRST GAME in Venezuela was almost my last. They figured since I'd just got there, I'd be too tired to pitch. So they put me in the outfield to get used to the way things went down there.

I looked around and saw this iron pipe out by the fence. I put that in my mind in case somebody hit the ball that way. I didn't want to trip on it.

A few minutes later the guy up at the plate really belted one and it rolled toward the iron pipe. I went hoofing after it and just as I reached for the ball, that old pipe moved.

I was looking at a boa constrictor.

I lit out of there so fast the papers the next morning said Jesse Owens was in Venezuela posing as Satchel Paige.

I didn't have no more troubles with pipes, I tell you, but snakes always plagued me when I played the outfield on that visit. A couple of games later we were tied going into the last of the ninth with the other club up to bat. They got a man on first and the second batter up struck out. The third batter hit a fly ball and I caught it. Just as I did, this small snake moved right by my feet.

I jumped back, laid down my glove, and picked up a stick and beat the devil out of that snake.

Only trouble was the guy on first tagged up and went all the way around to score the winning run while I was busy. The crowd chased me right out of the park and the manager of the club wouldn't pay me for that game.

The next time I was supposed to pitch, I got him aside. "You're gonna pay me double for this game or I don't throw," I told him.

He knew if I didn't pitch the fans would hang him. He paid up. So I didn't lose anything on that other game.

Toward the end of the season in Venezuela I started waking up every morning with some pain in my stomach. I figured it was because I was hungry and I'd run downstairs and toss some more of that good spiced-up food into me.

That did it.

One morning I woke up and somebody was fighting inside me. I couldn't lay still, the pain was so bad. I thought I was about to cash in. I rolled back and forth, moaning.

"Get me a doctor," I yelled. I yelled it again and again. Finally somebody heard me.

The doctor came and he poked me all over and looked inside me. Then he shook his head.

I'd caught the stomach miseries.

He didn't speak much English and that was about all he could tell me. He gave me some medicine and it seemed to help and then he left.

I laid there looking at the ceiling. My stomach still hurt so I couldn't play that day.

"What if I never can play again?" I suddenly thought.

I got scared. It got worse and worse the more I thought about it. I'd tasted the good living. Was I going to lose it?

I felt lost.

Then the manager of the club came in. He spoke the doctor's language and had talked to him.

"You got nothing to worry about," he told me. "The doc says you can go on doing anything. You'll just have to put up with that stomach. But it shouldn't hurt your pitching any."

Bad stomach and all, I jumped out of that bed and did a jig.

'Course, that was the end of all that spiced food and all that fried food I'd stoked up on. Since then I've lived on boiled chicken and greens, liked boiled broccoli or spinach or green peas. I do eat some broiled steak and baked fish, but not too often.

Usually I try to cook my own food so as not to get the poison in me.

I had so much trouble getting food the rest of the winter down below the border that I almost kissed the ground when I got back to the United States.

I went to some of the best doctors around, but none of them could come up with anything for me. Since then I've been pressed by the miseries and they're real miseries, too. And this gas is always bubbling up inside me. I'm not one of those hypochondriacs, and you better believe it. When I take a pill, there's a pain waiting down there just for it.

Usually it didn't affect my pitching, but sometimes it did get so bad I couldn't even go out to the ball park and if I did I couldn't throw like Ol' Satch.

That stomach of mine acted up the first game I pitched for the Crawfords to start the 1934 season. It was a bad one for it to happen in, too, because half the sports writers in the country was there watching me.

They were the guys who'd been hearing about me, but never saw me.

I got out on the mound and my stomach tried to work its way outside. I pitched and won, all right, but I gave up five hits even though there wasn't a run scored off me. But it was a real strain to get those last two strikeouts to end the game and I only had fourteen strikeouts all told.

Afterwards I ran over to those writers and apologized.

"Sure, I finished out in front," I told them, "but I don't know that I gave you too good a show. My stomach don't feel so hot."

But that stomach didn't slow me down enough to be anybody but the best in the league.

It seems funny but there were some of the fans who even got mad because I was pitching so good. I won't forget at one game I was on the bench between innings and I heard this pretty little gal behind me talking to her boy friend.

"Pitch and pose, pose and pitch, that's all he does," she complained. "It almost makes you mad."

o o o o o

Through the summer of 1934 I hardly had time to see Janet because of all the games I had to throw. I was always on the run.

One day I pitched a no-hitter for the Crawfords against the Homestead Grays. That was on July 4. I remember because somebody kept shooting off firecrackers every time I got another batter out. Those firecrackers still were popping when I ran out of the park, hopped into my car, and drove all night to Chicago. I got there just in time to beat Jim Trent and the Chicago American Giants one to nothing in twelve innings.

And that same day somebody said I was supposed to be pitching in Cleveland. Can you beat that?

Another time in 1934 I drove all night from Pittsburgh for a doubleheader against the Philadelphia Stars in Yankee Stadium. That didn't leave time to get a room so I just pulled the car of mine alongside the curb at 157th Street and fell right asleep with my radio going.

"You Mr. Paige?"

That woke me up. It was the batboy. The manager told him to find me and the kid was going up to everybody outside the park. I got into my uniform just in time to get that first pitch over the plate.

I was a little tired and didn't do as good as usual. We were tied one to one going into the last of the tenth and I got a little careless. The first two guys up bunted and got on base safe.

Those bunts woke me up. I beared down and fired nine straight strikes to the next three batters. In the eleventh we scored one and I closed the door in the last half of the inning.

I'd won me another, two to one. But it'd taken eleven innings after two days without any sleep except that nap in my car.

o   o   o   o   o

I was getting such good crowds at all those games that everybody watching the Negro leagues wanted me to stay for the 1934 East-West all-star game in the Chicago White Sox' park. The Negro leagues'd had their first all-star game in 1933, just like the major leaguers. But I hadn't been in that first game. I was new around the league then and I guess that's why they didn't name me, even if I was one of the top hands around.

But 1934 was something else. Everybody was voting for me and I was named to the East squad.

I can't say for sure how many there were in the stands, about twenty thousand I guess. Through the first five innings nobody cracked. It was nothing to nothing in the last of the sixth, when the first West batter up cracked a two-bagger. I'd been sunning myself out in the bullpen, but my manager wanted me in there now.

I headed for the mound and when I passed first base I ducked over toward the bench to toss my jacket in there. That's when I heard this guy in the stands.

"It's Paige. Good-bye ball game."

He didn't know how right he was.

Three men came up against me and three men died while

that runner stayed glued on second. In the next three innings, I faced only ten batters and none of them could score. We got a run in the seventh and it was good as a dozen.

We won that second all-star game. I got credit for the win, my first all-star win.

o   o   o   o   o

Chapter Twelve

IT WAS JUST ABOUT after I got back from the all-star game that Janet and me sat down to talk about getting married.

"Don't you think it's time we set a date?" she kept asking me.

"No need to rush into these things," I told her.

"Satchel, we can't just keep running around like you were just my guy and nothing else. Now you just make up your mind about that."

"What about all those times when I'm gone? You get mad now when I am. What're you gonna be doin' when we're married up?"

"We'll manage."

"You just remember there'll be times when I'm away for mighty long stretches."

"I'll remember."

"If you don't, we're gonna have troubles."

We decided on the end of October. The regular season'd be over then and it'd be before winter ball started.

I've been trying to forget that date for a long time now. I just don't like to think about that wedding anymore.

We were just like a lot of folks. We made a mistake and it never should have started at all.

We didn't find out different until it was too late. I was a wandering man then, but Janet was against all that wandering. She wanted a man who ran a store or something and came home every night, a guy who'd never leave her and if he had to go somewhere he'd be the kind who'd take her with him.

I wasn't that kind at all back in those days.

I wasn't going to run me no store and give up baseball.

Janet said she wouldn't make any noise about my wandering, but she was just kidding herself. When she told me that, I guess I kidded myself, too, believing her.

And I was kidding myself about something else. I thought I was ready to settle down. I found out different.

When I got those trips away from Pittsburgh, I wanted to go alone. I didn't want a wife tying me down in those towns I visited.

We were in for troubles.

But back in 1934 I didn't know that yet. Neither did Janet.

o   o   o   o   o

Janet got a preacher for October 26. That sounded okay to me.

Even if it hadn't sounded okay, there wasn't much I could do about it. I found out right then that a man sure loses his say-so when it comes time for him to get married.

It got me a little worried, but it was too late to do anything about it. I felt like I would have if I had a three and two count on Josh Gibson and the bases was loaded. Knowing how he could hit, you didn't want to let go of the ball, but you had to.

Gus Greenlee fixed it so we could have the wedding celebration at the grill.

I asked my old buddy, Bojangles Robinson, the tap dancer, to be my best man. We did some running on the town together and I figured he might as well be there to see the end of my running.

We were all set. All we needed was the preacher.

And one of those tranquilizing pills for me, but they weren't invented yet.

They had to go a long way to find a bigger wedding than mine.

We had to lock the door to keep the fans out. There were a bunch of fine-looking girls out there with the fans. They knew Ol' Satchel, too, but they wouldn't be getting to him anymore. At least I didn't think so the day I got married.

I remember sitting there in my brand new suit and wanting to yank my tie loose. Then the preacher was through and everybody was pounding me on the back and congratulating me and pecking Janet.

It went like that for about an hour, until Gus Greenlee quieted everybody down.

"Satchel won't be leaving us, don't worry about that," he yelled. "I got a new contract here for him." Gus and I'd agreed before to announce that I was signing a new two-year contract with the Crawfords right after the wedding. While they still were yelling and cheering, Gus and I sat down and signed the contract. Bojangles stood there and watched and right behind me was Janet. I looked up at her and she was all smiles.

After that we had us a party and the way it was going I just about forgot about getting Janet out of the grill. But I didn't forget altogether. We headed off on our honeymoon while the party still was going.

By the time we left, a lot of those folks there'd even forgotten why they came.

o   o   o   o   o

After that honeymoon, I started noticing a powerful lightness in my hip pocket. Married life was a mighty expensive thing and those paychecks of mine just weren't going as far as they used to.

And Janet and I were both used to eating and living pretty high.

"What do you think we should do?" she asked me.

"I'll go to see Gus. He'll give us more money."

But I guess Gus was mad or something like that. He turned me down flat.

Ol' Satch didn't get mad too many times back in those days, everything going so good. But I perked over right then and there.

Gus wouldn't give in.

All he said was something like "don't forget those games we got coming up next week."

I was so mad I went home and started throwing clothes into a suitcase.

"Where're we going?" Janet asked me.

"I don't know. We're just goin'."

"I don't want to leave."

I didn't pay any attention to that.

"But you haven't got a job and we haven't got any money," she said.

That pulled me up real quick.

But I wasn't stuck for an answer too long. A few days later a guy named Neil Churchill, who ran a car agency in Bismarck, North Dakota, got in touch with me. He sponsored a club in Bismarck and he wanted a top pitcher to finish out the 1934 season.

He came to the peak of the mountain.

I took him up on the offer quick. I wasn't going back to Gus, not after he turned me down on that raise.

Janet didn't want to go, but she gave in. I guess she wasn't ready to fight with me yet, with us just being married.

We left Pittsburgh, even though Gus had that two-year contract for me.

o o o o o

It wasn't until after I signed up with Mr. Churchill that I found out I was going to be playing with some white boys. For the first time since I'd started throwing, I was going to have some of them on my side. It seemed real funny. It looked like they couldn't hold out against me all the way after all.

I'd cracked another little chink in Jim Crow.

But when I got to Bismarck I found out everything wasn't all fine and smooth. I got a pretty cold shoulder. Mr. Churchill wanted me, but those white ballplayers weren't too sure they did. They just didn't know what Ol' Satch could do.

When they saw me pitch, they wanted me more than anybody.

But getting everybody in town to want me was something else. Most of the folks there were pretty nice, but there were some of those other kind, like you run into everywhere.

Because of them, it didn't look like such a hot idea having Janet with me. Those mean folks didn't want any colored people around. They didn't want us living by them.

"Sorry, we just don't have any room," or "we just rented the place."

That's what they told me, but when I'd pass those places later on, they still were empty.

Mr. Churchill came on my side then and started looking for me.

"I found you a place," he told me a couple of days later. "Don't get excited about it, though. It isn't much."

He was right. It was an old railroad freight car that they made into a bunk car for the work gangs. It was parked off on a siding.

But we didn't have anything else and there wasn't money left to go to another town.

We moved in.

"If you didn't go running all over the country we wouldn't have to live in places like this," Janet told me.

"You want to eat, don't you?"

She quieted down then.

But having to live like that ate at me. I got to shooting off my mouth at everyone because of it, trying to get even, I guess. I even got to riding my own ballplayers and those white boys didn't take too good to that.

While we were on the bench for our bats in one game, I really lit into three of them. They were my outfielders and the inning before they'd let so many fly balls drop around them that the club we were playing scored a run. On top of that, they weren't getting any hits.

"If you did that in the league I play in you'd get booted fast," I yelled at them.

They just walked away, but one of them muttered "dirty nigger" or something that sounded like that.

"I'm sure clean enough to be playing with your kind," I said. "Where would you high and mighty boys be without me?"

Nobody said anything and the batter up at the plate went out and I headed back out on the field.

While I was taking my warmup pitches the fans started yelling. I looked around to see what was happening. I didn't have any outfield. They were still in the dugout.

I was sure of one thing. They weren't going to make me give in. I just stood out there on the mound and yelled out, "Let's go. Play ball." My outfielders weren't about to play with me anymore and Mr. Churchill was having a fit.

The fans loved it. They thought it was a stunt.

I'd pulled plenty of stunts like that before, but this time it was serious business.

Mr. Churchill couldn't get the outfielders to go back out,

not after the way I'd talked to them. I wasn't budging either.

Because of the way the fans were carrying on, Mr. Churchill figured he'd better let me pitch without the outfield. He didn't need to worry. I had something to prove and something to drive me.

Three of those boys on the other team came up and three of them struck out.

"That'll show them who needs who," I muttered.

But I knew I couldn't get by striking out the other guys all the time and that meant I needed an outfield. Anyway, when you show how big you are, you can be pretty nice to the little guy.

I thought I was big stuff right then.

I apologized and my outfielders did the same. I guess they felt pretty bad about it, too. On the field, it's a lot easier to be open-minded. If you don't help each other it just hurts the pocketbook.

The next inning I had me an outfield again. I decided from then on out I'd be the quiet guy, like I'd always been before. The other guy can't tell what's going on in your head if you don't tell him, and those that don't know what's going on have the short end of the odds.

After that game, I didn't have any troubles in Bismarck.

o   o   o   o   o

Chapter Thirteen

WHEN BISMARCK CLOSED DOWN for the winter, Janet and me headed for the West Coast. Janet was glad to get out of Bismarck, but she still picked at me about moving around and not going back to Pittsburgh.

Even with her acting that way, I wasn't about to head back East. That winter ball through the rest of 1934 and into 1935 was something I was looking forward to. I was going to play against Dizzy Dean and his all-stars and old Diz was one boy I wanted to run up against.

They were saying Diz and me were about as alike as two tadpoles. We were both fast and slick. But Diz was in the majors and I was bouncing around the peanut circuit. If I was going to get the edge over him, I had to set him down in a little head-to-head baseball.

Janet and me caught up with Diz in Oklahoma City. We were going to play our first game there. Before the game, Diz got on some radio program and the announcer asked him about some of the stories they were telling about how good I was.

"He's got a great fast ball," Diz said, "but no curve."

Diz couldn't have made me madder if he'd wanted to.

That afternoon Diz and I met. I fired my fast ball right by his boys. Then Diz came up to the plate for the first time.

"Hear say you're goin' around tellin' people I ain't got a curve?" I yelled at him. Diz just grinned. "Well, then, you tell me what this is," I said.

I threw him a curve. He swung and missed. It was about the first one I'd ever thrown in a game up to then.

I threw him two more curves and he missed both of them, too, striking out.

"How's that for a guy who ain't got a curve ball?" I asked.

We had some more high old times on that trip, like the first time I pitched against Pepper Martin of St. Louis.

All the boys'd been telling me what a tough out he was.

That got me real curious, so every time a batter came up I asked, "You Mr. Martin?" Then this guy comes up and grins when I asked that and I knew I'd found Mr. Martin.

"They tell me you can hit," I said. He just grinned. "Then hit this." I threw my bee ball.

I only fired that bee ball three times before Mr. Martin struck out and went back to the dugout.

I got plenty of laughs out of that, but one of the biggest laughs I got was one day when I wasn't pitching and was playing right field and Pepper singled out to me. Old Pepper took a big turn at first and bluffed toward second. But I just fired that ball to first base and nabbed him. Was old Pepper sore.

By the time we got to the Coast and finished up playing each other, old Diz and I'd pitched in six games and I'd won four of them.

When we was saying good-bye, Diz came up to me and said, "You're a better pitcher'n I ever hope to be, Satch."

I guess Diz meant it because later on he had a whole bunch more nice things to say in a column he was writing in a Chicago paper.

"A bunch of the fellows get in a barber session the other day and they start to arguefy about the best pitcher they ever see," he wrote. "Some says Lefty Grove and Lefty Gomez and Walter Johnson and old Pete Alexander and Dazzy Vance. And they mention Lonnie Warneke and Van Mungo and Carl Hubbell and Johnny Corriden tells us about

Matty and he sure must of been great and some of the boys even say Old Diz is the best they ever see.

"But I see all them fellows but Matty and Johnson and I know who's the best pitcher I ever see and it's old Satchel Paige, that big lanky colored boy. Say, Old Diz is pretty fast back in 1933 and 1934, and you know my fast ball looks like a change of pace alongside that little pistol bullet old Satchel shoots up to the plate. And I really know something about it because for four, five years I tour around at the end of the season with all-star teams and I see plenty of Old Satch.

"He sure is a pistol. It's too bad those colored boys don't play in the big leagues because they sure got some great ball players. Anyway, that skinny old Satchel Paige with those long arms is my idea of the pitcher with the greatest stuff I ever saw."

You know, when I finished reading that stuff, I knew for sure old Diz was just about one of the smartest fellows I ever looked around for.

o   o   o   o   o

When you play baseball the way I played, you don't have much of a life of your own. You're on the field or you're traveling to get on the field someplace else. About the only times Janet and I ever had to ourselves was after the games.

"I never see you," she told me. "All I see is that old baseball."

"That old baseball is what's paying for that dress of yours."

"I don't care. I wish we had us that store we always used to talk about. Then we could go visiting and out when we wanted to and we wouldn't have to be riding all over the country."

I wasn't even surprised. She'd been picking at me so much

I guess I was kind of expecting her to pop off real loud. She got a lot worse when I quit letting her travel with me.

"I'm no storeman," I told her. "And there ain't any store that'll pay good enough so we can buy what we do."

"All I get to do is sit here in the hotel or sit out at the ball park. I just sit."

"I'm sorry, Babe," I said. I was starting to feel bad. No man wants his new wife to be unhappy. I just put the troubles we were starting to get into out of my mind. "We'll go dancing tonight. How's that?"

Janet smiled up real good after that.

That started us off on a real dancing kick. Now I always was a dancing man, but nothing like what Janet and I did that first year.

Sometimes I think I started leaving her at home after that just to rest up from all that dancing.

But that first trip out to the Coast was baseball and dancing and dancing and baseball.

Now that might sound like it'd be pretty tough on a man to play baseball, go dancing, and then get up to play again. But you got to remember I was only about twenty-eight then and when a man is strong enough to still be pitching in his fifties, why pitching and dancing in his twenties ain't anything.

I even made me some time for singing. I found three other guys on my club who could harmonize right well and they did some riding with Janet and me and we practiced our quarteting.

By the time we got 'way out West we were singing real good. We started in on a new song—"Let Me Call You Sweetheart" or something like that—but we hit some kinks.

I pulled the car over to the side of the road.

"There's a nice shady tree where we can relax," I told the boys. "Let's get over there and smooth this song out."

We just about had it down when we heard this siren roaring like crazy and right after that up came this sheriff's car.

"You Satchel Paige?" the sheriff asked me.

"That's me."

"Well, you got a couple of thousand fans waiting in the ball park for you. They've been waiting more'n an hour."

We'd forgot all about our ball game, we'd been so busy on that song.

'Course everybody heard about that and about how we were such good singers and out in Seattle they decided to put us on radio.

They made all kinds of plans for it and I started getting real excited. The four of us got to the radio station and they took us into the broadcasting booth a couple of minutes before air time.

I took one look at that mike and then I started feeling funny, feeling like I never had before. I tried to say something and I just squeaked. My three buddies were having just as much trouble.

Our musical careers ended right there, before we'd sang a note on the air.

o   o   o   o   o

Doing as good as I did against Diz and other guys like him kept sending my price tag even higher by 1935.

And the way prices were in those years, with that depression thing, I was living mighty high. Janet and I had cars and we had clothes. I threw that money around everywhere and still had some to send home to my Mom.

The sports writers loved it, too—me acting the big shot and living it up like that. They started talking about me like I wasn't even a real guy, like I was something out of a book.

They even began making up stories about me and having me say things I never said.

I didn't mind. The more they made up about me, the more the fans thought I was the only guy they really wanted to see.

Anyway, there were plenty of real things happening that would have made just as good reading so I sort of figured things evened out.

But not everything was real smooth for me. There was some trouble stirring around.

Back in Pittsburgh Gus Greenlee must have really been burned up by all I was doing out West. Anyway, I started hearing he was after me for jumping out on that contract and going to Bismarck. He was trying to get the Negro leagues to ban me.

Janet got pretty worried.

"We won't be able to go back," she said. "We'll just have to keep moving. Maybe we ought to get ahold of Gus and straighten things out."

"We don't need Gus," I said. "There're plenty of teams like Bismarck and like that club we barnstormed with against Dizzy Dean. They all want old Satch."

I didn't do anything about the noises Gus was making and when I heard the Negro leagues'd barred me for the 1935 season I just got ahold of Mr. Churchill and got me a piece of work.

Those Negro league owners were just spiting themselves, I figured. Everywhere I went those days I set attendance records. Some of them still stand.

There was plenty of green floating in and I was getting my share of it, but Gus and his pals weren't. They felt it, too, and don't you let anybody tell you different.

I had all the barnstorming offers I could handle. One semi-pro club even tried to hire me to pitch a spring exhibition game against the Pittsburgh Pirates.

The manager of that club scheduled a game with the Pirates and he figured he'd have a fair chance if he had him a pitcher. Then he heard I was available. He offered me five hundred for the game and I snapped it up.

Pie Traynor, the Pittsburgh manager, heard I was going to be firing against his boys and he swore he'd call off the game unless somebody pitched instead of me.

"Paige is too good for my boys at this stage of the training," he said. "Why, he might go out there and strike out sixteen or seventeen. Can you imagine what that would do to their morale?"

He had himself a point and I missed out on five hundred.

o   o   o   o   o

The summer of 1935 I was around Bismarck so much that I got to know a bunch of Indians up there real well. I think they were Sioux or something.

They took a real liking to me, too, and those Indians watched me good. They even gave me some snake oil. Seems there were all these poisonous snakes around there, like they had in Venezuela, and those Indians were afraid one of them might nip me, maybe one of them rattlesnakes.

When they gave me the oil, they said, "That's hot stuff. Don't use it on anything but snake bites."

"You sure it's hot?" I asked.

"Yes. Too hot for anything but snake bites."

Now that put me to thinking. Up in the North like where I was, it was just too cold for my liking. If that stuff was hot, it might be just what I needed to keep my arm loose.

So I tried it on my arm, even though those Indians said it would burn me up. It didn't. It was just fine and I started using it after every game.

Since then I always keep some of it in a jar and it kept

97

my arm nice and young. It's real fine oil, the best. The formula is a secret. I promised those Indians I wouldn't tell it, but I guess I'll put it in my will so folks will have it when I got no more need for it.

o o o o o

That Bismarck team of mine was doing so good against the teams up our way that we started looking around for some fresh bait.

We found it.

A guy named Ray Dumont was getting up the first national semi-pro tournament. We decided that was for us. We figured it would be a real plum, winning that first tournament.

The games were going to be played in Wichita, Kansas. They called it the National Baseball Congress tournament.

You never saw anything like Wichita. That whole town was baseball-crazy, and lots of them were crazy about Ol' Satch. They'd heard of him, and you better believe it.

Before we got that tournament started, before half those folks'd even seen me, some of them baseball managers was talking about keeping me out.

They wanted me out because I was too good.

A real big fight got going, with the fans wanting me to play and lots of the managers saying I was really a major leaguer and they couldn't match me with any of their white boys. They figured keeping me out would even the games up.

It might even up those games, but it sure would hurt the gate. And semi-pro or not, that gate was a mighty big thing. Anyway, the fans wouldn't have it. So I stayed for the tournament.

Those first few days was just like warming up for me. I won two games and struck out thirteen in the first and seventeen in the second one. Those seventeen strikeouts were a tournament record and it stood for a mighty long time.

Then we came up against a bunch of boys from Duncan, Oklahoma. Everybody was saying they were the club that could beat us.

But I just breezed along against those boys, winning three to one and striking out sixteen, just one less than my record. They got only five hits off me.

Most times that would have taken care of those Oklahomans, but that tournament was one of those double-elimination things. You know how those are. Even when you beat a team they ain't beaten. You got to knock them off again.

They came roaring back to play us again, this time for the championship.

There were ten thousand people out there to see that game—ten thousand for a couple of semi-pro clubs. But it was the championship and Ol' Satch was pitching.

I still had it a little tougher this time.

Not that they were doing too much with my bee ball and my trouble ball. That skinny arm of mine was flapping just as good as ever. But we weren't hitting. Going into the last of the seventh, we were leading only two to one.

Now one run is plenty for me, but I sure breathe easier when I got some to spare. I decided I'd better do something about it.

We got a couple on base in the last of the seventh and I was up.

I singled and drove both runners home. We scored another one to give us five and the Oklahomans got one more off me, but that was just charity. We won the first National Baseball Congress tournament, five to two.

I whiffed fourteen in that last game, the fourth one I'd won in the tournament without a loss. Those strikeouts gave me sixty for the tournament and twenty-five years later that still stood as the record for most strikeouts in a complete tournament.

They named me the most valuable player of the tournament.

And that was back in 1935. Thirteen years after that they were talking about naming me rookie of the year in the American League.

o   o   o   o   o

Chapter Fourteen

I GUESS 1935 was about the same year I hooked up with a Negro league all-star team that was barnstorming after the season was over. The league still hadn't canceled the ban on me, but all the boys were playing with me. That was mighty good news because I needed some work. We'd run out of games up at Bismarck so Neil Churchill and I'd parted.

That all-star club I joined was headed by Candy Jim Taylor. He still hadn't forgotten how I plunked a few of his boys back when he was with the St. Louis Stars, but he was happy to have me on his side. He was extra happy one day when we were playing a white all-star club.

The day before, I'd won my game, so I was riding the bench for this game. Our pitcher was stumbling something bad and in the seventh inning he set me to cussing by walking the bases full without anybody being out. Then that pitcher wound up and threw another ball.

I grabbed Candy Jim's arm. "You wanna get those men out, don't you?"

Jim nodded his head.

"That's all I wanna know."

I grabbed my glove and headed for the mound. Jim yelled at me to come back, but I didn't pay any attention to him. He ran out to the mound after me.

"Satch, you pitched yesterday," he told me. "You can't go again today."

"You wanna win?" I asked.

He just nodded again and handed me the ball.

"Jim, you hold up a finger for every out I get. I'll look over to keep up with things. I don't want to forget how many's out."

I busted loose that shooting star of mine three times and Candy Jim held up one finger. I threw three more and up went two fingers. Three more and Candy Jim made it three fingers and I walked back to the bench with the side struck out.

"One guy out there had me worried," I told him.

"Why's that?" he asked.

"He got a tip of it. But don't you worry. I'll see he don't do it again."

o   o   o   o   o

I pitched down around southern California through the rest of 1935, beating everybody. Then New Year's Eve popped up and I took the night off to celebrate. That celebration was so good I didn't think about any baseball for three days.

Then I got this offer to play up in Oakland, California. I'd never been up in northern California playing before this and I jumped. 'Course, if I wasn't getting paid, I wouldn't have jumped. But in those days, most everybody was paying for Ol' Satch.

When I got to Oakland, I ran into the same old thing I was running into everywhere. No matter how people talk about you, they still won't buy your reputation unless they see you or their friends see you or sports writers they know see you.

I was just going to have to prove what I could do all over again in Oakland, like I was always doing. When you weren't in the major leagues you had to keep proving it because nobody goes around keeping tab of barnstorming and Negro league records like they do the major league's.

The all-star team I was going to play had major leaguers from top to bottom except for one guy. And he was a pretty fair hand—a kid named Joe DiMaggio. He'd already been tapped to go to the New York Yankees for the 1936 season.

That team was one of the best potfuls of major leaguers I'd ever faced. It was known as Dick Bartell's All-Stars and besides Bartell at short and DiMaggio in the outfield they had Ernie Lombardi of Cincinnati catching, Gussie Suhr of Pittsburgh at first, Cookie Lavagetto of Pittsburgh at second, Johnny Vergez of the Philadelphia Phillies at third, Augie Galan of the Chicago Cubs and Bud Hafey of Pittsburgh in the outfield, and Johnny Babich of Brooklyn and Tony Freitas of Cincinnati pitching.

They didn't really worry me, though. I'd stopped Tommy Bridges and Schoolboy Rowe of Detroit and I'd whipped old "Bobo" Newsom of Washington already. Fact was, I'd won about seventeen in a row out there on the Coast, and that was against batters like Pepper Martin of St. Louis and Frank Demaree of the Chicago Cubs and Lou Gehrig of the Yankees and Charlie Gehringer of Detroit and the Waners from Pittsburgh. Gehringer was real tough for me, the toughest of all those stickers. You couldn't fool him. When they hit flat-footed they're the best hitters, and he sure stood there flat-footed. DiMaggio was good, but that Gehringer—he was real good.

The only thing that did worry me was my ball club. It was just a pickup club. I figured they wouldn't be much help at all at the plate and they probably'd be even worse out in the field.

If they didn't really wound me out in the field, I thought I'd be all right.

When I got out to the ball park, there was a good four thousand out there. I had Ebel Brooks from the New York

Yankee Black Sox to catch me, but he had about the only face I knew on our bench.

I didn't have any trouble in the first, but in the second Bud Hafey and Cookie Lavagetto pumped out a couple of doubles back to back and the major leaguers had a run. They got a hit off me in the third, then I closed the book.

In the fourth inning, our lead-off man got a walk and went to third on Ebel Brooks' single. I was up.

With my team of amateurs, I knew it had to be me or Brooks or nothing. And Brooks'd already batted.

I grabbed a bat and hustled up to the plate. I saw that first pitch coming up there. It looked like a watermelon. I swung and pounded out a single. A run scored and we'd tied the game, one to one.

All I had to do was hold them, hold them until we could get another run across.

The fifth, sixth, seventh, and eighth innings rolled by and they hadn't gotten another hit off me. But we couldn't dent the plate. I'd done everything I could. I'd slid into first trying to beat out a hit. I'd busted into second to break up a double play. Why, those two slides were more slides than I'd had for the whole season.

And when I wasn't batting or running, I was down at first trying to coach those plumbers playing with me on base.

Then it was the top of the ninth.

The first two guys up for us went down real easy.

Then old Ebel Brooks went walking up there, the only other boy on my club who could play even with the major leaguers. Brooks didn't let me down. He bombed one to the clubhouse and ended up on third with a triple.

I was up.

You could hear that crowd now. You could feel it. They knew if Ol' Satch got a run in it would be all over.

Everybody was fidgeting, everybody but me. There was only one thing I had to do. I just had to hit that ball.

In it came and I swung. It went off my bat like a shot, hugging the ground. Dick Bartell got over to it somehow and reached for the ball.

Then he fumbled it. But he jumped quick, grabbed it again and fired for first. Gus Suhr speared the ball but I knew I'd beaten the throw and Brooks'd scored. Then I heard the umpire yell:

"You're out."

I couldn't believe it.

I argued and argued, but you know how that came out. Mr. Blue won. I was out and the run didn't count, that was all there was to it. We were out in that inning.

In the last of the ninth, I still felt shaky and the major leaguers got a couple on base with one out. But I wasn't going to let that game get away from me. I reached way back and started firing my trouble ball. I struck out Hafey and Johnny Vergez.

If my run had counted, I'd have won in nine innings, two to one. But instead of winning I was going to have to pitch the tenth inning, all because of some dumb umpire who didn't know safe from out.

I was so mad my stomach started crying and I had to belch to ease the miseries. I'd pitched good enough to win in nine. I'd given up only those three hits and had me about a dozen strikeouts. Why, my bunch of sandlotters had six hits in those nine innings. But it wasn't enough.

We went down quick in the top of the tenth. I went out to the mound. I still was mad. And I felt the cold now. It was getting darker. I just had to hang on, just a little longer.

Somewhere I found that fast ball of mine again and got Ernie Lombardi and Augie Galan out of there. One more out, I thought. Dick Bartell was up.

He singled. That was the first hit off me since the third inning.

I still wasn't worried. Joe DiMaggio was up. Joe hadn't

caused me any trouble up to then. I'd hit him with a pitch in the third, but outside of that he'd grounded out to short, grounded out to second, and flied to center.

I cut loose with my fast ball and it was a strike, but Bartell stole second, just beating Brooks' throw down there.

I fired my bee ball again and it was strike two, but in that dusk it got away from Brooks and Bartell raced down to third.

But there were two strikes on DiMaggio.

I fired again and DiMaggio swung. It was a hopper to my left and I just couldn't get over to it. I did flick it and it rolled straight for my second baseman.

It looked like a sure out and the end of the inning.

Then I saw my second baseman. He stood there, looking half frozen. It seemed like an hour before that sandlotter moved, but finally he did. He grabbed the ball and fired to first, but DiMaggio beat the throw for an infield hit.

Bartell cut across the plate with the winning run.

I just stood there on the mound awhile. Finally I moved off the mound and walked by those major leaguers. DiMaggio was there grinning to beat all. He was talking to his teammates. I didn't hear all he said, but I did hear him say something like, "Now I know I can make it with the Yankees. I finally got a hit off Ol' Satch."

○ ○ ○ ○ ○

I guess I got more notice for losing that game than I did winning most of my other games.

In the Oakland *Journal*, Eddie Murphy wrote, "The greatest pitching attraction in the world is being passed up by scouts, club owners and managers only because the doors of organized baseball are closed to him. It is surprising a move is not planned to lift the bars and allow this fellow and other diamond greats of his race to prove their supremacy just as they would be allowed to do in boxing and many other sports.

"The writer refers to LeRoy 'Satchel' Paige. He lost yesterday by a two to one score in a ten-inning duel with Tony Freitas and Johnny Babich, two of the best young hurlers in the majors. But for the fact he was backed by only an ordinary bushball Negro club, he probably would have won with ease.

"After nearly a score of years covering Coast League games, it was the greatest two-man baseball team this reporter has seen as Paige and his battery mate, Ebel Brooks from the New York Yankee Black Sox, were the whole ball club."

Some other guy wrote, "Never was it more clearly demonstrated how important pitching is to a ball club. That is all the colored team had, yet the big leaguers were lucky to win by a two to one score in ten innings."

They still were talking about the game a few days later. And I'll be darned if old Connie Mack, boss of the old Philadelphia Athletics didn't tell somebody or other he'd give a hundred thousand for me if they'd let him use me.

All I had to be was white. . . .

o   o   o   o   o

Chapter Fifteen

AFTER THAT GAME, the talk about getting me in the major leagues really flew.

Finally, some of those sports writers came around and said the major league owners were even thinking of giving some of us tryouts and maybe letting us in the majors.

"I don't believe them owners," I told those writers. "If they wanted to try out colored ballplayers they'd take 'em to spring trainin' camps, same as the white boys."

"They're still saying they'll give you a chance to try out, though, Satch," a reporter said.

"This business of trying us out at the tail end of the season makes me laugh," I said. "What player who got a go of it in the Negro leagues can afford to give up his salary for a couple of weeks to get a trial with a major league team? I know I'm not about to do nothin' like that. It'd cost me a couple thousand dollars to report for a big league trial at the tag end of the season. Man, I need that money.

"No, sir. I'm not giving up any of that money just to make some owner look goodhearted. Anyway, I don't guess I'm a prospect anyway; not with me going on thirty. . . ."

The writers busted out laughing. Even then everybody was saying I was a hundred years more than I was. I guess when you're long and thin and sit quiet, they think you're ready for that embalming man.

"That's right, boys, I'm going on thirty and that probably makes me too old. Anyway, I'm probably drawin' more money right now than any other pitcher in baseball. What owner is goin' to pay that kind of money right now at my age. Even if I did jump, I don't think those white boys from the South'd stand it. They got ahold of somethin' bitter when they were little and they ain't been able to relax and smile at all the world since then."

That got plenty of play all over the newspapers.

But, like all that big talk before, it quieted down real quick. Those owners'd said some highearted things and then just shut up. They always like to talk nice but some of the worst medicine I ever swallowed came in some sweet-tasting candy.

o o o o o

While that major league talk still was going around, the Negro league owners decided to be nice to me again.

They wanted those fans I could pull.

At least that's what made Gus Greenlee get ahold of me, I figured.

"We've lifted the ban on you," he told me. "When can you rejoin the team?"

"I'll have to do some thinkin' on that," I told him.

I didn't have to do as much thinking as I thought. Janet jumped me quick about it when I told her.

"We'll have a place again," she told me.

"But the money. . . ."

"I don't care about that money. I want to settle someplace. I don't want all this traveling. You either go there or we're through, Satchel."

I'd seen that coming, I guess, ever since the first trip. Now it was sitting right in my lap. I should have just called it quits with Janet then, but I was still trying to hang on.

"We'll go," I told her. I figured that'd make her happy. I just didn't know.

I got ahold of Gus and told him I was coming back.

By then the idea of being in the Negro leagues again was beginning to look better to me. A man just likes to play in something that's organized and all set out for him. It keeps him from worrying about what's going to happen.

When I started acting happy about going back with Gus, Janet and me started hitting it off better than we had for months.

We even figured we'd take a few weeks off before joining up with the Crawfords.

But a trip took money, so I looked around for some quick jobs. I didn't get any of those, but I got a fat offer to pitch down in Puerto Rico.

It was a real fat one.

I forgot all about that trip with Janet.

"I got to leave you in a couple of days," I told her.

"You're what?" she yelled. "We're going on a trip."

"We'll just have to forget that trip."

"What do you mean, forget it?"

"I'm goin' down to Puerto Rico."

"Then I'll go with you."

"They ain't letting us take wives."

Janet didn't like it. You better believe it. But I went anyway.

o   o   o   o   o

When I got back to the Crawfords for the 1936 season, they didn't throw confetti out of a window and have a parade for me, but they were happy to see me, all right.

As happy as the fans and ballplayers were to see me, that was just about how unhappy Janet seemed.

"You finally got back," she said. "Did you have a good time without me?"

It was all over, that feeling we once had. She'd boiled all

winter at my being gone and when I got back she couldn't wait to start nibbling at me about it. One thing led to another and soon we were just waiting to fall apart.

"I told you when you married me there'd be times when I'd be gone a lot," I kept telling her.

But all she could think of was, "You didn't have to go off and leave me."

You can't convince a woman that argues like that. Fact is, you can't convince a woman about hardly anything. Once they put their minds on it, that's where their minds stay.

After that I didn't even try to smooth things out whenever the Crawfords went on the road. I just went. I was glad to get away.

And the Crawfords really traveled. With me around, every town in the country wanted to see them. When we weren't playing a league team, we were playing some town club or barnstorming club here and there.

And I was beating them all.

Even when you're beating everybody, there're still those shufflers who think they can knock that ball of yours all over the place. I ran into one of them in Dayton, Ohio. We were there playing a club called the Dayton Ducks or something like that.

This boy was the number four hitter on the Ducks and before the game he was standing with a whole bunch of people around him and just couldn't keep from flapping his mouth with that kind of audience.

"That tall, skinny guy ain't got enough meat to blow a fast ball by me," he was saying. "You just watch it. I'll send it clear out of the country."

Bigmouth came up against me in the second inning.

"Pump it in here, buddy, and watch it go," he yelled at me, still playing the big man.

I just laughed and called down to Josh Gibson, "What one'll you have now, Baby?"

"Fast ball, low and on the outside corner," Josh called back.

That's just where I put it, but bigmouth still swung and missed for strike one.

"What'll you have now?" I yelled at Josh.

"Fast ball over the middle."

I threw. Bigmouth had two strikes on him.

"What'll you have now, Josh?" I yelled again.

"Fast ball in the same place."

I kicked back, fired, and had me a strikeout.

The fans really rode old bigmouth and he wasn't doing any talking the rest of the game.

He wasn't doing any hitting, either.

o o o o o

Maybe it was because Janet and I were drifting apart that I got to thinking more and more of my Mom and the family back in Mobile. Not that I'd forgotten my Mom. It's just that when you're pitching everyday you ain't got time to think of much of anything.

I had been sending her money, to keep the food on the table, but I hadn't been home in a long time.

I decided to head home. I had a pocketful of money and a few days off between games.

That greeting they gave me was mighty strong stuff.

I guess everybody that kind of makes a name for themselves always thinks about how the folks back home are talking about him, about what a big man he is. And then when he does get back home and they all act like he's sort of a king, it just makes his head swell until it about pops.

Mom took that swelling down, quick.

"You been playin' any on Sundays?" she yelled at me as soon as I got in the house. It was the same old shotgun house she'd almost always lived in.

Chapter Sixteen

HOME ISN'T A PLACE you stay around too long when you're a barnstormer. I was back on the road, out-traveling any salesman, in no time.

Barnstorming against major leaguers brought me and a few of the other boys some big money. But the fellows who played only regular-season ball in the Negro leagues didn't have it so good.

The Negro league teams played to crowds that was nearly always colored and there wasn't enough of those fans so you could make real big money, like the major leagues.

That meant the Negro league teams couldn't pay most of the players real high.

And that's why when somebody waved a fat paycheck under the players' noses, a lot of them jumped.

In 1937, most of those checks was being waved by teams down in the islands and there was a whole flock of boys jumping Negro league contracts and heading down that way.

I wasn't the only player around who did some fast stepping in those days, and you better believe it.

At first, I didn't pay much attention to those boys from Haiti and the Dominican Republic. They had money, but not enough for Ol' Satch. I was one guy the Negro league teams would pay for, no matter what. I just mosied down to New Orleans and joined the Crawfords for spring training.

Everywhere we went down there we ran into these guys

from Haiti, scouting us and the Homestead Grays and the other clubs, looking for ballplayers.

"Haiti pirates, that's what they are," Gus Greenlee kept muttering.

And I guess he was right.

At one game they were sitting in a box watching us and Gus finally busted a gasket.

He stormed down to the courthouse and swore out a warrant and had them jailed for "conspiracy."

When the police was taking them away, Oscar Charleston, who managed the Crawfords for Gus, yelled, "I'd knock the insides out of you thieves if you weren't so little."

They took those two scouts down to a magistrate and one of them turned out to be nothing but a millionaire down in the Dominican Republic. The other guy was a fellow working in the Dominican consulate in New York.

The whole deal hurt Gus more than it did them. They were set free, but at the hearing they told how they'd just hired one of our speed ball pitchers, Ernest Carter, for eight weeks at seven hundred seventy-five. When some of the other players heard that, they went looking for those boys from the Dominican Republic.

It burned Gus up so he went to the State Department in Washington to see if something couldn't be done to stop the raids. They couldn't do anything.

I didn't pay a whole lot of attention to it. Money like they were giving Carter was just jingling stuff. It didn't interest me.

Then one afternoon this fellow comes up to me.

"I'm Dr. José Enrique Aybar," he rattled off. "I direct the baseball team in Ciudad Trujillo."

I'd heard of sick clubs and ballplayers that looked pretty sick, but I never knew there was one so sick it needed a doctor to manage it.

"What can I do for you, Doc?" I asked.

"We are interested in your pitching. President Trujillo has instructed me to obtain the best pitcher possible for his team and our scouts recommend you."

"I'm glad your scouts like me, but I figure I'll just stay with Gus Greenlee."

"We are very interested in winning," he told me. "We will give you thirty thousand American dollars for you and eight teammates and you may take what you feel is your share and divide the rest."

Now Ol' Satch was making good money but thirty thousand was more than three thousand apiece, even if I didn't skim some off for managing the whole thing. Even three thousand was mighty tempting when you figured guys like Carter were getting seven seventy-five for the eight weeks down there.

"Thirty thousand?" I asked.

"Yes. Thirty thousand."

"Do I get to see the money?" I asked then. I'd been roped in on too many of those big deals and then ended up without a penny and this kind of smelled like one of them. I wasn't going to jump a good job like I had with the Crawfords, not without some hard money in my pocket.

"I will be back tomorrow," he told me.

The next day he was back and handed me a bankbook. He'd put thirty thousand in that bank for me. I grabbed George Perkins, who'd become my catcher with the Crawfords after Josh Gibson went over to the Homestead Grays, and talked him into going down. It didn't take much talking, not at the price we were being paid.

We rounded up seven more players real quick and jumped for Ciudad Trujillo.

Now some of the papers said I paid back all Gus'd done for me by busting up his club, but like I said I wasn't the only one heading down to the islands like that.

Anyway, I didn't have any real contract with Gus then

and I had to look out for number one. Gus was feeling a money pinch, too, and the checks from him weren't what they used to be.

There were plenty of other guys down there with me, too, guys like Josh Gibson, Cool Papa Bell, Harry Williams, Schoolboy Griffin, Sam Bankhead, and Leroy Matlock.

Even with those guys jumping off, the Negro leagues didn't come close to busting up. That bust-up came when the major leagues started raiding Negro clubs and just giving them a few pennies or nothing and killing off attendance. If the major leagues'd turned the Negro leagues into a good minor league, those owners who squawked at me never would have gone out of business.

o   o   o   o   o

We got a hero's welcome for sure when we got to the island. They flew us in and that was some deal back in 1937 for a bunch of ballplayers to fly in for some games.

Those major league owners always was about twenty-five years too late on everything.

When I got there I found out Dr. Aybar wasn't just a ball club manager. He was dean of the University of Santo Domingo and deputy of the national congress.

The first thing he did was call a press conference.

Seems like some of those hungry peasants was crying because all that money was being spent on ballplayers and Dr. Aybar wanted to straighten things out.

"That amount," Dr. Ayber said, "was subscribed voluntarily by enthusiastic baseball fans of this district. Neither the president of the republic, Dr. Rafael Trujillo, nor the government had to intervene in the importation of the players."

There sure were a lot of doctors down there.

"Baseball in Trujillo City is not commercial," Dr. Aybar

went on, and you could see some of those reporters grin. "Money makes no difference. Baseball is spiritual in every aspect, as indulged in by Latin races.

"The importation of colored American players resulted from a desire on the part of the provinces to win. The Americans accepted the terms offered because the pay was much higher than that they were accustomed to receive in the Negro National League.

"They did not come by force, nor because they had been ousted from the league in the States. They came voluntarily. We would have imported white American players if the salaries of the white players had not been such that it was impossible for us to better them.

"This has been the biggest year in baseball ever seen here, because of peace, unity and goodwill brought to the republic by President Trujillo; which accounts for the fact that the Dominican people do not wish him to leave office."

Dr. Aybar didn't quit then. I could see he was one of those fellows who never stops once he starts talking.

"American baseball magnates, however, need not fear a repetition of what happened this year. If baseball is played here next year, it will be during the winter and spring months."

Then Dr. Aybar introduced us to the reporters and took all of us to one of the presidential plantations for a picnic.

One of the reporters got off with me when we were out there at the plantation.

"Trujillo runs the whole show down here," he told me, "and he wants a team so good it will win the championship. That'd be a real feather in his cap. You see, his chief rival is a strong man down in one of the provinces and that boy got a ball club, too. Trujillo won't like it if his club goes around losing to that other club," he warned.

That reporter scared me good. And I could see that

Trujillo, with those soldiers around him all the time, sure was a powerful man.

I started wishing I was home when all those soldiers started following us around everywhere we went and even stood out in front of our rooms at night.

We played around some down there and then we came up to this big game for the championship with the Estrellas de Oriente team. You'd have thought war was declared. We were guarded like we had the secret combination to Fort Knox.

Some of them guys the president had watching us would have made those bums back in the States look like school-teachers. They was that tough-looking. They all had guns and long knives stuck in their belts.

When we got to the park for the championship game, our manager got us all together before we went out on the field.

"You better win," he said.

"What'a you mean, we better win?" I asked.

"I mean just that. Take my advice and win."

But by the seventh inning we were a run behind and you could see Trujillo lining up his army. They began to look like a firing squad.

In the last of the seventh we scored two runs and went ahead, six to five.

You never saw Ol' Satch throw harder after that. I shut them out the last two innings and we'd won.

I hustled back to our hotel and the next morning we blowed out of there in a hurry.

We never did see Trujillo again. I ain't sorry.

o   o   o   o   o

Chapter Seventeen

WHEN I GOT BACK in the States, it was like I'd never left. The Negro league owners who'd been saying I was killing them and busting up their clubs smiled real pretty at me.

They wanted me. They wanted me so bad they developed the shortest memories you ever saw anywhere around about me jumping the Crawfords. Through that summer there were all the jobs I wanted and more, so many I couldn't get anywhere close to taking care of them.

And guys'd still call me up and offer me a piece of work.

"Sure," I'd tell them. "Just send me travelin' money."

They'd say they would and then advertise all over that I was pitching with their club. But they never sent the money so I never showed up. That happened all the time. That's how most of those stories about my jumping contracts got started.

'Course there were some games where maybe they sent me money or I said I'd go anyway and then didn't. But when you're on top and you got so many jobs going, you just might forget one or two.

Ball games wasn't all there was.

Being a number one pitcher made for a lot of socializing. But I was a solo act. Janet and me didn't go out and around together too much. We just kept falling apart, like we never knew each other.

Maybe we didn't.

Even without Janet, it was high living. Living like that is

when you forget how you grew up. You think you always were high society, always knew all the actors and singers and boxers and politicians. You don't remember you once never knew anybody and nobody knew you.

You change, nobody else does. And when you change, what you do and who you know changes. Before you know it you get sort of uptown. I know.

I remember once I was at this club and a waiter comes up.

"Mr. Paige, there are some old friends of yours from Mobile out in the lobby," he told me. "They'd like to see you."

"Who are they?" I asked.

The waiter gave me a couple of names I remembered but not real good.

"Tell them I left already and you didn't know it," I told the waiter.

Then I tried ducking out the back way, but one of those guys from Mobile'd come on inside.

"Hey, Satchel," he yelled and came hustling over to me. "Thought they said you weren't here."

"Oh, I've been here."

"Maybe you're too busy to see some of the old boys from home?" He sounded like someone'd hurt him.

"No, not Ol' Satch. Anytime you want me I'll be around. But right now I got some business downtown. You get ahold of me later, hear?"

I ducked out then and never thought anymore about it.

It took me a lot of years before I found out it was a mighty little man who did things that way.

o   o   o   o   o

I guess it was because I only thought of old number one in those days that I jumped to Mexico before the season was over. I didn't have anything to hold me back, not even

Janet anymore. So when a guy down there put a few bucks in my pocket—a few more than Gus Greenlee'd give me—I walked down to Mexico.

That burned Gus up—for the last time, I guess. He traded off my contract to the Newark Eagles. I never reported to them.

A few years later I couldn't remember for sure whether Newark got my contract or didn't. Some say they never had it. But I always heard different, so I guess Gus did sell me off.

Only he was selling a piece of paper and not the real stuff.

Whatever happened, I didn't pay much attention to it down in Mexico. I was running up and down that country.

And everywhere I went in Mexico I ran into Negro league players.

With all those guys I knew, it was real friendly down in Mexico, but I wasn't enjoying it like I should have. I had troubles getting the kinds of food I needed and my stomach miseries started up, smacking one another and burning up my insides.

It kept spreading and pretty soon every part of me was hurting, even my arm. But I figured it'd go away. Why, I'd never had a sore arm or anything like it, not in twelve years.

That was because I always took care of my weight and back muscles. Those muscles gave me balance. That kept my arm from getting strained, ever.

Keep your back strong and your stomach down and you'll have balance—and balance is what you need out there on the hill. They say too much exercise will get you. Back in those days I never did see where it'd get you. I saw where it made you, that's all. I kept moving from the minute I stepped on a ball field. I never did sit until I came back after the first inning. I started fielding bunts, then I'd hit to the infield, chase flies, or work out at third. But I never threw until every muscle, every single one, was all loosed up.

People told me to sit, not to work so hard. They said I'd break a finger.

I just told them my hands'd take care of themselves. With my hands, I could have played the infield if I didn't pitch.

When I got all loosed up, I got me a catcher and warmed up, but I never threw hard until I was sure every little muscle was fine and free. I never did throw a ball in all those years since 1926 until everything was loose and ready. I never threw them cold. No day. I took a bath, hot as I could stand it, when I got up in the morning and then I took one hotter than that after a game, so hot nobody else could stand it. Near boiling, that's how hot I took it. And it kept my arm from ever getting sore, and it kept my arm alive.

That and no fat kept all the strain off. And with me getting away from fat ain't any chore. All I had to do was keep moving. Keep moving and fat never'll settle anywhere.

Because of all that, I figured it'd go on forever and I'd never have a sore arm.

That's why I just kept throwing down there in Mexico after my arm started hurting.

I told my manager about my arm.

"It kind of burns in there and feels like somebody pinched off the blood," I told him.

"Take a few days off," he said.

"They expects me to pitch and I can't let those fans down. Anyway I'm gettin' paid by the game so I guess I'll just keep throwin'. It'll go away. I never had a twinge in my arm before. And I ain't gonna miss none of those paychecks just 'cause it's complainin' a little now."

Being greedy like that just about ended my career and just about cost me a couple or three thousand times the money I was making from those few games in Mexico.

I pitched four or five games in a row, trying to work that feeling out, but it got worse instead of better.

"I'll shake it," I kept telling my manager. "You can tell

my fast ball's just as quick as always. It just hurts some when I throw it."

"It sure doesn't look like you lost anything," he said. "But take this afternoon off. Maybe you just need a little rest."

I thought on it a minute, then decided I'd grab me a little rest. I went to my hotel and had a little of that tequila.

"That ought to burn what I got in my right arm out," I muttered. Man, but that stuff put a kick in you.

I headed for bed early that night, thinking the sleep might help, too. My arm didn't seem to be as sore as it had been, but it seemed a little stiffer. After the numb way it'd been feeling, some stiffness instead of that old soreness was mighty welcome.

I figured it was a sign of recovering.

The sun was way up when I woke up in the morning. It was going to be a good day, I thought, and sat up real quick. My stomach got sick with the pain that shot up my right arm.

Sweat popped out all over me. The pain wouldn't quit. I tried lifting my arm. I couldn't. I just sat there, sweating, hurting enough to want to cry, getting sicker in the stomach and getting scared—real scared.

My arm. I couldn't lift it.

o　o　o　o　o

The pain stayed so long it finally numbed my arm. Have you ever seen an old man, a real old one, one who hurts so he can hardly move and what he can move is so stiff it don't work very good? That was me. I sweated some more and bit into my lip, but I finally got my shirt on. I didn't even think of trying a coat.

I couldn't even think. Nothing like that ever'd happened to me before. I didn't know what to do so I did the only thing I really knew how to do. I went out to the ball park.

125

I didn't go to the locker room. I went straight out to the field. My club was already there. I walked over to the manager.

"Gimme a ball," I said.

"Where's your uniform?"

"Never mind that, just gimme a ball."

He picked one out of the ball bag and handed it to me.

"Hey," I yelled to one of the fielders. I cocked my arm back, but I couldn't even get it up to my shoulder. It was less than sidearm. It hurt like nothing'd ever hurt before, not even my stomach. I threw.

All I could see was white. Everything in me hurt. Then I could see clear again. The ball was only a few feet from me. My manager came running over.

"What's wrong, Satch? What's wrong? That ball went nowhere."

"It's my arm . . ."

He grabbed my arm and tried moving it around.

"Don't," I yelled. The pain'd cut clear through my head.

Again and again I tried to throw the ball. It was like I was a shot-putter. The ball'd bloop up a little and then drop, not going anywhere.

They took me back to my hotel and got about every doctor they had in Mexico City to look at me. They couldn't find anything and my arm ached and ached.

"It'll go away in a few days," I told my manager. And I kept telling myself that. But my arm just kept burning.

"Maybe you ought to go back to the States and get it looked at," my manager finally said. "You ain't doing any good here and you can't make any money not pitching."

That was the way with barnstormers. Once you couldn't make them any money, they didn't care about you. If you got hurt, there wasn't any pay because you weren't pitching.

I packed up that night and the next day headed back for

the States. I went to every doctor I'd heard of in most every city I'd been in.

They couldn't find anything.

Since they couldn't find anything, I figured that meant I'd be pitching again real soon. I was sure all I needed was a touch of rest.

But my arm didn't quit hurting. Finally I heard about this specialist. I was so numb then I don't even remember what town I went to see him in, but I remember him.

Oh, yes. I remember him. Real good. I remember him because after he was done poking me, and lifting my arm, and checking my back, he studied and thought for what seemed like an hour.

Then he turned and looked long at me.

"Satchel, I don't think you'll ever pitch again."

o   o   o   o   o

Chapter Eighteen

WHEN YOU BEEN AT THE TOP and hit the bottom, it's a mighty long fall. I know.

For a week I just sat in my hotel room, looking and sitting, then walking a little and then sitting and looking again. It'd been a long time since I'd thought about having nothing, about how it was to grow up in Mobile. Ten years can make for a lot of forgetting. Now I started remembering. I didn't want to go back, but baseball was the only thing that'd keep me away.

And when the arm won't come around, there ain't a lot you can do in baseball.

I thought maybe I could manage a ball club. I thought I could coach. But nobody was needing any managers. Nobody needed coaches all of a sudden.

Negro baseball was closing on me tight.

They wouldn't even take me for my name.

You'd figure they'd want my name. That'd still draw some fans. But they didn't want it.

They all seemed to be saying something like, "Well, Satch, you treated me pretty rough back in '35," or, "If you'd joined my club like you were supposed to in '36, if you'd taken care of me then, maybe I could take care of you now. But things are pretty rough right now. You know how it is?"

I just sat then. I didn't want to go nowhere. I didn't want to see nobody. I could see the end. Ten years of gravy and then nothing but an aching arm and aching stomach. Oh, I had my car and shotguns and fishing gear and clothes.

I had those, all right, and they are all mighty fine. But you got to make money to keep them and when you ain't making money and when you ain't saved any money, they go fast.

Mr. Pawnshop must have thought I was a burglar the way I kept coming back to see him with another shotgun or another suit.

I had to. A man got a way of getting used to eating and eating takes money.

As skinny as I was, you'd think I wouldn't need much food, and I guess I didn't before. But when a man got food he doesn't really want it. When he ain't got it and got no way to buy it, then all of a sudden he gets a big hunger.

By the time the winter meeting of the Negro leagues came around, I saw nothing ahead for me. My arm seemed dead for sure.

There wasn't anything working in my corner and everybody seemed to be stepping on me. Nobody knew me anymore.

I thought of going back to Janet then, but that wasn't any good. I knew if I couldn't keep her when I was a big man, I sure wasn't going to be able to keep her when I was a broken bum just wandering around looking for a piece of bread.

Anyway, my pride wouldn't let me crawl back to her.

I was beat. I knew it. There was no place to turn. I was a big man who was just falling into that old land where nobody knows you.

What I didn't know was right while I was sinking down lower than a man can sink, a couple of guys from Kansas City were fixing to grab me by the neck and hoist me up high.

About halfway through the winter meeting, I got a call.

"This is Satch," I said when I picked up the phone.

"Satch, this is J. L. Wilkinson. I own the Kansas City Monarchs. Remember me?"

I remembered good. I'd put in some time for Mr. Wilkinson after my Bismarck club'd cut him up a couple of times.

"Yes, sir, Mr. Wilkinson," I said.

"Satchel, Tom Baird, my partner, and I just got your contract from Newark. When can you report in Kansas City?"

I couldn't believe what I heard, but that phone wasn't lying.

"I can be there tomorrow," I said.

"Make it next week and meet me there."

When that phone clicked I didn't even hear it. I just sat there holding that receiver.

Finally I put it down.

I'd been dead. Now I was alive again. I didn't have an arm, but I didn't even think of that.

I had me a piece of work.

o   o   o   o   o

I didn't even bother telling Janet where I was going. Everything was over as far as I was concerned. I just packed and left.

When I got to Kansas City, I didn't give it even a half look when I drove through. I'd been around so much I didn't look at any place. They were all the same.

I got me a hotel that night, and the next day I went around to see Mr. Wilkinson and Mr. Baird.

They were mighty pleasant gentlemen. Later on, Mr. Wilkinson and me sat down to do some business talking.

"My arm still won't do any throwin'," I told him after we'd talked around a while.

"That's what we heard," Mr. Wilkinson said. "But maybe you can play some first base."

"That's fine with me. When do I join the Monarchs?"

Mr. Wilkinson was pretty quiet for a minute.

"You're not going to play with the Monarchs," Mr. Wilkinson said. "We've got a Monarch traveling team, a barnstorming team. We planned to send you up North on a tour with them."

"You don't want me with the Monarchs?"

"You couldn't pitch with that arm of yours," Mr. Wilkinson said, "and you haven't played first enough to hold it down in the Negro leagues."

That good feeling I'd had just sort of floated away. I'd been down and somehow I'd figured I'd jumped all the way back up. But I hadn't.

"How about it, Satch?" Mr. Wilkinson asked me.

"I guess that's how it will be," I said. "But if I ain't good enough for the Monarchs, why're you givin' me this job?"

"We think you're still big enough to pull the fans."

"My name ain't gonna lure that many fans."

Mr. Wilkinson was quiet for a minute.

"It'll lure enough," he finally said. "Anyway, I thought you needed a hand."

That's how Mr. Wilkinson was. I found that out later.

If you were down and needed a hand, he'd give you one. He was all the time hiring ballplayers that'd been great and were on their way downhill.

"They can still do some good," he used to say. "And they've done a lot for the Negro leagues and made us all some money so I'm just trying to pay them back a little."

And even if you weren't going down, just having a bad time, Mr. Wilkinson was a mighty patient man. He'd give you plenty of time to come back.

That's what he was doing for me back that day when he offered me a job with the traveling squad.

That's more than anybody else was doing.

o   o   o   o   o

It was traveling like I'd always traveled, only there was something different about it with the Monarch traveling team. I was still pulling some fans, but to the boys on my team I was just the old man without an arm anymore.

"Boy, I can remember when you . . ."

That's how they talked to me, like I was dead and buried.

Nobody said anything like, "You was great out there today." It always was, "I can remember . . ."

About the only one that didn't sound that way was Knut Joseph, the traveling club's manager and a real old-timer. We talked about my arm and my playing and what we could do.

"I guess I'll just have to hang on long as I can," I told him. "My name ain't gonna keep pullin' those fans if I can't fire my trouble ball anymore. Maybe if my first basing comes around, I can stick."

Knut'd just shake his head. "Your first basing ain't anything great. And you talk a better game'n you hit. But maybe we can work that arm of yours out."

I just shook my head. My arm wasn't hardly any better. I could throw the ball again, sure, but about all I could do was get it up to the plate or play first. I couldn't fire it any more. And you don't win ball games with just a weak first baseman's arm.

I guess it could have been worse. As long as I was making spending money things weren't all black, but I didn't see any more light coming my way.

o   o   o   o   o

We plowed through all that Northwest country, playing every town team we could find. I started doing some throwing in those games, but it was just a lot of fooling and only for an inning or two.

I pitched because Knut told me to. I guess he had to pitch me because all those people up there expected to see Ol' Satch.

They'd heard all the stories. Some of them even'd seen me. But what they saw in 1938 was something else.

"How'd he ever get anybody out?" I heard one kid ask his dad after I finished up a couple of innings.

Talk like that hurt you, deep inside. Everybody'd heard I was a fastballer and here I was throwing Alley Oops and bloopers and underhand and sidearm and any way I could to get the ball up to the plate and get it over, maybe even for a strike.

But even that made my arm ache like a tooth was busting every time I threw. And the balls I was throwing never would fool anybody in the Negro leagues, not without a fast ball to go with them. And those major leaguers I'd used to flatten would feast real good on that stuff.

But Knut kept after me and I kept pitching, one and two innings at a time. I didn't know it then, but Knut figured he might work my arm back into shape. If I'd had his confidence I'd never have lost any sleep.

But I lost plenty of sleep, from worry, from that aching arm, from that boiling stomach of mine.

I was feeling like that man sitting in a little cage in a prison, knowing that before long somebody is going to come along and tell him it's all over.

I'd seen guys like me before. They'd been boxing champs, living on top of the world. Then someone stopped them and the next thing you knew they were dead, alone in the dark somewhere.

I'd done just like them. I'd lived high, way up, but when I'd come to the end of the road I didn't have a quarter. Sure I'd known I was getting up there in age, as far as baseball players go, even before my arm went dead. But I'd still been only thirty-two and I'd figured there were a few more years, enough to salt some green away or get some money working for me in some business.

But it'd ended. Now I didn't have that arm to bring in the real big stuff. I didn't have the arm to make a killing so I'd have enough to get something going for me when I was through with baseball.

All I had was the Monarchs' number two team and a job wandering around the bushes. All I could do was hang on, hang on until they wouldn't pay to see me anymore. After that, I didn't know.

I just kept moving and I kept throwing and aching.

o o o o o

Every town was the same. I don't remember if we won or lost. I just remember guys hitting balls I tossed that wouldn't even have gotten into the batter's box against me a year before.

"It's no use," I told Knut. "I can't do anything with that ball. I might as well just play first."

"Keep throwing," Knut said. "What difference does it make? The fans still come out when we advertise that you'll throw. And those fans mean money in our pockets."

So I pitched and then I'd take my aching arm to a hotel and soak it in boiling water. I had to do that after every game I pitched those days. Otherwise, my arm'd have ached me to death.

We kept moving up North and I think we might even have gotten into Canada. I hadn't pitched for a few days and Knut told me it was my turn again. I went over to toss a couple of warmups before the game started. I'd been doing that before all the games. My arm always hurt more when I threw that first pitch so I always got that first one out of the way before the game. After that my arm got sort of numb and I could pitch a little without it stabbing enough to like to kill me.

I motioned my catcher and threw.

There wasn't any pain. I'd been expecting it so that when it didn't come it was like a bomb going off. I threw again.

There wasn't any pain.

"I'm gonna try a fast ball," I yelled at my catcher. He'd been crouched, waiting for me to pitch, but when I said that he stood up and just looked.

"You're gonna what?" he asked.

"You just get ready," I told him. "I'm gonna fire a fast ball."

It was like a dream. All I knew was that I was going to throw a fast ball, my first since Mexico. I started to rear back, then I stopped.

What if it went dead again? What if the pain came back? I just stood there.

"You gonna throw?" my catcher finally asked.

I looked at him. I took off my glove and rubbed the ball. I was afraid, like I'd never been. That fast ball either was going to be there or before long I'd be living that poor life in Mobile again. If the pain came back I wasn't any worse off than I'd been. If it didn't . . .

I kicked my leg up fast and threw. I didn't feel anything. The ball plopped into the catcher's mitt, not my bee ball, but I hadn't tried to throw as hard as I could.

I threw again and again and again.

My catcher didn't say anything. He just kept whipping the ball back to me and grinning, big as life.

I kept throwing. Knut Joseph ran over and just stood there watching. I kept throwing. I could feel the muscles tingle. I could feel that sweat, sweat that I hadn't felt in weeks because I hadn't been able to work hard enough to sweat.

It was a miracle, but my arm was alive.

"I can throw it again, Knut. I can throw it again."

We called Mr. Wilkinson that night and told him.

"You work yourself back into shape real easy," he warned me. "Don't strain that arm. You just stay with the club 'til the season's over and get back in shape. You'll join the Monarchs for the 1939 season."

o   o   o   o   o

The rest of 1938 and the winter of 1939 flew by like they was clouds. I played everywhere getting my arm back in shape, and none of it seemed real—playing in the islands, going out to the Coast, throwing and throwing and throwing like I always did. Then I joined the Monarchs.

After my arm first came back, I didn't know for sure I could blaze away until I got into some games and really had to.

I could.

That hummer of mine just sang a sweet song going across the plate. It was the finest music I'd ever heard.

I can't help laughing now when I think how I felt like a kid then, a kid starting all over again. Why, I was coming on thirty-three when I started my comeback. Most ballplayers were curling up then, but not Ol' Satch.

When everybody's calling you ageless, you got time for those comebacks.

It seems funny that my climbing back off the floor came about the same time my marriage with Janet went tumbling down for the final count. Later on, when she filed for divorce, she said I deserted her to go play with the Kansas City Monarchs. But I wouldn't call it deserting, exactly. We'd been split pretty good for a long time before that and it was just sort of a final parting. But I didn't fight Janet about it when she went hunting for a divorce. It was all something I wanted to forget then and still want to forget.

o   o   o   o   o

I'd thought I'd hit the top when I'd been with the Crawfords and Bismarck and when I'd won those national tournaments. But I really hit it with the Monarchs. I got so I was making eighteen, twenty, maybe even twenty-two thousand a year sometimes.

I made the Monarchs one of the richest clubs in baseball, too.

'Course, you don't make the big money unless you pitch real often, so I went back to throwing three, four times a week with the Monarchs, just like nothing'd ever happened to my arm.

The way it was coming around, you'd never have thought anything had happened to it.

When I wasn't pitching, I was going off fishing and hunting. I usually went alone, just like I went alone after my games and when I traveled.

A man who's got to stand out in the middle of thousands of people all the time, day after day and year after year, got to get him some alone time now and then.

That's how I felt.

I did so much shooting that my shotgun was just like a part of me. I could put that shot out about as straight as my fast ball. I busted those clay pigeons like they was nothing. I'd knock off about ninety-seven out of a hundred and beat some of the best talkers in baseball.

Lots of baseball men are mighty fine hunters and they got pretty good eyes for skeet, but there wasn't any of them that could stay up with Ol' Satch on the skeet ramble.

o   o   o   o   o

Chapter Nineteen

WORKING FOR MR. WILKINSON was something no man'd forget. He was as good a boss as you could ask for. And he was a real promoter. Some folks even called him the daddy of night baseball. 'Way back in 1930, he hooked up a bunch of spotlights on a truck and ran it up by a field, switched on them lights, and played a game at night. His ball clubs barnstormed all over the country, playing night games for the fans who had to work all day.

With those lights, Mr. Wilkinson's teams could get in an awful lot of baseball. I remember once we played three games in one day. We had a game in the morning and then another one in the afternoon and switched on the lights for a game that same night.

I pitched the morning game and won. I was going to rest in the afternoon, but we got into a little trouble and I relieved in about the seventh and pitched the last three innings. We won. That night I pitched the whole ball game and we won again. There ain't many who can say they won three games in one day. I know some ballplayers that don't win that many all season.

I was throwing so good that most people didn't even remember how I about disappeared from baseball because of my sore arm. When you're on top, folks don't remember your bad times, and when you slip they forget your good times.

The fans were coming out to see me like they always

had. In one six-game stretch in the East, I drew a hundred and five thousand customers. I pitched three to six innings in each one of those games.

They came out there to see my speed, and I had all of it back. I was throwing so hard that before the games the guys on the other teams'd pray, hoping that'd keep my bee ball from blowing them away.

With all that throwing, more people were talking about me than about any other pitcher—colored or white.

If they really'd wanted to know how good I was, they should have stepped into that batter's box against my trouble ball.

My pitching helped turn the Monarchs into as tough a team as the Homestead Grays, maybe tougher.

After the Crawfords kind of busted up, the old Washington Homestead Grays became the big team in the Negro leagues again and they won the Negro National League title in 1937, 1938, and 1939. In fact, they went ahead and won it in 1940, 1941, and 1942, too.

But with my sore arm just a bad dream, I started making the Monarchs the big name. I pitched them to the Negro American League title in 1939 and after that we racked up the championship in 1940, 1941, and 1942—just like the Grays.

o u o o o

That arm of mine never once bothered me during the 1939 season and in 1940, with a whole year of pitching behind me, I was even hotter. I must have won about forty ball games that season. After the season was over, I was ready to head anywhere and there were plenty of places for me to choose. Finally, I decided on Puerto Rico.

While I was down there, I met a gal named Lucy Figueroa. Lucy had a hankering to get into the United States and after we got friendly I gave her a hand. We came back in the spring of 1941.

Lots of folks tried to spread around the word that we were married and later on when they'd see her at the ball park when I was pitching, they wrote she was my wife. Janet even said Lucy and me were married when we got into divorce court later on, but there wasn't any truth to it. Lucy was a fine woman and we were good friends for a while in the States and that was it. Then I went my own way.

Even with seeing Lucy as much as I was when I got back from Puerto Rico, it seemed like all I did in the regular 1941 season was pitch. I pitched every day for thirty days running one time, and when I say I pitched thirty days running I mean with something on the ball. I don't mean just dropping it in there.

I had my worst time in 1941, too. It was in September and I was pitching with the Santo Domingo Stars, who'd picked me up when Mr. Wilkinson and Mr. Baird didn't need me anymore. My club was beating everybody around and we headed into Hartford, Connecticut, for a game and figured we'd have us another win.

We was real sure we'd win when we heard Hartford was using some high school boy to pitch against us.

"You don't want to cancel out, do you?" I asked the Hartford manager when we got in town. "We're liable to kill that boy."

"Don't you worry, Satch," he told me. "We'll be out there. Maybe you ought to worry. You're not as young as you used to be."

Now, it didn't even take a dumb fellow to know that, but I still was moving real good, even if I was thirty-five.

So we went ahead with the game and that kid pitched like he was Satchel Paige. Through the first seven innings he didn't give up a hit. I wasn't letting the Hartford boys score either, but I wasn't pitching no-hit ball.

In the eighth Hartford scored twice off me and that was it. That high school boy pitched a no-hitter against us and faced only twenty-nine batters, two more than a perfect game.

I gave up only eight hits and struck out eight, but it was nowhere near as good as that kid did.

You've never seen an old man if you didn't see me after the game. I ran back to the hotel and locked myself in my room.

"Maybe I'm over the hill?" I kept asking myself. It's a mighty bad feeling when a young punk cames along and does better than you and you know it. And you know you ain't young like you used to be so you don't have time to get any better.

For a couple of days I just moped around, but I had to pitch—my contract said so.

It didn't take me long to find out again I still could pump that ball. And I just kept pumping. Man, I didn't even realize for how long that would be. Fact is, I was still pitching long after everybody'd forgotten what that high school boy'd done against me.

o   o   o   o   o

By the time the 1942 season rolled around, people who knew Ol' Satch was beginning to think he'd changed.

I guess I had.

I'd been with the same club about four years and I hadn't jumped them once.

Before I went with the Monarchs, I hadn't thought anything about jumping contracts when I felt like it. I guess I never cared about much of anything except myself.

It'd made guys like Abe Saperstein, who ran the Harlem Globetrotters, and Gus Greenlee and Candy Jim Taylor and lots others mad at me because of that.

I might have gone on doing that, but after my arm went

dead and then came back I started thinking. I wasn't getting any younger and I figured it was about time to take care of some of the boys who was taking care of me. That was easy to do when the guy taking care of you was somebody like Mr. Wilkinson. And Mr. Baird, too. They made Kansas City a real fine home. I sort of settled there. The folks in Kansas City treated me like a king and you never saw a king of the walk if you didn't see Ol' Satch around Eighteenth and Vine in those days, rubber-necking all the girls walking by.

One night early in the 1942 season I was down that way and I stopped by a drugstore to get me some camera film. I walked up to the counter and this nice-looking gal came up to wait on me. I could tell right off that she didn't know who I was. That kind of bothered me. Everybody knew Ol' Satch around Kansas City, especially the gals.

"You got some one-twenty film?" I asked her real polite.

I just stood there waiting while she shuffled through a big stack of film. She came back to the counter without any.

"We don't have any one-twenty left in stock," she said. "Could you use something else?"

That boiled me over. First she didn't know me and now she was asking me if I could use any other kind of film when she could see the camera I was carrying around my neck wouldn't take anything but one-twenty.

"No. Just one-twenty," I snapped.

"Well, don't act so smart. It's just a twenty-three-dollar camera you got there 'cause I got one just like it."

There have been some that have seen Ol' Satch mad, but nothing like that. I guess when you're playing the peacock and somebody pulls a feather, you get a lot madder than when you ain't playing. I yelled for the manager. He knew who I was all right.

"Who's this girl you got here?" I asked. "She don't know anything."

"What's wrong?" the manager asked.

"This clerk of yours just don't know how to be nice to customers," I said.

"Miss Brown?" the manager asked.

That manager looked so upset I thought he was going to reach out and try and dust me off or something like that, just to make me feel better.

And that Miss Brown just didn't say anything. She'd of jumped in a hole if there'd been one around, I bet.

"Mr. Paige, if she insulted you we'll fire her right now. You just say the word."

Even as big a man as I thought I was those days, I didn't want anything like that happening, not to a gal who was as fine a looker as that Miss Brown.

"No, sir. You don't have to fire anyone. But maybe she'll have some manners after this."

That ended it. But the next day I couldn't wait until I got back to that drugstore. I went hustling inside and saw her. She was down at the end of the counter and another clerk was up near the door.

"Where's that half-smart girl?" I asked the clerk. I said it loud enough so Miss Brown could hear it. She did and came up and waited on me.

Every couple of days I'd go back to the drugstore and always ask for that half-smart girl. I figured maybe by kidding her like that she wouldn't be mad at me for what happened that first night.

A man can't go around having good-looking gals mad at him.

I could tell by the way she was acting that she wasn't mad any longer. After I was sure of that, I went up to her one night when there weren't any customers around.

"What's your first name?" I asked.

"Lahoma," she said.

"Well, Lahoma, because you're so smart, I'd just like to have dinner with you."

"I'd like to have dinner with you, too," she said.

That was the first date I had with Lahoma. We had plenty more and I spent money squiring her around like I'd invented it.

But I didn't run out of green. Why, with what I was making, I had to find me new ways to spend my money. I took up china and antique collecting and I ain't really ever quit. That was one thing that took my fancy and kept it.

I don't even know how much it all cost. One guy said all that stuff I'd bought the first couple of years I was collecting was worth about twenty thousand. It sure didn't cost that much, but it cost enough. The most I ever paid for one piece was three hundred dollars for a great big Meissen drinking stein.

I got me some Chinese vases that also cost me a big penny and I got a complete set of Wedgwood and Sèvres French china and Royal Vienna dishes. And I bought me some of that Eighteenth Century Chippendale and some Queen Anne pieces for the dining room. I got me a big Chinese cabinet and some Fischer Hungarian plates to put inside it. Those plates cost about fifty dollars each.

It might seem funny for a baseball player and wanderer like me to start collecting china and antiques and all that stuff.

But it was a sign. It was a sign that that poor little colored boy in Mobile had grown up to be a big money-maker. It proved how high I'd climbed—how I'd gone from a place where sometimes we didn't have money even to buy a little piece of meat to go with the greens to a place where I could buy the best stuff or the oldest and most expensive stuff if I just took a liking to it.

I could have bought that real expensive, modern furniture,

Satchel Paige takes one of his long, slow strolls
for the Cleveland Indians in 1948.

Paige pitching for the West against the East
during the Negro American League's twenty-ninth East-West
All-Star game at the Yankee Stadium, New York, August 17, 1961.
Satch, fifty-five years old, held the East
to a single in the three innings he pitched. *Wide World Photos*.

Pitching for the Miami Marlins against the Montreal Royals, April 30, 1956. He allowed four hits and no runs in the seven innings he pitched. *Wide World Photos.*

With the St. Louis Browns in 1952. *Wide World Photos.*

With the Kansas City Monarchs.

Paige talking with Roy Campanella during the East-West game August 17, 1961. *Photo by Don Rice, New York* Herald Tribune.

With Bill Veeck, who brought Paige into the major leagues with the Cleveland Indians in 1948. *Staff Photograph, St. Louis* Post-Dispatch.

Paige stands fifth from right, middle row,
in this picture of the 1948 pennant-winning Cleveland Indians.

Paige relaxes in an easy chair, waiting
to be called in an emergency, with
the St. Louis Browns in 1952.
Wide World Photos.

Striving for a hit with
the Kansas City Monarchs
in 1940.

A tremendous swing results in a strike for Paige,
with the Cleveland Indians in 1948.
Photograph by Arthur A. Somers.

The huntsman
with one of his favorite dogs
in Kansas City, Missouri.

Putting on the finishing touches
during his careful dressing program
after a game with the Cleveland Indians
J. H. Wilson, Jr., Springfield, Illinois.

Shirley Long *(left)*, Satchel Paige's stepdaughter; Satch holding his daughter Lula Ouida Paige; and his wife Lahoma. *Courtesy of United Artists Corporation.*

ssed for his cavalry sergeant role he movie *The Wonderful Country,* ed in Durango, Mexico, in 1959. *rtesy of United Artists Corporation.*

Paige with two St. Louis admirers. *Staff Photograph, St. Louis* Post-Dispatch.

Autographing
for young fans
in Chicago in 1955.
*Photo by Don Rice,
New York* Herald Tribune

A copy of Paige's birth record,
obtained by Ralph B. Chandler,
publisher of the Mobile
(Alabama) *Press-Register*.
The spelling of the family name
was changed sometime
after Satchel's birth.
United Press International.

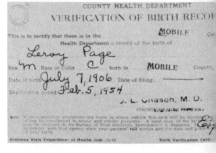

but when people look at that they just say, "My, that's beautiful." They never seem to say, "Boy, you must have had to spend plenty to get that," and then think, "He sure must be up in the big time if he can afford an antique like that."

People always think antiques and real good china come high. And the man who got them is sitting 'way uptown.

Every time I look at that collection of mine, I got something to remind me of how far I'd come, something to prove that pitching day after day all year round was worth something.

I drove those big cars for the same reason I collected antiques and china. A man can owe a lot of money on a car, but if he's driving the biggest and reddest car around, people think he's sitting mighty pretty.

There was only one trouble with my cars. They was fast. Since I always seemed to be a little late getting where I had to go, I let them run and when you let them run they got just about enough power to fly.

Those Kansas City policemen arrested me so many times for speeding they must have been thinking about giving me wholesale rates on tickets.

Speeding was one thing I've never gotten out of my system.

I had me so many court appearances on speeding tickets I couldn't keep them all straight. It even got so I'd miss one of them every so often because of that.

But the judges didn't issue any warrants to arrest me.

They'd just say, "This has happened before with Satchel and it'll happen again. He'll be back in court."

I was.

o   o   o   o   o

Chapter Twenty

DURING THE 1942 season I buzzed my bee ball by the batters until the Monarchs'd won their fourth straight pennant in the four years since I'd joined the club. That set us up to play the kings of Negro baseball, the Homestead Grays.

Nobody was giving us much of a chance to push over the Grays, but they didn't know just how many good ballplayers we had—guys like Johnny O'Neil on first and Jim Greene catching and Willie Brown in center field and Bonnie Serrell at second and Bill Simms in left field and Ted Strong in right.

People started changing their minds about us pretty quick. We knocked off the Grays in the first three games of that best four out of seven series. I was in all three of those games. Now we were after winning that World Series in four straight games. There weren't many people around baseball who thought anybody could do that to the Grays.

The night before that fourth game, I drove back over to Pittsburgh.

I'd been staying there each night and driving about three hundred miles each way to our games in Philadelphia. As much as I was thinking about the series, there was a mighty nice gal over there that I just had to see.

It wasn't Janet. That'd been over for a long time.

Going back and forth like that really wasn't much of a drive for a man who likes cars the way I do and for a man who got a nice, powerful piece of machinery to zip around in.

But I always had to make good time.

When the morning of that fourth game came around, I hopped in my car a little earlier for that trip back to Philadelphia.

I started earlier because the last thing I wanted to do was miss that fourth game. I was scheduled to start again and was all set on doing me a little winning.

I really stepped on the gas and was clipping right along when I heard this siren while I was busting through Lancaster. It was a cop. I pulled over and he came right up beside me.

"You're under arrest for speeding," he said to me.

"But I got to pitch a ball game over in Philadelphia—the World Series."

"All you got to do is see a justice of the peace," he said, and took me to town. We stopped in front of a barbershop and the officer told me to get out.

"I don't have any time for haircuts," I said.

"Just mind your tongue," he said. "The justice of the peace is the barber."

We went inside and the justice was cutting somebody's hair.

"You'll have to wait," he said.

Well, I could tell there wasn't any use arguing anymore so I just sat and waited until he finished snipping.

Then he came over, wiping his hands on his apron.

"What is it?" he asked the officer.

"Speeding."

He turned and looked at me. "Guilty or not guilty?" he asked.

All I could think about was getting out of there. If I got stuck much longer, I'd miss the whole game.

"Guilty," I said.

"That'll be three dollars."

I threw that money at him and got out of there quick. It's just a good thing that cop didn't follow me anymore. If he had, he'd of found out that speeding I was doing before was just snail-walking when you looked at what I did the rest of the way to Philadelphia.

Even as fast as I was going, I didn't get to the ball park until the fourth inning and we were behind, five to four, then. I jumped into a uniform and ran out there. My manager sent me in there real quick. I didn't even have time to warm up. I just went out there and replaced Jack Matchett.

There was two Grays on base and two outs. I knew I wasn't warmed up enough to pitch yet, so I tried picking off that runner on first about ten times until I'd gotten loosed up. Then I looked in at my catcher, got my signal, and started firing. I struck out the batter for the third out in the last of the fourth inning.

Going into the seventh inning, we still was behind by that five to four score. Then the roof fell in on Ted Wright of the Grays, who'd been pitching since the second inning. We scored two runs in the seventh to go ahead and three more in the eighth for icing. While all that was going on, I kept pitching no-hit, no-run ball. I didn't give up a hit or a run for the five and one-third innings I pitched.

We had us the World Championship in four straight games.

I couldn't help needling Josh Gibson of the Grays.

"How's that, big man," I yelled to him from the mound.

Josh wasn't talking.

But I was, plenty. Sometimes it seems to me like that was the best day I ever had pitching.

Maybe it was, but when a fellow has pitched two thousand or more games there's a lot of best days.

o   o   o   o   o

There was more and more baseball after the regular season ended. I just never seemed to tire. They already was starting to call me ageless. There ain't anybody that's thirty-six that's ageless, but that's what they called me. But I've got to admit that I had to rest a little more and I got to taking it easier than I used to. When I was on the bench I didn't even get up for a drink of water. I was sort of the eternal rester.

Just resting like that don't get it alone. I had to make sure I kept my belly down and my legs in shape and avoided hurry-ups, which is what kills a lot of pitchers. And I never strained anything. That's because I used three sets of those little biceps in my arm when I pitched. Overhand I used one. 'Way out sideways used another and up from the ground used another. That's why my arm never did get tired.

I was lucky it didn't get tired because it was getting plenty of work. I was everywhere. It seems funny how you can't remember some things for sure, but I think that was about the same year that I decided I'd better skip going down to the islands or anywhere around there. The war was popping pretty good and I figured there was some of those fascists down there and they'd rather shoot at you with a gun than swing at you with a bat.

I didn't need those islands for playing baseball. There was plenty of games in the States, enough so I kept on pitching the year round.

A lot of those games was at Army camps. All those colored boys in the Army wanted to see me and I had to do a lot of pitching to keep them happy. And where those colored boys were, there was white boys, a lot of them who'd never seen Ol' Satch before.

I showed them plenty and you'd better believe it. They did

a lot of talking, too, just like folks always'd done. They'd wonder if I was better than this and that guy and what I'd have done if I'd been in the majors. Of course some of those guys shot off their mouths about me being a clown, a show-off, and not a real pitcher. I always ran into folks like that, too. After some of them got real noisy about my being over-rated, Lefty Gomez of the New York Yankees got in my corner.

"That's bunk about Satchel being an overrated pitcher," he told some reporter. "I pitched against him many a time on the Coast in exhibition games and he was great. Paige could win in any league consistently. And don't forget he was pitching three or four times a week. If he had the rest a big leaguer gets, I don't know what club could beat him. He has been gifted with a great throwing arm that has been able to take a lot of punishment. I wish I always had his control."

That quieted down the talkers for a while.

o　o　o　o　o

When you stay around as long as Ol' Satch, you got to change your style of pitching, just to keep those batters guessing wrong. I started throwing a curve and a few of them trick pitches more and more. I thought that'd save my arm for my old age. I didn't try a fast curve. I never broke it off sharp. I might have cracked a bone in my wrist if I did. Just slow curves, that's all I threw. Slow ones to fool the batters.

And those batters couldn't believe it from me, not after all those fast balls I'd thrown in seventeen years. I used that slow curve for strike three when I had the batter three balls and two strikes. Right at the first of the 1943 season I got about seventeen strikeouts on men waiting in that three and two spot for the fast one and then getting a slow curve.

Those batters'd get so tangled up waiting for that slow curve that I got to figuring on how I could make it even slower.

The idea came to me in a game, when the guy at bat was all tightened up waiting for my fast ball. I knew he'd swing as soon as I just barely moved. So when I stretched, I paused just a little longer with my arms above my head. Then I threw my left foot forward but I didn't come around with my arm right away. I put that foot of mine down, stopping for a second, before the ball left my hand.

When my foot hit the ground that boy started swinging, so by the time I came around with the whip he was 'way off stride and couldn't get anywhere near the ball.

I had me a strikeout.

The manager of the other team stirred up a lot of dust protesting about that pitch and saying it was illegal. But the umpire said there wasn't anything in the rules against it. After the argument was over, he came walking out to see me.

"What was that pitch, Satch?" he asked me.

I thought on it a minute.

"I guess you got to call it my hesitation pitch."

"You hesitated for sure," he said. "Man, I never saw anything like it."

Tell you the truth, I hadn't either up to then. But later on that pitch really caused a stir in the major leagues. I got real famous with that hesitation pitch. I'd just bring my arm around a little behind my foot to throw those batters off so they'd be swinging at nothing. Then when those batters were off balance like that I'd go ahead and let go of the ball.

I practiced on that hesitation plenty, polishing it up, and before long I got so I could get it right over the heart of the plate as good as my fast one.

But you can't get by on speed and hesitation pitches alone. You've got to out-think a batter, too. When you out-think him, then you can take chances. And it's taking chances that brings the fans to the park.

I took plenty of chances, like one game when we were playing Josh Gibson's club. Before the game Josh and I got together and got to arguing, friendly-like, over who was the best, me at pitching or him at hitting.

"I'll bet you five dollars I strike you out in this game," I said.

"It's a bet."

Going into the last couple of innings, I guess it was the last inning, I was ahead by one run but I still hadn't struck big Josh out.

I got the first two batters out and it looked like I'd lose the bet for sure because there were three guys up before Josh was due to bat again. There weren't three guys anywhere that could get on base against me one after another when I had my stuff working and I had it working that day.

So I walked all three of those guys.

My manager, Frank Duncan, came running out to me. He was mighty upset.

"What're you trying to do?" Duncan yelled. "If Josh hits we lose."

"Don't worry about Josh," I said. "He's not gonna do anything. I'm telling you so."

Duncan went back to the bench. He couldn't have done anything else because only Ol' Satch could handle Josh and he knew it.

I wound up and stuck my foot way up in the air. It hid the ball and almost hid me, too. Then I fired.

"Strike one," the umpire yelled and you should have seen Josh. The way he was looking you could tell that ball must have looked like a white line to him.

I fired again and I had two strikes on Josh.

One more to go. I knew it. Josh knew it. The crowd knew it. It was so tense you could feel everything jingling.

I took one look around the infield and then threw fast. It was strike three.

Josh threw that bat of his four thousand feet and stomped off the field. I don't think he ever paid me that five dollars, but that didn't matter. It was just something to strike out Josh like that after I'd told him I would.

o   o   o   o   o

Along about July of 1943 I pulled into Chicago for a special ball game. A bunch of folks there decided to have a Satchel Paige Day at Wrigley Field. I was going to pitch for the Memphis Red Sox against the New York Cubans in the game they were going to play.

A couple of days before the game, I picked up a paper and right there in it was this article saying how Janet Howard Paige had filed for divorce against me in Chicago.

I knew Janet'd been living there, but I can't remember having seen her since we busted up back in 1939.

Janet said she'd filed the divorce because I'd deserted her on April 17, 1939, and married Lucy Figueroa in Puerto Rico in 1940. Like I'd said, there wasn't any truth to that business of my marrying Lucy, and Janet was just trying to make things look bad, I figured. Janet also said how I was making about forty thousand a year, had me property valued at twenty-five thousand in Kansas City, and that my china and antiques were worth thirty thousand. I only wished that was so.

I called up a lawyer real quick, but before I went over to see him, I got ahold of Janet. I figured she'd be after some alimony or something and I wasn't wrong. After I found out what she wanted, I hopped over to see my lawyer.

"I talked with Janet about a settlement," I told him.

"How much does she want?"

"Something like a hundred a week during the baseball season and fifty a week the rest of the year."

"That's quite a sum," my lawyer said. He did some figuring. "Well, I guess we can figure fifteen weeks of baseball at a hundred a week and thirty-seven weeks at fifty a week. That's three thousand three hundred and fifty every year."

I just kind of groaned.

"What'd you say?" he asked me.

"I just said, 'Oh, my,'" I told him, and just sank back into my chair. That was some chunk, big enough so it'd cut real deep into my living. And it wouldn't leave me hardly enough to take care of a gal like Lahoma.

"Maybe we can figure something else out," my lawyer said. "Don't you worry about it. You just take care of that ball game tomorrow and I'll take care of the divorce."

That's when I first remembered that game again.

o   o   o   o   o

Twenty-five thousand fans showed up at Wrigley Field just for me. I didn't disappoint them. Before I finished up my five innings, I struck out seven Cubans. And I didn't give them a hit or a run. Why, those Cubans didn't even get the ball out of the infield against me.

After we batted in the last half of the fifth, the game was stopped for a few minutes, with us ahead, one to nothing. The players all sat down and I was called out to home plate. They gave me a whole bunch of stuff, like luggage and that. I hauled that stuff off the field and they got the game going again. Porter Moss took over for me and you could tell he wasn't going to let anybody take that win away from me.

He set them down in the sixth, seventh, eighth, and ninth, and gave up only two hits.

The crowd really went wild and came rushing on the field. The cops couldn't hold them back. We ran, but I didn't get too far. Some man stepped out in front of me and blocked the way. He held out a piece of paper and I reached out for a pencil. I figured he wanted my autograph.

"I don't want your autograph, Satchel," he told me. "This is a summons for a divorce court appearance."

That's some way to celebrate Satchel Paige Day, was all I could think. I took the paper and just stood there. Then a bunch of folks were all around me. I don't know how many autographs I signed. Time just wasn't moving.

You just don't expect to have everything going your way like they do on a special day and then have it cut right off by a divorce summons.

Finally the fans were gone. So was the summons. I looked around me. There were plenty of pieces of paper, but no summons. I guess somewhere today there's some guy with my autograph on my divorce summons.

They had the hearing on August 4, 1943. I think the judge was a man named Benjamin Epstein.

I'd won a lot of decisions in the past, but this was one I lost bad. Janet got her divorce on the grounds of desertion and the judge told me I had to give her fifteen hundred cash as a lump settlement and three hundred in attorney's fees. At least it was better than that three thousand three hundred and fifty a year I was afraid I was going to get hit for.

When it was all over, I didn't feel anything. Janet and I'd busted up so long before, there just wasn't anything left to feel. All I could think about was that there wasn't anything blocking me from seeing Lahoma all I wanted.

o   o   o   o   o

The next time I was in Kansas City after that I raced that buggy of mine over to Lahoma's.

"I'm a free man," I told her.

"I read about it."

She looked real happy about it and we started seeing the town like nobody ever'd done before. I could tell she was the gal for me. I'd never met anybody like her and that slowed me down like no gal'd ever slowed me down before.

"You hardly say anything and always act real shy," she'd tell me.

I guess with Lahoma maybe I was.

There were a lot of things I wanted to tell her, but it took me forever before I even got up enough nerve to tell her I liked her.

When Ol' Satch ain't got nerve, you know he's been struck.

Finally, one night I got her out for dinner and after we were done I gulped down a drink quick. I figured that might help me ask her what I wanted to ask. But it didn't, so I had me another one.

That helped some.

"If you'll be my best girl, I'll be your best boy," I finally blurted out. That wasn't what I'd wanted to say, but I'd said at least that much.

"You know I will, Satchel," she told me.

Getting into the major leagues didn't make me feel any better than I did that day. Lahoma was from Stillwater, Oklahoma, and came to Kansas City a few years before I met her. She'd been married before, too, and she had her a little girl named Shirley Long. Shirley was about three in 1943. Back in those days Lahoma was all ears when I told her about all the places I'd been. She never really'd been out of Oklahoma except when she moved to Kansas City, and that was like going East for her.

"You ain't ever traveled?" I asked her.

"No. I haven't been anywhere."

"Well, if you behave yourself and don't get half smart with me, I'll give you a trip."

She just laughed.

I gave her that trip. Lahoma went to New York and then to Los Angeles and got to see most of the country.

o   o   o   o   o

As much as you like to spend all your time just fishing and hunting and looking after your girl friend, you got to pay the bills.

I had to go back to work real quick after that trip back to Kansas City.

There were games everywhere and I tried to pitch in most of them, like the fans wanted. But even with that arm of mine, I couldn't go every day. That didn't stop the promoters. They'd always announce I was going to pitch, even if I wasn't. That got big crowds out, but it made a lot of people mad when I didn't show up.

One game like that was in Pittsburgh.

I'd pitched about the three days in a row before we got to Pittsburgh for a game in Forbes Field against the Homestead Grays. Everybody on my club knew I wasn't supposed to pitch, but the promoter still ran ads saying I was going to.

"What should I do?" I asked my manager, Frank Duncan.

"Nothing. You aren't scheduled to pitch and that's it."

So I just stayed in the locker room. I wasn't going to work that tired arm of mine and risk another sore arm just to make some promoter rich.

But that didn't make any difference to the writers.

One of them wrote the next day, "LeRoy (Satchel) Paige made suckers out of ten thousand people last night at Forbes Field. He made 'em turn out . . . stand in line . . . and then crane their necks like a flock of kangaroos, looking for him after they had paid out their hard-earned dough to see him pitch against the Homestead Grays.

"The 'Great Satchel' . . . the man who has received more

than any other player in the history of Negro baseball for doing less . . . didn't feel like putting on his uniform. He didn't feel like giving the fans who had trudged out to Forbes Field a 'break.' So he just lolled around in the dressing room while his mates were out on the field taking a shellacking from the Homestead Grays."

I didn't argue any. It never does any good when you got to argue against guys who got something sour in their stomach.

o   o   o   o   o

Chapter Twenty-One

WHEN THE 1943 East-West game came around, I was still the biggest name in the Negro leagues. I led all the players in total votes for a spot on the West's all-star team. I had my chance to become the first pitcher in the Negro leagues to get me a win for both the West and East teams. I'd gotten credit for that win by the East in the second all-star game back in 1934.

The way they were selling tickets for that game, it looked like I'd have more people watching me try to stop the East than there ever'd been at any of the other East-West games.

Those days during the war Negro baseball was drawing more fans than it ever did. Everybody had money and everybody was looking around for entertainment and they found plenty in Negro baseball. Even the white folks was coming out big. They'd heard about me and about Josh Gibson and about guys like us and they knew there'd be a good show whenever we were out there.

Knowing all those fans would be paying big money to see the all-star game got me to thinking about how I could make an extra dollar. I figured those owners ought to give a poor boy like Ol' Satch a bonus for the game. Without me, that East-West game wouldn't draw two-thirds the people it would if I was playing. The way I looked at it, there wasn't anything that said I had to make those owners any richer. The only person I had to make richer was me.

I decided to tell the league I was going to hold out unless

they gave me a bonus. Just so they wouldn't go high-hat on me, I got ahold of Josh Gibson. He was about as big a drawer as I was and with both of us out, that all-star game'd be in real bad shape.

"They got to come through with some extra money for us if we both hold out," I told him. "How about it?"

"I don't like to go against the league," Josh said.

"We ain't goin' against the league. We're just makin' us some extra money. If we don't make it, somebody else will."

Josh decided to go along with me and we both went to see our league presidents to tell them we weren't playing unless they came through with an extra two hundred dollars for both of us.

"I'm not gonna pitch unless I get two hundred extra," I told Doc Martin, the president of the Negro American League. "Josh Gibson won't play either."

Doc Martin almost fell out of his chair.

But he knew there wouldn't be hardly anybody out at the game unless Josh and me was there. He gave in. Tom Wilson, president of the National League, gave in to Josh, too.

'Course, I didn't go around telling anybody about it.

It just wouldn't have been good if people thought I was greedy.

o   o   o   o   o

After I got that guarantee for the extra money, I headed for Comiskey Park in Chicago for the game. I was sitting in the locker room getting ready when Mr. Wilkinson came in.

"You should see that crowd out there, Satchel," he told me.

I went out and looked.

There sure was a crowd out there. It was fifty-one thousand seven hundred twenty-three. A couple of guys I knew snuck in and weren't counted. They even had to turn about ten thousand away.

It was a real circus and I knew just how to put on a three-ring show for them. I played a little pepper ball and went out and worked at third base, just flapping around and getting all those muscles nice and loose.

Then I threw a little.

After I was done warming up, I went to the bench and pulled on my jacket and buttoned it up so it'd keep it hot in there, letting the heat build up high. I could feel everything relaxing and that's how I wanted it. When you go out against a team like the East all-stars—guys like Josh Gibson, Cool Papa Bell, Buck Leonard—you got to be relaxed. If you're tight or nervous for a minute, you're liable to be a hundred runs behind before you get going smooth.

I started the game and breezed through my innings without allowing a hit. We scored one run in the last of the second and I had me a one to nothing lead when that three-inning limit in the All-Star game made me quit for the day.

Lefty McKinnis of Birmingham replaced me on the mound. He didn't let me down. He went through his three innings almost as good as me and while he was pitching, we'd got another run. Then Theolic (Fireball) Smith came in to pitch for us in the last three innings and I figured we were in.

He blazed along in the seventh and eighth and it looked like we were going to win us a one-hitter. Going into the top of the ninth we still were ahead, two to nothing.

He got the first two guys out in the ninth. That brought up Buck Leonard and he picked on one of Fireball's quickies and put it in the left field stands for a home run. We were only ahead two to one. And Josh Gibson was up next.

On the first pitch, Josh swung. He didn't get under it enough or the game would have been tied. Instead he almost tore the glove off Jesse Williams' hand at second and was on first with a single. Howard Easterling of the Homesteads followed Gibson with another single and the East had the tying and winning runs on base with two out.

I wanted to run out there. It was my game. I wanted to do something. I couldn't.

But Frank Duncan, our manager, did. He took Fireball out of there and put in Porter Moss. Dick Harris, the East's manager and one of the top hitters in the league, also made a change. He put himself in to bat as a pinch hitter.

It seemed like it took forever for Moss to pitch. Then he threw. Harris swung. The ball shot off his bat, but it was arcing up and out to center field. Willard Brown caught it. The West'd ended the East's three-year string and I'd gotten the victory.

o   o   o   o   o

When you're in a war, you can't just go ahead and play baseball, even if you want to get your hands on all the money you can. You got to help out in the war some way or other. I'd registered for the draft like everyone else and'd even moved my birth date up to September 1908, instead of July 1906, but they still never called me. So after the 1943 season was over I did a lot of helping out for the soldiers. You know, going out to the camps and hospitals and things like that.

I made one of those visits when I was out in San Diego. Somebody told me that some wounded soldiers that'd come home on a hospital ship heard I was in town and wanted to see me. I hurried down to the docks.

I went on the ship and I was so close I could touch them and the doctors told me to go and talk.

Those wounded boys'd lay on their stretchers and say, "I heard tell of you when I was a baby." They'd reach out their hands and feel my right arm and'd ask how it hung on there after all those years pitching. They'd ask me how come I'd pitched a hundred fifty games a year between here and Latin America so many years—and all kinds of questions like that. White boys and colored boys said it was a long time since they'd seen me and did I still have that fast ball.

You always feel kind of quiet after you leave those boys.

A few days later in Frisco I went to another soldier hospital and saw a House of David boy I'd pitched against barnstorming. Last time I'd seen him he was playing. Now he didn't look the same. I had to hold up his head so he could see me. He couldn't talk hardly at all, but he wanted me to tell him about games we'd had. They always said I'd been a big talker when I wanted to, but I sure talked to that House of David boy that day like I never talked before.

I had those wounded boys on my mind all the time.

Then a couple weeks later I was in Hot Springs when they unloaded a bunch of those boys from a train. They were just pieces of men.

That's when I finally decided I had to do something for them. That winter I got the idea of playing the 1944 East-West all-star game for those soldiers.

I told some of the managers and owners that we ought to give them soldiers ten thousand dollars from the game.

The only answer I could get was that they'd think about it the rest of the season.

I just let it ride for the time being.

o   o   o   o   o

I finished out the winter and didn't say anymore right away about that charity game. I just kept pitching. I could tell I was slowing down a little, especially after I took a couple of weeks off before the regular 1944 season started. When I got ready to play again, it was real tough. My arm never bothered me, but I was weak in the knees. I could feel it. But I knew they'd be all right in another couple of weeks. All I had to do was get in condition.

But back a few years before that, I never got out of condition, no matter what I did.

I still had my trouble ball, though. And I could do the same old thing with that ball that I could do five years before. Only, like I said, I couldn't do it as long. But that's still something for a guy who was thirty-seven and'd been pitching for more than eighteen years, ain't it?

Through the first part of the season, I still hadn't heard anymore about playing the East-West game for the soldiers. So when they started talking about picking the teams for the All-Star game, I told the reporters about my idea of giving ten thousand dollars to some war charity.

You'd have thought all the owners in Negro baseball'd agree with that and want to play the East-West game for the soldiers, but it wasn't that way at all.

Doc Martin, the president of the Negro American League, checked with the owners, I guess, and he said the National League turned the idea down flat. He told some reporter how most of the Negro league teams relied on the East-West game to finish in the black. He said without that game they'd lose money every year.

I couldn't buy that, not with the way fans were pouring out for all the games those days, and I said so. I got mad and said all the money from the game should go to the soldiers, not just ten thousand dollars.

That got even more dander up.

I guess that's why Doc Martin started telling folks that I'd asked him for a percentage of the gate of the East-West game for myself and'd told him if I didn't get it I wouldn't play in the game, just like the year before. He said that it wasn't until they turned me down that I asked them to play the game for charity.

He knew better. I didn't want any money for playing that

game. Like I'd said, I'd gotten the idea about playing for the soldiers that winter.

When it looked like that charity game was out for sure, I called up some reporters.

"If they don't play this game for charity," I told them, "I'm gonna lead a walkout and they won't have any East-West game."

But I didn't get any help from the players. I figure maybe those owners were putting the pressure on them to keep quiet. Most of the players didn't have that big name like me and couldn't buck the owners like I could.

For a few days after I threatened that walkout I didn't say anything else, but a lot of reporters said plenty.

One of them wrote, "Paige's desire to play the East-West game for a war charity is commendable and the Negro league owners' comments about him as a result of his stand are inexcusable. There is little or no doubt in the minds of seasoned observers that Paige and Paige alone, with his colorful characteristics, has raised Negro professional baseball to its present high plane. Paige, they say, was responsible more than anyone else for putting these games in such parks as the Polo Grounds, Griffith Stadium and other big league parks. Which, they point out, would make resentment on the part of other players, as cited by Dr. J. B. Martin, a rather short-sighted attitude. They have ridden the crest of prosperity and popularity along with the great Satch."

After that I kept pushing, but the closer we got to the day of the game, the more it looked like they weren't going to play it for the soldiers. That's when I told the reporters I was going to take a walk for GI Joe. Martin said they'd play without me and I was banned from the game.

Every reporter in the country must have called me after that.

"Sure I'd like to be in the twelfth All-Star game," I told them. "Last year there was fifty-one thousand in Comiskey

Park and this year there'll probably be more. And a pitcher like me likes that. But not unless it's for the soldiers this time.

"I told the owners that Negro baseball has growed up. Our leagues have got big. We can afford to do like white baseball with the money it gets on its big all-star day."

That wasn't all I told those reporters. I told them how twenty years before Negro baseball players had to sleep on their suitcases, go hungry, and play in little splinter parks for a hundred and twenty-five a month and expenses.

"Twenty years ago no white faces were in the stands when I was out there on the mound lookin' in," I said. "Now it's awful close some Sundays in New York and Cincinnati and Philadelphia whether there's more colored than white. Lots of white faces lookin' over from the stands in Louisville and New Orleans nowadays, too. Fans all holler the same at a ball game.

"I said to the owners I take notice when I used to go South with a ball club that I didn't do no autographin' for any white fans. Now, some days, seems I do as much for white as for Negro. I'd like to pitch in this all-star game thinkin' it was for white and Negro boys in the South Pacific.

"With all I done, I figure I got the right now to tell the owners how they should toss around that money from the East-West game.

"In the hard days I went from club to club in Negro ball and pitched every day, day after day, to build it up. I worked when anybody wanted me to and I worked oftener and oftener because people had paid money to see me and you shouldn't disappoint 'em. I made money for the owners that way, so I think they ought to let me spend a little of their money for the soldiers."

Those owners still said no. That meant it had to be no for me, too.

I sat out the game, but the West still won. There were about forty thousand people out there, too, I think. That wasn't one of those record crowds like I got out, but it still was plenty. Lots of people just don't seem to care what they're doing if they got their own entertaining to worry about. But the soldiers knew how I felt. You can't win all them fights, but you got to try.

o   o   o   o   o

Chapter Twenty-Two

YOU CAN'T KEEP SWINGING when a fight's all over, so after the East-West game I just put all that disputing out of my mind. I went back to pitching, picking up that money that was rolling in free and easy all over the country. I bought a couple of cars and some more shotguns and a mess of hunting dogs and all the fishing gear you could get your hands on.

Lahoma kept telling me to save a little of that money. Lahoma wasn't just going around smiling and being my girl friend. She had a real business head on her and tried to get me to keep my money all straightened out.

But with Ol' Satch, that was a pretty tough job in those days.

"Satchel, you ought to save some money, maybe even invest in some real estate," she'd tell me.

I'd just nod and then go out and buy me another suit or one of those flashy ties or trade for a new car. She had a time with me, that's for sure, but she kept trying to get me to save up some.

But I couldn't see it.

I figured I still had four or five years left before I had to start worrying so I didn't pay any attention to what'd happen when my arm couldn't bring home a paycheck. I went on living high, way high.

Lahoma got real worried and asked Mr. Wilkinson to try and get me to save some money. Finally, they talked me into buying war bonds and save up a little bit that way.

"Okay," I said. "If you think I'd better. You buy them for me, Mr. Wilkinson."

After that Mr. Wilkinson kept a little money back and bought me a couple of bonds each month. Seems like they were five hundred dollar bonds or something like that.

The only thing was, every time he gave me one of those bonds, it seemed like I was a little short then and I'd cash it in that same day.

Then I hit this time when I didn't have any money or any bonds and needed some money bad for a car payment.

I hustled over to Lahoma's house.

"You call Mr. Wilkinson and see if you can get me an advance," I told her.

"You mean you're broke again?" Lahoma asked me.

"I jus' need a little advance," I said.

"Why don't you cash a war bond then and not bother Mr. Wilkinson?"

I didn't say anything.

"Why don't you?" she asked again.

"I don't have 'em. I'd cashed 'em the day Mr. Wilkinson got 'em for me."

If you didn't see Lahoma that day, you'll never know just how upset she can get. She finally got over it and then she just started in all over again trying to get me to invest in something. Finally I bought me some property in Kansas City. It was a great big house on Twelfth Street there, and there was plenty of room for all my dogs, antiques, guns, fishing equipment, and cars, and I still had rooms left to rent out.

'Course, there wasn't too much rent. I always seemed to be running into some old buddies who needed a room but didn't have money to pay for it.

"I'll send it to you later when I make a buck," they'd all tell me.

I'm still waiting.

But at least I'd invested some of my money in something.

"No matter what happens, you'll have that to fall back on," Lahoma told me.

She was a real businesswoman. I guess that's when I decided for sure I'd better marry up with her before too long. You don't find good business managers that look as good as Lahoma too often.

o   o   o   o   o

My dogs weren't the only animals I kept around my house. I bought me a couple hundred chickens for the back yard and turned the place into a sort of downtown chicken ranch. And just to make things real easy when I got hungry, I bought me a cow and put it out there.

You never saw anything like it with all those chickens and that cow and my twelve hunting dogs running around out there.

Nobody around my house said anything, even though I was living right downtown in Kansas City.

They'd just come around for eggs.

But one day this man comes up to the door and knocks away. I didn't answer for a while, figuring he might go away. But he was a real sticker. He just kept pounding.

Finally, I answered the door.

"You Satchel Paige?" he asked.

"Yes, sir."

"Mr. Paige, I'm from the city zoning board. We heard you're keeping animals here in violation of city zoning laws. Is that true?"

"No, sir. Not Ol' Satch," I said.

He looked like he wanted to believe me, but just then my cow came wandering around the side of the house. You probably won't believe it, but there that cow was.

That was the end of my chickens and cow. But they let me keep my dogs. I was mighty glad of that. They were the finest hunting dogs around.

'Course, with the regular 1945 season on, I wasn't around that house too much, but this fellow who lived free at the house took care of my dogs while I was gone.

o   o   o   o   o

We had us a good season in 1945. We had about the same old team that'd won a lot of those pennants for us and we'd added a couple of players or so. About the best of the lot was a college boy, a kid named Jackie Robinson. I'd never heard of him before, but he was pretty good— quick on his feet and a good hand at the plate. But I didn't get to know him real well. When Ol' Satch pitched, he didn't need a lot of help from anybody and so I didn't pay too much attention to those other boys on the team, especially those rookies.

After the season was over, the Monarchs busted up again like always, some heading down to the islands and the others every which way. I busted out to the West Coast and joined up with an all-star team. We were playing against a bunch of major leaguers headed up by my old buddy, Bobby Feller. While I was out there I began hearing all these rumors flying around about getting some colored boys into the major leagues.

I'd been hearing talk like that all through the 1945 season. But if there was anything to it, I didn't know about it. None of those white owners were coming to me about getting in the big time. But a lot of reporters came to see me. They figured if the rumors were true, I'd be the first guy to know. They were wrong.

But with all of them reporters coming around to ask me about it, I got that old bug real bad again. I knew I was old, the way baseball men figured it, but I didn't think I was too old.

"I'm just prayin' I get into the big show before my speed ball loosens," I told those reporters.

It wasn't too long before I heard for sure what was starting all those rumors. Branch Rickey of the Brooklyn Dodgers'd been scouting some Negro league players.

Even with Branch Rickey out scouting, I wasn't believing that any colored boys were going to be signed. I'd been hearing about the white boys scouting colored ballplayers for twenty years but I didn't see any of them playing in the major leagues. I was thinking there might never be any.

○   ○   ○   ○   ○

I found out just how wrong I was while I was still out on the West Coast in October of 1945.

Branch Rickey told the world he'd signed Jackie Robinson off the Monarchs and assigned him to the Montreal Royals of the International League. Almost twenty years after I fired my first trouble ball as a full-time professional, Jim Crow'd gotten busted on the nose.

I hadn't thought it'd ever happen, but it had. The colored ballplayer'd made his first dent in organized baseball.

After all those years of fighting, it'd finally happened.

It hadn't happened to me, but it'd happened. They'd signed my old teammate, Jackie Robinson.

Somehow I'd always figured it'd be me. But it hadn't. Maybe it'd happened too late and everybody figured I was too old. Maybe that was why it was Jackie and not me.

Anyway, those major league owners knew I wouldn't start out with any minor league team like Jackie was. They'd have had to put me right in the majors and that might have caused a revolution because the high-priced white boys up there wouldn't have had a chance to get used to the idea that way.

Some of them weren't taking too good to the idea even though Jackie was going to the minors.

But signing Jackie like they did still hurt me deep down. I'd been the guy who'd started all that big talk about letting us in the big time. I'd been the one who'd opened up the major league parks to the colored teams. I'd been the one who the white boys wanted to barnstorm against. I'd been the one who everybody'd said should be in the majors. But Jackie'd been the first one signed by the white boys and he'd probably be the first one in the majors.

When you hurt like I was hurting, hurting like you do when somebody you love dies or something dies inside you, you go hunting for someone to ease that hurt.

There was only one person who could do that for me. That was Lahoma.

"They took that kid off our team and didn't even look at me," I told her.

"He's young, Satchel. Maybe that's why."

"He's no Satchel Paige."

"Everybody knows that, Satchel. But Jackie did all right with the Monarchs. And if they let one colored player into their leagues, they'll be letting others. Maybe the major leaguers'll come to you."

"They'll have to come real pretty-like. They've been puttin' me off too long to just wiggle their fingers at me now."

"Don't you go sounding like you're sour. When they come for you, you know you'll go. You've been wanting it real bad for too long not to."

"Well, it still was me that ought to have been first."

o o o o o

Through the whole winter everybody kept writing about Jackie and how great it was. It almost seemed like they'd forgot Ol' Satch.

But the barnstorming teams hadn't forgotten me and there were as many jobs as I'd ever had.

I just kept pitching and reading. I figured Rickey'd told about Jackie going to Montreal back in October to give the boys a chance to get used to the idea.

I got used to the idea too.

But Mr. Wilkinson and Mr. Baird didn't. Oh, they were happy, all right. They were too fine gentlemen not to be. They wanted to see the colored ballplayers get ahead. But they were burned up at the way it'd happened. The Dodgers'd just signed Jackie without giving them anything for him. And Mr. Wilkinson and Mr. Baird were afraid if other major league teams did that too, it'd kill off Negro baseball. They were right. When the best ballplayers were gone, the fans stopped coming out.

Mr. Wilkinson and Mr. Baird and me and a lot of others could see the handwriting in 1945, but it took a couple more years before it really got bad. When that happened, even Ol' Satch had to think about moving.

o o o o o

By the time the 1946 season opened, everybody in baseball was sitting tense to see how Jackie worked out. He didn't let anybody down. I wouldn't put him on my all-time great team, but he had plenty in him and that first season he burned up the International League.

But he wasn't the only one getting in the papers.

I gave those reporters plenty to write about in 1946, too.

I was still throwing lightning and it struck down a lot of teams, enough to make it pretty easy for the Monarchs to win the first and second half championships in our league. That put us in the World Series against the Newark Eagles.

While we were winning the pennant, I rolled up a record of twenty-one wins and no losses in league play. That's not too bad for a man who's pushed past forty. Only trouble was, I had to pitch so often I didn't dare go nine innings at any one time through the first half of the season.

That got people to saying I was too old to pitch.

"Don't let 'em tell you I'm too old to throw in baseball," I'd tell them. "I'm not old—only forty. And forty, even fifty, ain't old if your arms and legs are twenty."

And I just went on pitching those three, four, and five innings.

And you just remember that guys like Dizzy Dean, who used to pitch against me, were announcing ball games, not playing in them.

Even with me throwing like that, I still wasn't getting any bites from the major leagues. Maybe I'd never get in the majors, I kept thinking, but if I didn't it wasn't going to be because I couldn't carry my weight.

"I can't understand it, Satch," Frank Duncan, my manager, told me. "You could go in the major leagues right now the way you're pitching."

That's just how I felt. And I figured if I'd gotten the break ten years before that Jackie Robinson'd had, I'd have rated with the all-time greats.

o   o   o   o   o

Pitching in as many different places as I did made it kind of hard getting around fast enough in a car, so Mr. Wilkinson and Mr. Baird bought a Cessna 140 airplane for me. It was a two-passenger job and Mr. Wilkinson's son, Dick, flew it. Dick'd been an Army captain and flier in World War II and'd gotten shot down over the Ploesti oil fields on his twenty-seventh mission. He was some flier.

They called that bird *Satchel Paige* and put my name on both sides. I guess I was the first pitcher ever to have his club buy him his own plane for traveling.

"You can make more playing dates now," Mr. Wilkinson told me after they bought the plane and brought it to Kansas City.

"When do we start?" I asked.

"Tomorrow. You'll pitch three innings in our game here tonight and then Dick'll fly you to Madison, Wisconsin. You'll pitch three innings there the next day."

"You just get me to that bird," I said.

Dick flew me to Madison that next morning. It was a real smooth hop and beat that long car-driving. And it meant I'd have two paychecks instead of just one. You can't beat that.

After I was through on the field in Madison, I just sort of lazed around the locker room. As fast as that bird went, I didn't figure there was any need to hurry.

But about an hour after the game I got a call from Dick.

"There's a storm brewing, Satch," he told me. "If you don't hurry we won't be able to make it out of here and back to Kansas City."

I'd never been worried about storms before so I didn't see any reason to worry now. I just didn't know airplanes.

I took my time and got out to the airport kind of late.

"We'll be in for some rough weather," Dick said, "but we can make it."

"That old weather don't scare Satch," I said. "It's just a lot of noise. Let's get that bird going."

"It'll be rough, Satch. There's a big storm in our way."

"I've seen storms before."

Dick just shook his head at me and we got into that bird and up we went.

Man, when we hit that storm, Dick had me upside down half the time.

"You tryin' to kill me?" I yelled at him. "Get me out of here!"

He finally did. We got to Kansas City but it took us a good hour longer than it had going up.

When I got my feet on the ground I was the happiest man in the world.

"I ain't ever flyin' in one of those little birds again," I told Dick.

"That wasn't anything, Satch. Just a little rough weather."

"It may not be anything to you, but for Ol' Satch it's the end."

"But you've got another game tomorrow out in Oklahoma. We've got to fly to get there on time."

"Not me."

"Satch, they're paying you five hundred for that game. You going to miss that?"

"I ain't flyin' again," I said, but that five hundred was mighty tempting. "Maybe we can drive tonight?"

"You know we can't, Satch. What about it? You want me to call them and tell them you're skipping that five hundred?"

Dick sure knew my weak spot. I gave in.

So the next day I climbed back in that little bird again and we headed out.

It was fine flying going out and I started figuring maybe I'd been wrong about flying.

"We got any storms?" I asked Dick after the game, when we were ready to head back.

"Nothing in the way," Dick said.

"Well, let's get goin' then," I said.

I was feeling pretty happy, but it didn't last long.

"What's that black stuff?" I yelped when we were about halfway home. Black stuff was splattering all over the windows.

"We've got an oil leak," Dick told me. "Don't worry. It's nothing."

I did plenty of worrying, all the way home. That oil was flying all around me and I knew how my car burned up when that oil was all gone. I figured the same thing'd happen with an airplane. And when you burn out way up in the sky, there ain't any place to go but down.

I got scared right to death.

But we made it back to Kansas City.

"I'll never fly in that little plane again," I told Dick. This time he couldn't talk me out of it. I stuck by what I said.

They had to sell that bird after only two trips.

A few months later, they got me to do some flying again, but it wasn't in one of those little birds. It was a big job, with lots of motors.

When we dropped down for the landing, I saw all these fire trucks and ambulances and all racing alongside us and making all kinds of noises.

We landed real smooth so I never figured they were there because they thought we were in trouble.

I turned to Mr. Wilkinson. "Man, look at all them fire trucks and ambulances blowing those sirens just to honor Ol' Satch."

"I guess that is why they're here," Mr. Wilkinson said.

It wasn't until I left the Monarchs that he told me that at first the pilot couldn't get the wheels down and that's why they called those trucks and ambulances. But that pilot finally got them down before we had to land so everything went real smooth. They weren't going to tell us players until just before we landed, and when the wheels dropped down they didn't have to tell us anything.

If they had told us back then, I'd never have flown in any plane again, big or little.

o   o   o   o   o

When we were getting near the end of the regular 1946 season, some of those talkers started saying louder than ever how I couldn't go nine innings anymore. That's because I still hadn't pitched a full nine all the way up through most of August.

I didn't want the major leagues to think that, so I told old Frank Duncan I wanted to go the distance when we played the Indianapolis Clowns in St. Louis on August 1. We had a double-header with them and if we won one of those games, we'd clinch the second half pennant and qualify automatically for the World Series.

The games were in what they used to call Sportsman's Park there.

"You pitch the second game, Satch," Frank told me. "We'll have some shadows then and that fast ball of yours'll be real hard to follow then."

That was fine with me and I just lazed around in the locker room during the first game.

I was kind of dozing when the boys came in to rest after the opener.

"Did we take the pennant?" I yelled at them.

"They beat us, three to two," someone said.

"Don't you worry none," I answered. "Ol' Satch'll get it for us in this next game."

I buzzed right by the first nine men, getting them on only twenty-five pitches and I went the whole way just as strong. The Clowns, with old Goose Tatum dancing around on first for them, got only six hits off me and I struck out about a dozen. I won six to one.

A couple of reporters came in to talk after the game.

"That's your first complete game of the year, isn't it, Satch?" one of them asked.

"That's right," I said. "There were all those folks in the stands and I just wanted to let 'em know Ol' Satch still had it."

"What's next, Satch? You going to the majors?"

"I never worry about what's next. If they call me, I'm always ready to pitch. But right now I think I'll just loaf around 'til it's time to meet those Newark Eagles in the World Series."

o   o   o   o   o

It seemed funny to walk down to the bullpen and sit there when the first game of the 1946 Negro World Series opened in New York at the Polo Grounds. I'd almost always been a starter before. Time'd made me a reliever, a short-inning man. But there was plenty of relief work in the World Series with Newark.

Those boys had guys like Larry Doby and Monte Irvin, who later made the major leagues, and they could work a pitcher over. We couldn't stop them, even with our hot-shots like Henry Thompson, who beat me into the major leagues with the old St. Louis Browns and then really made his mark with the old New York Giants. Newark won that Negro World Series, four games to three.

o   o   o   o   o

Chapter Twenty-Three

THROUGHOUT THE REST OF 1946 and into 1947 I kept thinking I'd get a bite from the major leagues, but I didn't even have anybody snap and miss.

Some clubs talked to me, but my salary was more than they could pay.

They still kept sending scouts around and those boys'd take a long look at me and then come up after the game and say, "Satch, I couldn't see a soul out there but you." They were right. I remember one eleven-inning stretch when I struck out eighteen batters.

But they didn't take me, not even after Jackie Robinson was called up to the old Brooklyn Dodgers in 1947 as the first Negro in the majors.

That was my right. I should have been there. I got those boys thinking about having Negroes in the majors, but when they get one, it wasn't me.

That bothered me plenty, but I wasn't going to fold up and quit. I promised myself I'd keep throwing until somebody figured they needed me bad in the major leagues. Before that arm of mine gave out, I was going to taste that major league living.

Lahoma made sure I kept thinking that way, too. If I forgot for just a minute, she'd be there reminding me.

A man just can't let a gal who takes care of him like that get away. And the only way to make sure a gal doesn't get away is to marry her.

I thought about that all through the 1947 season, but I guess since I was seeing her real regular I just never did anything about it. Then I signed up to barnstorm against Bob Feller's major league all-stars out on the West Coast in October. That meant I had to leave Lahoma for a couple of months and I didn't like that idea at all.

I went over to see Lahoma.

"I'm gonna pitch against Bobby Feller out on the Coast," I told her.

"That's wonderful, Satchel."

"You know what I'm gonna do when I leave?"

"No. What?" she asked.

"I'm gonna take you with me. We're gonna get married."

I got me a big kiss.

o o o o o

We didn't tell hardly anybody what we were doing and on October 12, 1947, we ran over to Hays, Kansas, and got married.

You talk about the best things you've ever done. Man, when you get somebody like Lahoma in your corner you can win them all.

She gave me that settled-down life I never had before.

And she gave me a family. Don't let anybody tell you I ain't always thinking about them, no matter how I act.

But when I first became a family man, when we had our first baby, it really staggered Ol' Satch.

It was just like trying to hit a change of pace after the pitcher'd been throwing nothing but blazers. You're thrown all off stride. There ain't a man alive that won't tell you that first baby don't do that.

Not that you don't love them. It's just that your life goes and changes so. You trade in that standing up to dance for sitting down to baby-watch.

That's what I did when Pamela Jean was born in 1948.

I was proud as anybody over that first kid. She was a real dandy, just like all the rest of mine.

Lahoma and me were like somebody with a new toy. At least I was like that until Pamela started crying real loud for the first time.

A man who ain't heard a baby cry in his house for about thirty years don't remember just how upsetting that can be.

"Is she dying?" I asked Lahoma. I was that worried.

"Don't be silly. She's just hungry."

That must have been a powerful hunger. Pamela was bawling so loud I was afraid the neighbors'd call the police and tell them I was murdering somebody. They didn't. They knew babies a lot better than me.

After a couple of weeks I kind of got used to that baby stuff. I thought I had it all figured out.

I guess I wasn't as smart as I thought.

When Lahoma was up and around real good, I told her it was time to do some celebrating.

"Let's go dancin'," I told her.

"We can't go off and leave the baby. You know that."

Maybe I didn't. I guess I just figured babies took care of themselves.

"We just got to sit here?" I asked.

"What do you want us to do?"

If I'd known, I'd have told her.

"I guess we'll just stay home," I said.

"Well, since you've got to stay anyway, I'll run down to the store and get some groceries. You mind Pamela."

And Lahoma left me, left me with that little baby.

I picked her up, but it wasn't anything like picking up a baseball. I still think she was going to break.

I've pitched in some pretty tough games, but I never was anywhere as near tired after those games as I was by the time Lahoma got home.

By the time we had our second child, I was a pretty old hand at babies. I could have even written a book about it.

That second baby was another girl. She was born in 1949 and we named her Carolyn Lahoma.

I guess I sort of spoiled Carolyn. You know how it is. You remember all the bad things you did with your first baby and so you try not to do them with the second. Only trouble is you try so hard you usually end up being too good and go and spoil them. But Carolyn got over it. She had to. We had other kids coming along that we had to pay some attention to.

The next one was in 1951. That was Linda Sue.

I was just as glad to have Linda Sue as I was about the first ones. Little girls are mighty cute things, just like big girls.

But I was beginning to wonder if I'd ever have me a boy. There ain't any daddy around that don't want a boy.

I didn't have to wait too long. About a year later, in 1952, I had me a son, Robert LeRoy. He's built just like me. I don't know for sure if he will be a pitcher. A daddy likes to think his boy is going to be what he is, but he never knows. And Robert ain't got big enough for me to tell if he can throw like me. It'll be something if he can. Nobody else is ever been able to.

Robert's like me in one way for sure. When things don't go his way, he can get mighty mad. I remember when he was about six or seven and he'd gone to the store for some candy.

He came back crying to beat all and kicking at the ground and the door and everything.

"That mean old store man wouldn't sell me a candy bar because I only had four pennies and it cost five," he yelled and started crying and kicking all over again.

I didn't say anything. I just gave him another penny and

sent him back to the store. If there's anybody that knows what I should have said then, they better come around and see me. Maybe they better go around and see everybody. Ain't many daddies I know that got an answer for a little boy who wants something and don't know why he can't have it.

When that happens you'd just better help that boy out. You don't want him keeping that hunger for something and maybe ending up in reform school because he stole it. You don't want that to happen, especially if you know what it's like when it does happen.

Lahoma and me didn't have any more kids until 1958, when Lula Ouida was born. After Lula was born, I guess we figured it'd be easier counting those kids if we had an even half-dozen. Anyway we had our sixth child and fifth girl in 1960. We named her Rita Jean.

Man, if there are anymore, I don't know what we'll do for names. I'm just about all out.

When those first kids got a little older, it was even nicer having them around. They'd run off and fetch things for the old man so he didn't have to upset his thinking by getting out of a chair.

And they helped Lahoma keep track of where I put things.

I was never any good at that myself but with them around, all I had to do was yell, "Pamela, where's that letter I got from that promoter in North Carolina," and she'd run and get it and bring it to me.

All the other kids did that way too.

Robert was a real good one at helping. I guess he wants to be like his daddy and just follows me around whenever I'm home.

And he's like me about cars. He always wants to help me wash mine. He'll go get the hose for me and wet down the car and then help me rub. He don't say much but he's always right there beside me.

The way those kids act, I'm getting so I wouldn't trade them for all the stuff I had before put together.

o   o   o   o   o

Before the kids came, Lahoma saw more baseball than most sports writers. That's because I still was pitching so much. It got so sometimes she wouldn't go to the games because she'd seen so many. She'd go to a movie and then meet me afterwards.

We'd go to some good restaurant and then go dancing. We did that all the time until the kids came. It was like a year-long honeymoon.

We really lived it up on the West Coast when we first got out there after being married. We had us a few days off before the major leaguers got out there and we saw everything and went everywhere.

But you always got to go back to work.

"You make sure they know you're out there," Lahoma told me when my first game out there came up.

If that's what the wife wanted, that's just what I was going to do.

A man bites off more trouble than he can chew when he doesn't do what his wife wants. You better believe it.

o   o   o   o   o

I was playing with a club called the Kansas City Royals and our first game was in Wrigley Field in Los Angeles.

I was going to be playing against guys like Feller, who'd won twenty games in 1947 for Cleveland; Ewell Blackwell, who'd had a no-hitter and won twenty-two and lost only eight and won sixteen in a row at one stretch for Cincinnati;

Ralph Kiner, who'd hit .313 for Pittsburgh and'd tied Johnny Mize for the National League home run title with fifty-one; Andy Pafko of the Chicago Cubs, who'd hit .302; Bob Lemon of Cleveland, who'd hit .321 and won eleven and lost five pitching; and Bob Dillinger, who'd hit .294 for the old St. Louis Browns.

That was a fine crew, but the papers weren't calling any of them a wonder man like they were me.

I wasn't even supposed to pitch that first game. Dan Bankhead, who'd been pulled up by the Brooklyn Dodgers for a few games in 1947, was going to pitch. But he didn't show up.

When I saw all those folks out in the stands, I decided I'd better pitch. You don't make about fifteen thousand mad when you want them to come out the next time.

I put on my uniform and headed for the field.

Feller and I both went the first four innings.

I struck out seven of those major league all-stars, including Ralph Kiner, while Feller was striking out only two of my boys. But I got saddled with the loss. The all-stars got a run off me in the fourth, even though I gave up only two hits. They got another run in the top of the seventh off my reliever. We got one in the last of the seventh, but it didn't do us any good. We lost, two to one.

Four days later we played Feller in Wrigley Field again, and his boys beat us two to one again. But this time I really outdid Feller.

We both went the first five innings and Feller gave up three hits and one run and struck out five. They got to me for three hits, too, but I didn't give a run and fanned eight. I was leading, one to nothing, when I left after the fifth. But Feller's boys got runs in the sixth and seventh and beat us.

Against those tough major leagues, real all-stars, I had me fifteen strikeouts in nine innings and'd given up only five hits and one run. Feller'd given up seven hits and one run and fanned only seven in those same innings.

You never heard such talk. All those writers out on the Coast couldn't believe I wasn't in the majors, the way I was showing.

I couldn't understand it either.

I took my boys against Ewell Blackwell and his all-stars a couple of times the next week and I ran my strikeout record to twenty-nine in eighteen innings against those Major Leaguers. People started saying how I was better and faster'n both Feller and Blackwell.

That gave Bob Feller an idea. He was down in Mexico City with his boys and he got ahold of me. He figured a challenge game between us for a full nine innings'd give the papers a lot more to write about. That'd let them say we were going to settle all that talk about who was best. And a play-off challenge game like that was a sure bet to get out the fans. I told him it was okay with me.

We set up the game for November 2 in Los Angeles. Feller told the papers I might have an edge on him in those few innings we'd pitched against each other, but I was too old to stand up against him if I tried to go the full nine innings.

Everybody played up that challenge game big. I couldn't help grinning every time I read about it. Some challenge game, I thought. The fans didn't know it, but it was just a way for Feller and me to get a few more out for one last game and then pack and head someplace else.

And I was going to get a good price for that game. About five hundred, maybe more if the crowd was real good. A honeymooner like me could use that kind of money.

But the more they wrote about the game, the more it began to look like everybody'd figure what Feller'd said was really the truth if I didn't pitch real strong for nine innings. Some of those reporters were saying I was so old I probably couldn't even go nine, much less win. I couldn't believe they really figured that way, not after twenty years of pitching, top pitching.

That game stopped being just any old game for me then. I decided it was time for those writers out there to see a man who still could throw, throw hard enough to tear the glove off a catcher's hand. All I had to do was go nine, I kept thinking. Sure, I was pushing into my forties, but they thought I was fifty and even if they believed that, it never seemed to worry them before.

Those writers knew I still could throw. All I had to do was remind them. Then they wouldn't be thinking I was through, too old to stand up to the major leaguers.

By the time the game came up, I'd really worked myself up over it. I drove out to the ball park and smoked about five cigarettes just getting there. When I got to the locker room, I got me an arm rubdown, getting all loosed up. When that arm was loose, it could swing forever.

It seemed like I'd been using it forever, too. Long enough to get away from Mobile and from patched pants and old shirts and from truant officers and judges and reformatories. That old arm'd taken me from catfish to steak. Because of that arm people'd said I'd of been a sure Hall of Famer if I'd been pitching in the majors. I figured maybe I'd still get into the majors.

After that rubdown, after those hot juices in me'd stopped running, I got into my uniform and put on a couple of pair of socks so my legs wouldn't look so skinny. I didn't like them yelling that I looked like a crane, so I used those two pair of socks to pad out my legs.

"Hurry up, Satch," one of my teammates yelled. He and the rest of the guys started running out to the field. I never could understand why folks always hurried so. A man's got to go slow to go long and far.

○   ○   ○   ○   ○

I didn't take any warmups until I got out on the field to pitch the top of the first inning. Then I burned a few in to my catcher, Joe Greene. They popped against his mitt. I still had that old speed and the way I felt I'd have it for nine innings.

I was throwing my last warmup when Peanuts Lowrey of the Chicago Cubs came up to stand by the plate. I really kicked one in there then, just to scare him. The umpire took one look at that pitch and yelled for us to start playing.

I was ready. I fired my hard one and kept firing it. Lowrey struck out. The next two guys went down just as easy. Feller didn't get by as good as I'd done. We jumped on him for three straight hits in the last of the first and had us a one to nothing lead. In the top of the second, I set down the all-stars one, two, three and then my catcher, Joe Greene, busted one of Feller's fast balls out of the park for a home run. We were ahead, two to nothing, after just two innings.

That made me feel so good that I didn't even pitch careful when I went out there for the third inning. Bob Sturgeon of the Chicago Cubs pounded a double against the top of the fence. I think it was Roy Partee of the Boston Red Sox up next. I wasn't sure. I never could see any reason to remember every name. All I needed to know was how to get the ball over the plate. All I needed to know was that I had to go careful with that man on second base.

I threw and the batter swung and missed. I threw again and had me strike two. I fired a third time and had me a strikeout.

One out and Sturgeon still was on second.

Bobby Feller came up next and I threw three strikes past him.

Two were out.

Peanuts Lowrey was up for the second time and I struck him out for the second time.

I'd fanned the side and left Sturgeon out there on second.

In the last of the third, Feller and his infield fell apart. Two errors and four hits gave us four more runs and a six to nothing lead.

I coasted along after that and only beared down when I had to—like after Bob Lemon doubled in the fourth and after singles in the seventh and ninth.

My boys got me two more runs, too, and when it was over I'd won, eight to nothing.

I'd gone the nine innings. I'd shut out the all-stars. I'd given up only four hits. And I'd struck out fifteen major leaguers, some of the best in the business. Fifteen. Only three less than the major league record Feller'd set.

Feller'd gotten only about five strikeouts against my boys.

That sure tasted good, real good after all that talk about the challenge game. But boy was I tired. And my stomach hurt, hurt like it always did. And my feet were sore.

But I'd showed them.

In the locker room, somebody got out a bottle, but I just gulped me some beer. My old stomach howled when I did, but it was always howling anyway. The second beer went down easier.

"Hey, Satch," somebody yelled at me, "we really got something to celebrate about. Them all-stars couldn't get out of the second division in our league."

"They sure couldn't if Ol' Satch was pitchin' 'gainst them every day," I said.

o   o   o   o   o

I didn't bother getting out of my uniform until everybody else'd left. It felt good just sitting there. Better each day.

I'd shown them out there, but as tired as I was I couldn't

help wondering how many more years I could keep doing it. I'd gotten to wondering that more and more. They'd been asking me for four or five years when I was going to quit, but I just kept on winning, winning more games each year than most pitchers win in two or three. But now I was beginning to feel the soreness.

I started to get up to head for the shower when the locker room boy came over.

"Here's a towel for you, Mr. Paige," he said.

He handed me the towel and just stood there.

"You want something, boy?" I asked him.

"Mr. Paige, they got Jackie Robinson in the major leagues and they brought up some of those other guys, but they're nothing like you. Why, you're kind of like Babe Ruth. How come they took those guys and not you?"

That was one question I'd been hearing a hundred times that year. I didn't really know the answer, but I'd come up with one, just so nobody'd be sorry for me.

"Son, there's a lot of major league teams that'd like to have me," I told him. "They've been wantin' me for years. But my price is too high. I write my own ticket. I goes when and where I like. There ain't too many major leaguers makin' what I make and that's the truth."

I'd said it time after time. I guess in a way it was the truth, but that old major league bug was biting me harder than ever and I was looking around for an offer.

"Maybe somebody'll offer you enough one of these days, Mr. Paige," the boy said.

"Maybe."

o   o   o   o   o

After I left the Coast, some guy I knew out there mailed me a column signed by Vincent X. Flaherty that ran in one of the Los Angeles papers. He'd written it after I beat

Blackwell, but I hadn't seen it. Flaherty couldn't figure out why the majors hadn't grabbed me either. And he said some real nice things about me.

"The eternal Satchel Paige shuffled out there on Wrigley Field the other night and gave the customers a pretty fair sample of the stuff that makes him one of the most remarkable figures in baseball history," he wrote.

"Paige was pitching against Ewell Blackwell, the San Dimas (California) boy who became the major league's outstanding pitcher. Blackwell, who worked wonders with the second division Cincinnati Reds, however, had to saw a second fiddle when old Satch started going.

"The remarkable Paige was throwing against a pretty representative group of major leaguers. But all he did was strut out there and strike out nine of them in four innings. He pitched to 'em like he owned 'em.

"I have been watching Paige for quite a while. He was pitching before Lefty Gomez or Carl Hubbell came into prominence, and long after they departed from the scene, the old boy is still pitching.

"It was a good six or seven years ago when I saw Paige pitching around the East. They said poor old Satch had lost his fast ball, but he was getting by on cunning and his great control. They said he was pitching to hitters' weaknesses. Whatever he was pitching to, all I know is the fact that nobody was doing a great deal of hitting against him.

"It was like that the other night.

"Never was poor old Satch better than he was the other night. The fast ball that supposedly deserted him and bequeathed him to the old gentlemen's home, was cracking across the plate. And those major league stars were taking toe-holds and not getting a loud foul off of him.

"Paige still has a good fast ball. Don't let anyone kid you. He has what the profession calls a 'sneaky' fast one. He lets it go with that easy motion of his and before the hitter knows it the ball is right up there before he can get his bat around.

"Paige gives him that number one, and then he wraps number two around the corners of the plate. He pulls the string on his pitches and gives 'em the soft stuff. But he is forevermore giving 'em something they don't expect. He can make a hitter think he's throwing a curve, and a fast one zips across the plate. And when they're expecting a swift number, up comes a lot of fluff. He is like a crafty boxer out there. He never lets the hitter get set and strives to keep them off balance.

"Ten years from now it wouldn't be astonishing if Paige were still out there throwing. He has an indestructible arm that seems to defy the wear and tear of time. . . ."

Ten years from now, I thought after reading that column. That would be 1957 and I'd be better than fifty years old.

I figured right then that I'd just settle for three or four more years. I didn't realize I'd still be pitching long after that ten-year time limit.

o o o o o

Chapter Twenty-Four

THE REST OF THAT WINTER they filled up those sports pages all over the country with stories about how I was still good enough to be in the majors.

But nothing happened. When it didn't, I went back to the Kansas City Monarchs. Only just Mr. Baird was my boss there now. Mr. Wilkinson'd decided to kind of retire. But Mr. Wilkinson being gone wasn't the biggest thing that was different that season.

What was different was that I was making a lot less money.

After Jackie Robinson'd gotten into the major leagues, folks'd started forgetting all about Negro baseball. All those old fans were only watching the major league teams and Jackie. It kept getting worse every time the major league teams signed up another colored boy.

The worse it got, the less I got since I usually was paid a percentage of the gate on top of my regular salary.

Even with me going on forty-two, the way I was throwing I still felt I was too young to take any cut in pay. You don't want to settle for less until you know for sure you just can't get that big money anymore.

And it began to look like the only way I could stay in that big money was to get in the majors. I looked and looked, but I couldn't see any doors open for me.

The longer that old door stayed shut, the more worried I got.

Then it happened. When the biggest thing in your life happens you ain't got words big enough to say it. So I guess you just say it happens.

I'd been barnstorming out of town. I'd done a lot of that after Mr. Wilkinson left the Monarchs. When I got back to town there was this letter from Abe Saperstein, the guy who ran the Harlem Globetrotters.

Bill Veeck, who headed up the Cleveland Indians, had asked Abe to scout around for some pitching help. His ball club was trying for the pennant and they needed somebody to help out on the mound.

Abe scouted around a lot and I guess he figured the Negro leagues was the best place to find some quick help.

And as old as I was, there still wasn't anybody in the Negro leagues that could throw better than me. Abe knew that.

He recommended me to the Indians and Mr. Veeck wanted me to come up for a tryout. Abe's letter asked me to call him and let him know when I could be there.

I called quick.

After twenty-two years of throwing, I was going to get a crack at the major leagues.

Lahoma and me danced all over the house.

"You'll do it, Satchel," Lahoma kept telling me. "You know you can."

o   o   o   o   o

I got to Cleveland on July 7, 1948. That was my forty-second birthday and I was about to get me the best birthday present I'd ever had. Mr. Veeck told me to go in the locker room and get on a uniform while he was getting Lou Boudreau, the Indians' manager.

I didn't feel anything. I was just numb, I guess.

When I got out on the field, Lou Boudreau was there in

his uniform. Mr. Veeck and Abe Saperstein were there, too.

"Can you still throw like you used to?" Mr. Lou asked me.

"I got as fast a ball as anybody pitchin' now, but I got to admit it's not half as fast as it used to be. But I can still pitch it where I want to."

"Can you do that against major leaguers?" Mr. Lou asked.

"Don't you worry about that. The plate's the same size up here."

Mr. Lou just grinned.

"Why don't you catch Satch for about ten minutes and then bat against him," Mr. Veeck told Mr. Lou.

Mr. Lou nodded.

"Maybe you want to warm up first, Satch?" Mr. Lou asked me.

"Yeah, I'd like that."

"Why don't you take a lap around the gravel track, maybe run about fifty paces and then walk fifty like my boys do?"

I looked around that big ball park. But if that was what Mr. Lou wanted me to do, I'd try it. I ran about seventy-five yards and that ball park looked bigger than ever. I stopped and went back.

"You know, Mr. Lou, this is an awful big ball park," I said. "I guess I just won't run after all."

"You think you're warmed up enough?" he asked me.

"I sure am."

Mr. Lou got him a catcher's mitt and went behind the plate. I just tossed a couple real easy and then I started firing. I wasn't thinking. I wasn't trying to get in the majors. I wasn't doing anything except just pitching, like I'd always done.

That was the one thing I really knew how to do.

Finally, Mr. Lou told me I'd thrown enough and I walked up to home plate.

"That's some control, Satch," he told me. "You didn't miss the strike zone more'n four times out of fifty. Those that missed were only an inch or two off the plate, too. Let's see if you can do that good when I try hitting against you now."

"You want me to shag the balls, Lou?" Mr. Veeck said.

"If you want to," Mr. Lou answered. "Get over in right field. After seeing Satch's stuff, I don't think I'm going to pull many balls to left."

He didn't either. After we were done, he told me to go on in the clubhouse. When I walked away, Mr. Lou and Mr. Veeck were up close, real close, jawing away like everything.

A few minutes later Mr. Veeck came in the locker room.

"Lou thinks you can help the club," he told me. "Let's go down to the office and sign a contract."

It was just like that. Just that easy. As easy as it'd been for me to pitch all those years.

I was in the major leagues. The old man'd made it.

I signed that contract real quick. I was going to get a year's salary for only a half-year of ball.

After I'd signed up, Mr. Veeck grinned.

"Satch," he told me, "I'm just sorry you didn't come up in your prime. You'd have been one of the greatest right-handers baseball has ever known if you had."

o   o   o   o   o

Not everybody was happy that I'd gotten into the major leagues. Most were, but there were some who said it was just a cheap publicity stunt. Maybe Mr. Veeck did want some publicity, but he wanted a pitcher, too. There was only one guy around who could fill both orders. That was Ol' Satch.

Some people wrote some mighty nice things after I signed, like the story Tom Meany of New York wrote. He said, "As far as I'm concerned, the signing of Satchel Paige to a Cleveland contract is far more interesting than was the news when Branch Rickey broke the baseball color line by signing Jackie Robinson to a Montreal contract. It was inevitable that the bigotry which kept Negroes out of organized ball would be beaten back, but I'd never heard of Robinson at that time. With Paige it's different. The Satchmo has been a baseball legend for a long time, a Paul Bunyan in technicolor. More fabulous tales have been told of Satchel's pitching ability than of any pitcher in organized baseball. . . ."

About a day after I signed, Mr. Veeck called a press conference. "We signed Satchel in accordance with our policy of getting the best available material no matter the cost," he said. "We are convinced he is the best available player who has a chance to help us win the pennant."

When Mr. Veeck said he didn't care about the cost, I guess he meant it. I didn't get no bonus, but I got that good contract. And I think Abe Saperstein got fifteen thousand for finding me. When I heard that I couldn't help thinking that Mr. Wilkinson and Mr. Baird ought to get something. They'd sponsored me ever since my arm'd gone dead and I figured they ought to get something for that.

I told Mr. Veeck how I felt and he agreed. He was a mighty fair man.

He gave Mr. Wilkinson and Mr. Baird five thousand to split.

That was five thousand more than Branch Rickey gave them for Jackie Robinson when he took him from the Monarchs.

o o o o o

It wasn't until the day after I signed that I started feeling things. I knew the Indians weren't the Monarchs, but I'd still be out there with a ball in my hand and the fellow at the plate'd have a bat in his hand.

Maybe they'd knock me all over the place, but I was going to have to see them do it.

I was starting my major league career with one thing in my favor, anyway. I wasn't afraid of anybody I'd see in that batter's box. I'd been around too long for that.

I wasn't as fast as I used to be, but I was a better pitcher. If I couldn't overpower them, I'd outcute them.

I didn't feel bad about not having all my speed anymore. I was happy over still being able to throw. Why, guys I used to pitch against, guys like Waite Hoyt, Lefty Grove, Lonnie Warneke, Dizzy Dean, and Carl Hubbell, weren't even around anymore.

But Ol' Satch was.

I was just starting, starting years after those guys hung up their gloves.

I'd waited a long time to pitch in the major leagues, but I couldn't have asked for a better setting when I got my first chance. It was on July 9, and the Cleveland Indians were playing the St. Louis Browns in Cleveland's Municipal Stadium.

There were about thirty-five thousand in those stands and lots of them were there just hoping they'd get to see me. I didn't let them down.

Bob Lemon started for us and he didn't have it. He got behind, four to one, after three and a half innings, and they pinch-hit for him in the last of the fourth. A couple of the other boys and me'd been warming up out in the bullpen in the last half of the fourth and when we were ready to start the fifth, Lou Boudreau signaled for me.

It seemed like a mighty long walk from the bullpen to the pitcher's mound. I didn't go fast. No reason wearing myself out just walking.

I just shuffled along and every time I shuffled the stands busted loose like they never was so happy to see anyone in their life.

I'd pitched before a lot more than that a lot of times and I'd heard more noise, but there still were a pretty good bunch of cheerers out there for just an old Friday night game.

When I got to the infield, out came all these photographers. There must have been ten of them, popping flashbulbs in my face.

They tried crawling over one another to get pictures of me. It was such a mess I just dropped my mouth open and stopped and stood there for a minute. The chief umpire, Bill McGowan, didn't chase those photographers off the field like he was supposed to.

He must of thought history was being made so he just let them shoot away.

I guess maybe history was being made. I was only about ten feet away from being the first Negro ever to plant a spike on an American League pitching mound.

Lou Boudreau was on the mound waiting for me. He handed me the ball and said something.

I don't know what it was. I wasn't hearing too good. I don't even think I heard those fans any more, but folks tell me they were making even more noise now that I'd gotten to the mound.

I threw my first warmup pitch and all those flashbulbs popped again. You'd have thought I was the new President or something.

The photographers finally cleared out of the way and Chuck Stevens, the Browns' first baseman, stepped up to the plate to open the fifth.

This was it.

I felt those nerves. They were jumping every which way.

I didn't feel loose at all. I guess I wasn't. I threw and Stevens singled.

Then the nerves were all gone. I was pitching and I'd been doing that too long to be nervous in a game.

201

Gerry Priddy came up and I fired my hard one. He bunted and Stevens went to second while we were getting Priddy out at first.

There was one out, but the Browns had a runner in scoring position. Whitey Platt was up. I gave him my overhand pitch and my sidearmer and my underhander and my hesitation. He struck out.

When Zack Taylor, the Browns' manager, saw what I could do with that hesitation pitch, he protested. But Mr. McGowan said it was legal.

Al Zarilla came up with two out and Stevens still on second. I just fired, like I'd always been firing, and got him to fly out to right field for the third out.

We didn't score in the last of the fifth.

In the top of the sixth, Dick Kokos singled off me and went to second when one of my boys fumbled around with the ball. Roy Partee was up next and cracked the ball good, but right into a line-drive double play. Eddie Pellagrini flied out to end the inning.

Mr. Lou pinch-hit for me in the last of the sixth. I was through for the night. I hadn't set no records, but I'd done what the Indians was paying me for. I'd gotten the side out without giving up any runs in the fifth and sixth innings.

o   o   o   o   o

It wasn't much after that game that Will Harridge, president of the American League, banned my hesitation pitch.

He said he'd never seen a pitch like that. He said I was tricking the batters and umpires—having the batters swinging at balls when all the time I had the ball in my hand; having the umpires calling strikes when the catcher thumped his glove, making them lie.

The first time Mr. Harridge saw that pitch of mine, he

must have grabbed a rule book and thumbed all through it, but couldn't find anything in those rules against it. But he didn't like those batters falling all over the plate swinging at nothing. And he didn't like me making liars out of the umpires. So he decided I couldn't use that hesitation any more.

Man, I almost got worried. I was afraid if I showed any of my other tricks he might ban them too. I figured I'd better not throw any of that trick stuff, just throw that plain stuff like Bobby Feller and Ewell Blackwell and those other boys.

I guess Mr. Harridge didn't want me to show up those boys who were young enough to be my sons.

I didn't mind, though. It was pretty tough on those boys having to play against somebody like me. They hadn't had to get by like I'd had to. They'd had expensive coaches and guys like that to teach them how to throw. They didn't have to figure things out for themselves.

They had those trainers to rub them down all the time. And they'd gotten plenty of rest between games. They hadn't had to come up with those trick pitches just to rest their arms and work out the tiredness. They never had to pitch every day for a month at a time or play the whole year round.

I guess that makes a difference. And Will Harridge must have known I was a little too smart for those kids in the major leagues and he didn't want to see me fool them too much.

So even if it wasn't in the rule book, he called my hesitation illegal. He didn't want to cause none of them kids who came up against me any hardships.

I figured I'd just have to get out there and confuse those kids with ordinary stuff.

○　○　○　○　○

It was about a week before they banned my hesitation pitch that I got a chance to pitch in my second game. It wasn't a regular game, but an exhibition game against the Brooklyn Dodgers on July 14. And there were almost sixty-five thousand in Municipal Stadium to see it.

I went in after the Dodgers and us were all tied up three and three after six innings.

I needed only twelve pitches to get that side out. I used my old corkscrew windup and it really floored them. I whiffed Gil Hodges on four tosses, fanned Erv Palica on three curves, and struck out Tom Brown on five tosses.

I retired the side in order in the eighth, too, and we finally won the game in the eleventh, four to three.

After that, I knew I was in. I only wished Lahoma'd been there to see it, but the baby was keeping her busy and she wasn't going to be able to get up and see me until the end of the month.

○　○　○　○　○

That next day after the exhibition game, Mr. Lou sent me in to pitch again. If Mr. Lou thought I was too old, he sure didn't show it, calling on me only a day after I'd pitched that exhibition game.

We were playing a double-header in Philadelphia against the Athletics and we won the first game, six to one. If we won the second game, we'd have us a league lead of two and a half games and we could use a little breathing room.

We pushed ahead, four to two, after five and a half innings in that second game, but we couldn't stand that good living. Philadelphia started getting to Bob Lemon in the last of the sixth. They got a run in, and then Mr. Lou decided it was time for Ol' Satch.

I got us out of trouble quick and we went into the seventh still ahead, four to three.

We got us another run in the top of the seventh and I was ready to just ride home and protect that win for Bob Lemon.

But you don't just ride in the majors, not even if you're a Walter Johnson or a Dizzy Dean or a Bob Feller or a Satchel Paige.

Ferris Fain doubled off me in the last of the seventh and then Hank Majeski smashed my trouble ball on the left field roof. That tied the score.

I just shook my head. Those things happen. But they weren't going to happen to me any more in that game, I was going to make sure of that.

My boys got me a lead back right off the bat in the eighth. Ken Keltner belted out a home run and I was ahead, six to five, going into the last of the eighth. I put down the A's real fast then and in the ninth we got two more runs. With that eight to five lead, I just whipped right by the A's in the last of the ninth.

I'd gotten my first major league win, eight to five, and I'd given up only one more hit after that home run. The A's had only three hits for those three and a third innings I'd pitched.

I was one and zero in the majors, one and zero against guys who were in knee pants or weren't even born when I'd started pitching.

I kept rolling, too. About a week later I got the call again. We were playing before a capacity crowd of better than sixty-eight thousand in Yankee Stadium in New York. We were still leading the league, but that didn't scare the Yankees.

Going into the last of the sixth, we were behind, six to

five. That's when they sent me in to keep the Yankees from getting farther ahead. I didn't let them in the two innings I pitched. I put them down with only one hit in the sixth and seventh innings and in the seventh I struck out Joe DiMaggio, too. Joe'd belted a grand slam home run off Bobby Feller in the fifth, but he only got air off me.

It wasn't enough, though. We didn't score anymore, and the Yankees won by that six to five score.

But I'd run my string to seven and a third innings against the major leaguers while giving up only two earned runs with those two innings of shutout ball—and Lahoma saw it. She'd just gotten there that afternoon by plane. She was going to spend the night visiting and then fly back to take care of our baby.

After the game, we went out celebrating like we hadn't since the baby came. It was our first chance to celebrate over me being in the majors.

The next morning Lahoma and me got up early so we could have more time together before she had to leave.

When I looked out the window and saw all those clouds in the sky, I knew we'd have more time together than I'd figured.

"I know about weather and those clouds say 'no game,'" I told Lahoma.

"Then you can stay with me until I have to leave," she said.

That's just what I did.

We just sat around talking and watching that rain come down. It came down so hard they called off the ball game. I heard it on the radio.

"That's just what I told you," I said to Lahoma.

Then it was time for Lahoma to leave and I had to say good-bye to her again. That's the way it is when you're a traveling man.

After I left her, I headed for the train station. The Indians were leaving New York and heading for Boston. That rained-out game was the last one we were supposed to play in New York on that trip.

I guess I got kind of mixed up without my teammates with me. Anyway, I went to the wrong station. By the time I found that out and got over to the right one, the Indians' train'd left.

I'd just missed that old train.

But I caught me a bird over to Boston and headed up to see Mr. Lou.

"It's very nice of you to decide to join us," was all he'd say to me.

That's when I found out how they did things in the majors. Those boys just don't have heads of their own, I guess. Even if it's raining like everything, they got to go out to the ball park and wait until somebody tells them to go home.

Mr. Lou fined me for not coming out to the park and missing that train.

I didn't mind the fine. That's the way they did it in the majors. What made me kind of sore was they wouldn't pay me back for that ticket I'd bought for the airplane over to Boston.

o   o   o   o   o

Chapter Twenty-Five

IT WASN'T MUCH AFTER I'd missed that train that Mr. Lou came up to me and asked me if I could start.

"Sure I can start," I told him.

"Are you sure?" he asked me.

"Sure, I'm sure. I always started before."

"I know that, Satch. But all these boys are topnotchers up here."

"That's what I always played against."

Then old Bill McKechnie, one of our coaches, came in on my side and that seemed to satisfy Mr. Lou.

"You want me to give you any advice on how to pace yourself?" Mr. Lou asked me.

"No. I'll just pitch it my way. I always have."

"You can lose it like you want to," he told me and walked off.

I guess I'd upset him, but he didn't change his mind about starting me. On August 2, he told the papers I'd pitch the next day against the Washington Senators in Municipal Stadium.

Going into that game, I'd been used eight times in relief, winning one and losing one.

I'd pitched eighteen innings against those major leaguers and'd given up only four earned runs.

Nine more innings against them wasn't anything to fret about.

Everybody seemed to forget all about the pennant race

when Mr. Lou announced I was going to start. But I didn't. A win for us in our game with the Senators and a loss for Philadelphia in its game with Chicago would move us into a first-place tie in the league with the A's. Boston and New York could tie, too, if they won their games. We all were one game behind Philadelphia.

It was a big game, getting late in the season like it was. Every game was a big one.

You don't play around in the major leagues and I wasn't about to start the first time I got a chance to go all the way.

That first chance was something to see, all right. With everybody knowing I was going to pitch, better than seventy-two thousand came out to the ball park.

That was the biggest night crowd in Cleveland baseball history and it stood until I beat it myself a couple of weeks later.

For a few minutes out there, it looked like I was going to let all those people down. I got one out in the first inning, but then my control left me flat. I walked two batters and Ed Stewart slammed a triple off me and gave Washington a two to nothing lead before we'd even got to bat.

"Don't worry none," I told Mr. Lou after I got the side out. "That ol' control ain't gonna be missing anymore. You just leave me in there."

That's just what Mr. Lou did. Even if he'd wanted to take me out, I don't think he'd have done it that early—not with all those folks out there to see me.

I settled down pretty good after that.

We got back one run in the last of the fourth, but Washington squeezed across a run in the top of the fifth. My boys tied it up, three and three, with two runs in the last of the fifth. Then in the last of the sixth we scored again and I was ahead, four to three.

We got a rally going in the last of the seventh and Mr. Lou sent in a pinch-hitter for me. The pinch-hitter didn't do anything, but we still got another run and were ahead, five to three.

Ed Klieman relieved me and held the Senators scoreless in the eighth and ninth and I had me my second win of the year, five to three, even if I hadn't gone all nine.

I'd given up seven hits and after walking those two in the first inning, I walked only two more and got me six strike-outs.

And when I heard that Philadelphia'd lost to Chicago, I got a grin on me that didn't quit for a week. I'd pitched us into first place in the American League, even if we had to share it with Philadelphia, Boston, and New York that day. Boston'd beat St. Louis and New York'd beat Detroit.

o o o o o

That pennant race was really getting tough and we all felt it. Mr. Lou wasn't playing any of the amateurs because of the way it was going, but he was playing Ol' Satch plenty.

Five days after I got that first start, he called me in to relieve in the first game of a double-header against the New York Yankees. I went in to pitch the top of the eighth with the score tied six and six and held the Yanks while we were getting two runs and got credit for my third win against one loss, eight to six.

When we won the second game of that double-header, that kept us in first place by six percentage points.

You don't have to be no pencil whiz to see how much every one of those games meant. But Ol' Satch wasn't letting the pressure buckle him. I was pushing, pushing to show good my first chance in the major leagues.

But pitching that way wasn't any vacation. My stomach troubles were getting to me real often. Sometimes it got so I thought I couldn't throw that ball. I remember once we were

playing Washington and I was out on the mound. My
catcher, Jim Hegan, signaled for a fast ball and I shook
him off. I had to. Those pains was hurting so I couldn't
throw the ball. Then Jim signaled for a curve ball. I still
had to shake him off. He signaled for my letup and I shook
him off again.

I just had to wait until things quieted down inside me.

Jim came stomping out from the batter's box.

"Satch," he said, "I've given you everything and you don't
want them. What's the matter?"

"Man, I got the miseries in my stomach and Lefty Weis-
man ain't here to help me."

Lefty was the Cleveland trainer and he was out sick himself that day.

But Jim called into the dugout and Bob Lemon came
running out with Lefty's little black bag.

"What does Lefty usually give you, Satch?" Bob asked me.

"Somethin' white."

Bob fished around in that bag and finally came up with
one of those white pills for me. I swallowed it down and
it wasn't no time before my stomach got real peaceable and
I was ready to pitch again.

'Course, Jim Hegan called me a hypochondriac and told
me that for all he knew that white pill could have been a
cure for dandruff.

But I knew better. That pill was white, just like the ones
Lefty gave me. And it quieted them pains, didn't it?

o   o   o   o   o

After that first start of mine, it seemed like it was forever
before they ever got around to starting me again. But that
was the way it was in the majors. You just didn't pitch
every day the year round like I'd done before.

That took a lot of getting used to. For a long time just

sitting around like that wore me out. I'd get so tired just sitting I'd have to sneak into the locker room and take a little snooze.

I was in there one day, stretched out on the rubbing table, kind of dozing, when my old buddy Dizzy Dean came in. He shook me awake.

"What's the matter, boy, you tired from overwork?" he asked me.

"Diz, I'm tired from underwork. This is the first time in twenty years I've gone four or five days without pitching."

But that didn't last too long. With the pennant race tightening up like it did, Mr. Lou started using me more and more.

We'd dropped out of first place again and Mr. Lou gave me the job of getting us back in there on August 13. We were playing a night game in Chicago at Comiskey Park.

That park held a lot of old memories for me and a lot of folks'd seen me pitch there. A big chunk of those same folks, people who'd seen me throw my best against Negro leaguers, came out to see how I threw against major leaguers. They busted down a big gate trying to get in there to see me.

We had a crowd of about fifty-one thousand, the largest ever to see a night game in Chicago.

Nobody could have given me any better news than that. In my first start in the majors, I'd drawn the largest night crowd ever in Cleveland. Now, for my second start, I'd done the same thing in Chicago.

Ol' Satch could draw the fans, and you'd better believe it.

Now all I had to do was show them I still could throw, throw for nine innings.

But nine innings in this league was a long way. I'd found that out against Washington.

I went easy, real easy, not trying to burn that fast ball by the batters. I just tried to put it where I figured it'd do the most good.

The first four innings went by without us or Chicago scoring. That ball was flowing out of my hand just like it was some water. And I wasn't wasting any pitches. I hadn't walked a man in those first four innings. I was bearing down. I wanted that win, just as bad as anybody. It'd put us back in first place.

Larry Doby, our center fielder, gave me a hand in the top of the fifth inning. He tripled and scored a couple of minutes later when Jim Hegan, my catcher, hit a fly.

I had me a one to nothing lead.

I nursed that through the last of the fifth, the sixth, and the seventh. We weren't scoring anymore and I just kept praying my arm wouldn't tire out on me.

In the top of the eighth I got some breathing room. Ken Keltner, our third baseman, singled and got sacrificed to second. Then Dale Mitchell, our left fielder, singled him home.

That gave me two runs to work on.

That mob watching went wild, even though we were playing in the Chicago ball park. They were there for me, that was for sure.

I didn't let them down in the eighth. I set down those White Sox again real quick. I'd given up only three hits in the first eight innings.

"Don't worry, boys, we got them now," I said when we got to the bench for the top of the ninth.

They weren't worrying. My boys picked up three more runs in the top of the ninth and I had me a five to nothing lead.

I figured I was as good as home. I got the first man up real easy. I had one out.

But I wasn't home. Luke Appling singled and Pat Seerey singled. There were men on first and third and only one out.

I wasn't real worried about losing, but I didn't want to get taken out of there. I wanted that complete game.

I walked back to the resin bag and dusted my hands. I rubbed the ball. I wasn't nervous. I'd been in holes like this before. I just wanted to get those next two batters to fidgeting.

I must have. I got Aaron Robinson and Ralph Hodgin out real easy.

I had my first complete game.

And it was a shutout—a shutout in only my second start. We'd won five to nothing and I'd given up only five hits. I hadn't walked a man. That put us back into the American League lead.

"It looks like when they need that stopper, need that big game to get back into first place, you're the one, Satch," a reporter told me after the game.

It sure was funny how serious that reporter was when he said that—like nobody'd ever known it before. What he didn't know was that for about twenty years reporters'd been saying that.

But that reporter didn't bother me. What bothered me was those guys who were saying that I was just lucky to get that shutout.

That's why my next start—when I shut out those White Sox again and gave Cleveland a tie for the American League team record of four shutouts in a row—was the game I thought was the biggest in my career.

And that covers a lot of ground.

That second shutout even convinced the umpires. Bill Summers and Art Passarella hopped in my corner and stayed there.

"How can you rate him?" Bill told one reporter. "There are few better pitchers in baseball today. Maybe there aren't any. And there are few with more stuff. He has a slider that cracks like a whip and a curve that explodes. And he is plenty fast. Is there anything else?"

And Art told those writers, "There's a rocking chair if

ever there was one. That old boy's around the plate all the time and calling balls and strikes for him's a breeze. I was behind the plate in that shutout he worked in Chicago and I never had an easier game in my life."

o   o   o   o   o

You could feel that pennant tension every time you went into our locker room those last few days in August. It'd been twenty-eight years since Cleveland'd gotten in a World Series.

When I first heard it'd been twenty-eight years, I couldn't hardly believe it. Why, that was even before I started playing professionally, and the way most people'd always talked it didn't seem to me like baseball'd even been invented before I began tossing my trouble ball.

I tried to help those boys out when the pressure was deep like it was, but they were all so tied up they couldn't hear anybody.

I figured maybe my pitching'd snap them out of it and I got a chance on August 30. We'd dropped two games behind the Boston Red Sox and we were in third place when Mr. Lou sent me in there to straighten out the team.

That's just what I did.

I stopped the Washington Senators on seven hits and we won, ten to one. I had me a two-hitter going into the eighth and gave up only one extra-base hit for my sixth win against one loss. Boston didn't play that night and we were only one and a half games out of first place.

That pennant race kept going like that right up to the wire. Then it ended—ended with us and Boston tied for first place.

They set a play-off game and Gene Bearden went out to pitch it for us. I was ready in the bullpen just in case Gene got into any trouble against Boston, but Gene didn't need my help that day. We won the play-off and that gave us the

American League pennant. We were in the World Series against the Boston Braves.

It was Cleveland's first pennant in twenty-eight years and they hadn't done it until Ol' Satch came around and won them six games while losing only one down the stretch drive.

That's why they were saying I'd gotten more fame in three months than most pitchers do in ten years in the major leagues.

I got it because I won, and because the fans wanted to see me. I didn't get it because I was just a publicity stunt Bill Veeck was trying to pull off.

When Bill signed me, he knew what he was doing.

I showed he knew.

o o o o o

Chapter Twenty-Six

LOTS OF PEOPLE have to wait a long time to get their life's ambitions. I wasn't any different. Oh, that big money'd come early, but getting into the major leagues took a long time.

And that same season I finally made the majors, I stood a chance of satisfying another ambition—playing in a World Series.

That was up to Mr. Lou, but the way I'd thrown for him I was sure he'd use me.

Even though I knew I was with a World Series team, it still kind of surprised me. You can't help being surprised when so many things happen in only three months. I'd made it to the top. I'd proved what I could do, to guys like Gene Bearden and Bob Lemon, who'd expected to see an old man with a handle bar mustache after Mr. Veeck signed me.

I did have a mustache, but not an old man's mustache, when they first saw me, but I'd clipped that off after I'd asked Mr. Veeck if he thought I should shave it.

"You can keep it if you want to," he told me, "but nobody else on my team has one."

I didn't either after that.

Without that mustache and with my trouble ball still causing troubles, I was just another kid on the team when the World Series against Boston started.

I almost didn't even get into the ball park for that first game. The gatekeeper wouldn't let me through. He didn't recognize me.

"I'm a ballplayer," I told him.

He just didn't listen.

Finally, one of my teammates came along and got me in.

The way that first game turned out, I could have stayed outside. Bobby Feller started and he didn't need help from me or anybody, even though he lost to Johnny Sain, one to nothing.

In the second game, Bob Lemon started for us and I just relaxed out there in the bullpen. I was doing my best not to wear myself out with any extra exercise like moving, just in case Mr. Lou did want me.

The fans sure wanted me, even those Boston fans. They were yelling, "We want Satchel."

I didn't let that excite me, as bad as I wanted to get in the World Series. I just relaxed in a chair out there in the bullpen, talking to the fans. One of them leaned over the rail and handed me a hot dog. I took it and broke off a piece of meat and picked off the skin. I had to watch my diet. I couldn't eat skin. It's bad for you. I just kept peeling and chewing.

A man had to do something when he wasn't pitching.

Then Lemon started having some troubles.

"Satch," somebody called, "Lou wants you to warm up."

"I can see him," I said, "and he can see me if he wants to look around. When he wants me to warm up he'll let me know."

I finished off that last piece of hot dog and threw the roll away and kicked those pieces of skin away from me.

Lemon was really staggering now, even if he was ahead.

"Maybe you'd better start throwing," somebody else said.

I finally started getting excited. Maybe it was my chance. But Mr. Lou still hadn't signaled for me so I tried to play it cool.

I dug a package of cigarettes out of my jacket, lit one, and blew smoke.

"Now I'm all warmed up," I told those guys sitting around me.

I still felt that excitement and I almost jumped out of my uniform when Mr. Lou turned around and signaled me to start warming up.

But I held myself down. No man likes for the whole world to see how he's churning inside.

I got up real slow and started lobbing the ball in there. Maybe it's my chance, I kept thinking.

But Lemon got ahold of himself and I sat down, trying to act like it didn't matter.

I couldn't keep that sad look off my face, though. I'd wanted in there awfully bad.

I didn't get another chance in that second game. Lemon finished up strong and had him an eight-hit, four to one victory. That evened the World Series at one game apiece.

We only had a little bit of a party after getting that first World Series win. That's because we had to catch a train right off to get back to Cleveland, where we were going to play the third game.

On the train Mr. Lou told the reporters that Gene Bearden was going to pitch the third game. He didn't say who'd pitch the fourth game, but I kind of thought it would be me, so I was real loose on the train. I got into a kidding match with Spud Goldstein, the club's traveling secretary.

"How about a lower, Spud?" I asked him.

"We have nothing but roomettes on our train," Spud said. He sounded about as proud as a man with his first boy child. "Remember, Mr. Paige, you are with a big league club now."

I looked at him real serious. "If you boys ain't all careful, you all are gonna give me a swelled head."

Mr. Lou came along then and slapped me friendly-like.

"If Lemon hadn't settled down, Satch, you'd of probably been in your first World Series," he told me.

I figured for sure I'd make that fourth game then.

It just shows you how you can't always figure on things.

o   o   o   o   o

In the third game, Gene Bearden made it look like we never were going to need a relief pitcher. He shut out Boston, two to nothing, on five hits and gave us a two to one edge in the Series.

I was getting itchy. That fourth game had to be mine. I was sure of that.

Then Mr. Lou announced that Steve Gromek was going to pitch.

I felt sick.

When Steve beat Boston, two to one, and gave us a three to one lead, I started pressing. One more win for us and the World Series'd be all over.

"How 'bout startin' me next game?" I asked Mr. Lou.

A lot of sports writers were asking that now, too. So were the fans.

But Mr. Lou didn't say anything.

Then he announced that Bobby Feller was going to pitch and I was really troubled. Bobby was a mighty good hand and if he didn't need any relief help, that meant I'd miss pitching in the World Series.

Knowing Bobby, I figured he probably wouldn't need any help, even with him having only three days rest.

I felt low as anybody ever felt.

The papers were on my side. They kept asking why Mr. Lou was pitching Bobby instead of me.

"Satchel deserves to pitch," one reporter wrote. "Not only is he rested, but he earned the right with his tremendous pitching during the 1948 season. His six victories were the key factor in getting the Indians into the American League play-off. Without those victories, there would not have been a play-off and Cleveland would not have been in the World Series."

But Mr. Lou didn't change his mind. He went ahead and started Feller on October 10 in Municipal Stadium.

I didn't want Bobby to get hit, but I guess deep down I was pulling against my own team. I wanted in that World Series awfully bad. I didn't show it. I didn't want anybody saying I was against my own team.

Before the game, I just talked free and easy with the reporters.

"Man, it took me a long time to get here, but it was worth it," I told them. "This is one of the biggest thrills I ever had, and you better believe it. If I get a chance to pitch, believe me, I'm gonna show the Braves some stuff they never saw before."

"You sure take things good, Satch," one of them told me.

"Ain't any other way to take it," I said.

"Aren't you nervous?"

"I've been in these things before. Not in these leagues. In the Negro leagues. I've been with the Kansas City Monarchs when they played in the World Series. Some of these other boys may be nervous, but I'm used to it."

They all started leaving. It was about game time.

"Good luck," one of them yelled.

"Luck? Luck is my middle name."

I only hoped it was. It looked like it was going to take luck to get me in the World Series.

o   o   o   o   o

Bobby wasn't sharp like he should have been. The Braves clipped him for three runs in the first inning, but Mr. Lou left him in there.

I just sat in the bullpen hoping and hoping.

We got back a run in the last of the first, but Boston got to Bobby for another run in the third. That gave them a four to one lead. Bobby seemed to settle down then and when we got four runs in the last of the fourth to go ahead, five to four, I thought it was all over for me.

I didn't even have hope left.

In the sixth Boston tied the score, five and five, by scoring one. But I still was a long way from getting in the game.

Why? All I could do was ask myself, "Why?" It was the same why I used to ask myself when I couldn't get into the major leagues. There never was an answer.

Then came the top of the seventh.

Tommy Holmes of Boston led off against Bobby with a single. Mr. Lou signaled the bullpen and Ed Klieman, Russ Christopher, and me got up and started warming up.

Alvin Dark sacrificed Holmes to second and then Earl Torgeson singled, driving home Holmes to break the five-all tie.

Mr. Lou went stomping to the mound.

This was it, I thought. I threw harder and harder.

Mr. Lou waved to the bullpen. I jerked around. Then I sunk all inside me. He was waving in Ed Klieman.

I kept throwing. But I didn't want to. For about the first time in my life I didn't feel like throwing.

Ed Klieman must not have either. He walked two and gave up a single. Mr. Lou went to the mound again. I had a chance again. I lost it again.

Mr. Lou waved in Russ Christopher.

Why?

The fans wondered too. They kept chanting, "We want Satchel."

I was the only one left out in the bullpen throwing. I guess that's why Mr. Lou called on me when Russ gave up two singles in a row and Boston had six runs in for the inning and an eleven to five lead.

Maybe that's why he called me in. Or maybe it was because we already were so far behind.

When I walked out there the fans started cheering. There

were better than eighty-six thousand out there watching and they yelled louder than they had any other time in the World Series up to then.

"I just hope Mr. Lou is hearing them," I muttered.

Then I forgot about Mr. Lou and the fans and everything. I had me a pitching job to do.

There was a man on first and only one out.

I guess everybody figured the game was over, but I wasn't going to let up. I was mighty serious out there, but I still gave them some fun. I didn't mean to, but the umpires thought I was trying to trick those Boston boys.

I spit on my fingers, just to get the dryness out, and then wiped my hand off on my uniform. But George Barr, the umpire behind the plate, must have been worried by that. He called for the ball to make sure I wasn't going to try to throw a spitter.

Ol' Satch threw a lot of things, but my natural stuff was always good enough. I didn't need any spit to help out.

Warren Spahn was up and I threw. It was ball one.

Then I stretched and held my arms still for a minute about halfway through my delivery, but before I could throw, out came George Barr.

He had a little talk for me on how you're supposed to throw in one continuous motion. Mr. Lou came running over to help me out. Then Bill Summers, another umpire, came over, I guess to even up the sides.

They finally left and let me pitch. I got Warren Spahn out of there. There were two outs with a man on first.

Tommy Holmes came up again, for the second time in the inning. I started my delivery to Tommy and reached way up high, then brought my hands down against my chest and rested a moment. That was all legal, but Billy Grieve, another umpire, came running over.

"Balk, balk," he yelled. "You wiggled the fingers of your glove. It's a balk."

They moved Eddie Stanky, who was that runner on first, down to second. I didn't have anything to say, but it made me so mad I gave Tommy Holmes my real trouble ball and got him out quick, ending the inning.

That finished my show. Mr. Lou took me out after that. We lost, by that same eleven to five score, but that didn't bother me any. I'd been in a World Series.

Sure, I'd pitched only two-thirds of an inning, but it was the first a colored boy'd ever pitched in a World Series. I didn't even feel mad at Mr. Lou any more because of that.

o   o   o   o   o

We won the World Series in the sixth game, beating the Boston Braves, four to three.

After it was over, there were parties and press meetings and everything like I'd never seen before. All the reporters had the same thing to ask me, "Will you be back with the Indians in 1949?"

"That's up to the boss," I told them. "As far as I'm concerned, Ol' Satch'll be back. The way I'm feeling, I figure I got at least three more years of baseball left, anyway, and there ain't much left for me to do but pitch."

I was telling those writers I thought I had me only three or four years left, but I wasn't believing it anymore. I was feeling like I could go on forever. And I kept living it up like those baseball paychecks'd be coming in forever. I didn't save a penny of that 1948 money for my old age. I put me three new cars in my garage, bought me a new boat and motor, and a couple more shotguns and some more hunting dogs.

Lahoma tried to keep me from doing it, but she couldn't hold me down altogether. I was smelling that major league money and it was filling up my head so I couldn't even hear her. But she kept after me and finally she did get me to buy another house, a real fine one on East Twenty-eighth Street in Kansas City.

Those two houses would have been mighty good investments if I could of kept both of them. But I just couldn't slow down that spending and when the money got a little short again, I had to sell that first house on Twelfth Street.

Stocking away money for when you get old was something I still hadn't learned. It just seemed like I never was going to get too old to pitch.

o   o   o   o   o

Chapter Twenty-Seven

AFTER THE WORLD SERIES, I barnstormed for a while. I had me more games than one man could take care of. Everybody wanted me to play for them. They wanted the guy who'd pulled more fans than about anybody since Babe Ruth.

Finally I got home to Kansas City for a few days rest. But when you got a wife and a family and a house, you don't rest. Married folks'll know what I mean.

"There's some plumbing that's not working, Satchel," Lahoma'd tell me. "And that back door needs fixing. And maybe you ought to wash the cars."

Lahoma kept after me but I liked it. I like fooling around the house and fixing things myself. No matter what they say, I don't sleep all the time. I like keeping busy, keeping moving. A man rusts sitting in one spot, and if you don't rust you can keep going long after the other guy stops.

I still had plenty of time for fishing and hunting and dancing. Doing that kept me in shape between seasons, especially that dancing. You got to watch your legs and I stayed loose and easy in the legs with dancing. Mambo, cha-cha, shoe-and-shuffle—anything. I won prizes.

And that ain't too bad for a body who's getting near that halfway point on a hundred like I was.

When I stayed in shape like that, all I had to do to be ready for a new season was just shake hands with my catcher.

'Course, there were a lot of other things I did to keep going. I had me a whole system. Some sports guy on the East coast heard me talking about them once and then he went and turned them into a bunch of rules for me on how to stay young.

I just adopted them.

Those rules for staying young are mighty good for anybody:

Avoid fried meats which angry up the blood.

If your stomach disputes you, lie down and pacify it with cool thoughts.

Keep the juices flowing by jangling around gently as you move.

Go very light on the vices, such as carrying on in society —the social ramble ain't restful.

Avoid running at all times.

And don't look back. Something might be gaining on you.

That last one that fellow wrote was my real rule. When you look back, you know how long you've been going and that just might stop you from going any farther. And with me, there was an awful lot to look back on. So I didn't. That let me keep on going, and keeping going more than anything else made Ol' Satch the reputation he had.

That and a good fast ball.

○ ○ ○ ○ ○

On February 14, 1949, I got my contract from the Indians for the 1949 season. I signed it quick.

I just fooled around home until it was time to head for spring training.

Even with what I'd done in 1948, there were some guys there that didn't believe in Ol' Satch.

Right off the bat the first day I was out, a guy came up to me and said, "Hear you got control."

"You didn't hear no lie," I said.

"How many strikes do you think you can throw outa, say, ten pitches?"

"Maybe not over eight or nine. I ain't throwed since October."

"A Coke says you can't throw eight," that boy told me. "Man, you got a bet."

Jim Hegan put his shinguard down to serve as a plate.

"I can throw a thousand outa a thousand over that big old thing, Jim," I told him. "Put a baseball cap down there. That's all the plate Ol' Satch needs."

There were a bunch of new guys standing around and I heard one of them ask, "Is he kiddin'?"

"Sonny boy, you can get yourself a Coke free for nothin' if you think I'm kiddin'," I told him.

I pumped a couple of times and threw a sidearm curve. It was a strike.

"I gotta give you that one," the guy I'd bet with said.

"You're getting generous in your old age," I said.

"Look who's talking about old age," Bob Lemon yelled at me.

"You talk like you pitch, Bob," I gibed at him. "Loud, but not smart. What'a you know about anybody's age?"

"All I know," Lemon told me, "is there was a guy on

that barnstorming team of yours last winter and he told me he was forty-seven and you called him 'son.'"

I just started pitching again. I ran up seven strikes out of nine with one to go to win my bet.

I really tied myself into a knot and unwound. Then I stopped. Then I threw my hesitation pitch. It popped across the plate.

"You want the Coke now or later?" that boy asked me.

That showing got all the new boys talking about my control and it was only the first day of camp.

They'd never seen anything like my bat-dodger and my hesitation pitch. But what really surprised them was my fast ball.

When we were in the locker room after working out that day, that was all they were talking about—my blazer.

"Satch, what're you gonna do when you can't throw that fast ball anymore?" one of the rookies asked me. "You gonna start to work on a slider or something like that just to be ready?"

"Man," I said, "I'm not on my way into baseball. I'm on my way out. What I can't throw now I'll never have to throw. When that fast ball is gone, Ol' Satch will be gone right with it."

o Ō ō ʋ ʋ

I just kind of loafed through spring training. I wasn't against exercising and I wasn't tired. I just didn't want to get tired. When I'm called into a game in a tight spot, I need everything I got—arm, head, eyes, and legs. I don't want to walk in there wishing I wasn't so tired. So I try to keep from getting tired.

But as careful as I was, I had troubles. My stomach kept coming up and hitting me like it hadn't since my arm went dead. I didn't tell anybody; I didn't want them to think

I was making excuses, not after just one season in the major leagues.

But those miseries were sapping my strength. I was a sick man and it started getting to my pitching after the 1949 season started.

When it did, people began to wonder about Ol' Satch. I was wondering, too. I made one start and pitched a seven-hitter, but I lost. That was early in the season, about April. I tried some relieving, but I didn't do too hot at that, either. I still hadn't won a game and'd lost two going into the end of May.

But I had to keep throwing.

When it started getting hotter in May, my stomach miseries quieted down a little. I started feeling stronger again.

"I think I'm straightened out," I told Lahoma. "But I don't know how to show the boss. I don't want to tell him about my miseries. He might just drop me because of that, the way I've been going."

"Just start throwing harder in the bullpen," Lahoma said. "Maybe he'll hear the word if you do."

Lahoma always was coming in to save me. For somebody who didn't throw a baseball, she was about the best reliever you ever saw.

I did what she said and before long it worked. I was told I was going to start May 29.

That was the chance I needed. I made the most of it. I had to go eleven innings, but I beat the Chicago White Sox, two to one. That gave me a one–two record. I was back on the track. I was sure of it.

They weren't going to be saying good-bye to me for some time yet, I figured.

The Indians used me a lot through June and July and by August 7 I had me four wins and five losses, winning three and losing three after that eleven-inning game.

That wasn't bad pitching, especially the way the Indians

were going. We were World Champions, but in 1949 we were playing second fiddle to the New York Yankees. Nobody could figure it out. We had about the same team. We'd even got Early Wynn to help us out pitching. But we weren't clicking.

Some said it was because I wasn't doing what I'd done in 1948. Maybe that was it.

And that just showed what I'd meant to the club the year before.

Whatever was wrong, we weren't moving like we should have been.

And then just to make things worse for me, my miseries came back.

It got so I couldn't go more than two or three innings at a time. I couldn't win another ball game. I finished the year with four wins and seven losses.

"I don't know what'll happen," I told Lahoma.

"Did they say they'd send you another contract?" she asked.

"Yes. Only what good will it do if my miseries don't go away? I won't be able to do anybody any good."

"Then you go see a doctor."

"They never helped before."

"Maybe they will this time. You just get over to a doctor."

I went to see the doctor. He checked me all over.

"Nothing wrong, there," he told me. "Let me take a look in your mouth." He looked and looked. "That just might be part of your trouble. Your teeth are in pretty bad shape."

He sent me to a dentist.

"They'll have to come out—all of them," he told me.

"How'll I eat?"

"I'll put in false teeth."

"Store teeth?"

"Well, not quite that, Satchel. You'll think they're your own after you see them."

I didn't like that idea at all, but the dentist was sure it'd help my stomach and my stomach needed help.

When your whole life may be depending on your stomach, you don't worry about having no teeth. You'll do about anything, even if you got to put a bunch of sticks in your mouth.

"Go ahead," I told the dentist.

He pulled them all. He'd take out about four of them every time I went out to see him. That first time was almost the last.

"I don't care if I never pitch," I told Lahoma. "I ain't gonna go through that again."

Lahoma just looked at me.

"And if you don't pitch, what're you going to do?" she finally asked.

I couldn't say anything to that.

I just went ahead and let that dentist do some more pulling. When he was done I had an old sunken hole for a mouth and nothing to chomp food with.

"How do you like it now?" I asked Lahoma, but she couldn't hardly understand me because I was talking so funny.

But talking wasn't the worst part. All that soup and mush I had to eat because I didn't have any teeth was what was bad.

I had so much of that soup and mush I just sort of sloshed around inside every time I moved.

And I couldn't tell if my stomach was getting any better. My mouth was hurting so much no other hurt could get through to me.

Then everything inside my mouth healed up and that dentist put in them store teeth.

I felt like somebody'd shoved a baseball bat in my mouth.

But, you know something, I got used to them. And I could chew better than I ever could before.

After I got used to them, I didn't do any thinking on how good I could chew. I just sat and prayed that old stomach of mine was going to be better.

I just sat and sweated.

But those pains weren't coming back like they used to. They were there, but not like they'd been all through the last season.

I knew it was good enough to pitch, maybe like I'd done in 1948.

I knew there'd be no more doubling over with that pain while I was out in the bullpen.

I was ready.

I wasn't even worried about Mr. Veeck selling out and pulling out of Cleveland.

I was sure I'd be getting that same old twenty-five-thousand-dollar contract for 1949, especially after I wrote off and told Mr. Lou how my stomach troubles was all over now that I'd pulled all my teeth.

Then I got my contract. They'd cut me twenty-five per cent, down to about nineteen thousand.

"What'll I do?" I asked Lahoma.

"Maybe we'd better see Mr. Wilkinson. He'll know. Maybe he can tell us what to do."

I got ahold of Mr. Wilkinson. He was at home. He spent most of his time there since he'd sold out his share of the Monarchs and'd retired.

"How are you going to be, with your teeth gone?" Mr. Wilkinson asked me right off after I went to see him.

"I'm gonna be fine."

"Then you'd better accept. Negro baseball and barnstorming aren't what they used to be, not with the major leagues open now. You'd be better off with that steady job. Maybe you'd make more barnstorming, but maybe you wouldn't."

"I'll sign the contract, then," I said.

"Call them up and let them know," he told me. "You've

ad that contract a couple of weeks now without letting them know anything. It might be better to call."

I called Hank Greenberg. He was general manager and ran things after Mr. Veeck left.

It all seemed settled—until Hank Greenberg called me back in almost no time and told me Lou Boudreau said he couldn't use me.

I didn't hardly believe it. But the next day, January 29, 1950, when the papers came out with the story, I had to believe it.

"Paige reportedly has played his last game for the Cleveland Indians," the papers said. "Older players will have to make way for rookies, Hank Greenberg, general manager, says."

That was it. Just a few lines in the paper and I was out of the majors, out after only two years—two years it'd taken me twenty-two years to get.

And I had me a wife and two kids to take care of and no job.

Things look mighty black when you get in that shape.

But I wasn't through. I still could throw.

I called Mr. Wilkinson.

"Can you get me some work?" I asked him. "I ought to be worth somethin' barnstorming after those two years in the major leagues."

And I figured maybe barnstorming would give those other major league teams a chance to look at me. I figured if they looked it wouldn't take too long before one of them would be signing me up.

"Do you want to hook up with a team?" Mr. Wilkinson asked me.

"No. I don't want'a get tied down. I want to stay loose so those big boys can call me if they want me."

"I'll see what I can do about booking you independent, then," Mr. Wilkinson told me.

I went home and waited.

Waiting is the worst part. It always is. After a couple of days I got jumpy and was ready to run off to any old place.

But Mr. Wilkinson was running things and he didn't let me just grab at anything.

And he got ahold of guys like Eddie Gottlieb of Philadelphia and Abe Saperstein, who were a couple of pretty fair promoters and real sharps, to help him look for jobs for me.

With all those boys looking, pitching offers started coming in fast.

"It looks like you have some good jobs coming up, Satchel," he told me.

"When do I start?"

"In a couple of days. I've gotten ahold of a reporter and he wants to come around to talk to you. It'll help us get more bookings. You going to be home?"

"I'll be here. I got to stay home and baby-sit with my two girls 'til Lahoma gets home."

Mr. Wilkinson and the reporter came around about an hour later. That reporter had a photographer with him and they wanted to take pictures of me every which way. Photographers always were doing that. They figured I ought to look funny in pictures and they did everything to make me look that way.

It'd gotten so I couldn't convince anybody I wasn't sort of a clown.

I kind of had to let my babies roll around for themselves while that photographer was doing all that shooting, but they didn't seem to mind.

After that photographer was done, the reporter started in on me. It'd been two years since the American League'd bounced my hesitation pitch, but he still wanted to talk about that.

I never could figure out reporters. They always seemed

to be going back, wanting to know about how this and that happened. But it gets your name in the papers.

That pays off.

"How'd you feel when they said your hesitation pitch was illegal?" he asked me.

"They never did say it was illegal. I guess that trouble popped up when I had those hitters swingin' at the ball 'fore I pitched it. Bobby Feller got to toyin' with that hesitation pitch and he did pretty good with it last year. Got away with it pretty good, too."

"What'd you do after they stopped you from throwing it?"

"Oh, I had a lot of different pitches—change of pace, sidearm, everything. I had to have 'em, pitchin' every day like I used to do. I didn't know I could throw overhanded until I got up there and really had to. The hitters didn't like that sidearm pitch so I got to pitchin' overhand and saved the sidearm for the clutch."

"How's your stomach trouble now?"

"No trouble at all. Last year it was mighty bad. When I was on the bench or out in the bullpen I always had to have me a bottle of Bisodol right by me for when those miseries hit. But I still don't know why Lou Boudreau didn't use me as a starter those days I was feeling good. What I do know is that my luck was running real low because I usually got that relief call when I was feelin' low. I'm not gripin'. I'm just tellin' you."

"How was it relieving up there?"

"Seems like I always came up when Joe DiMaggio or Ted Williams was up. Joe and Ted were the hardest to pitch to. You can pitch a little better to Joe than you can to Ted. You can make Joe hit to left field, but Ted, he has power to all sides. Ted's power is from the waist up. He got strong arms and powerful wrists. That Ted was the greatest, him and Josh Gibson. They didn't have any weaknesses. Joe was great, too, but you could throw him outside and say a little prayer. That Dom DiMaggio was tough, too.

"I remember one game against the Red Sox when I went in with a six-run lead. But it disappeared real fast except for one run and there was a couple of runners on base. Dom DiMaggio was up and I was a mighty nervous man. But I tricked him. I got him three balls and two strikes and then I could see he was all set for the fast one so I gave him the curve. Struck him out."

o o o o o

Maybe going from the major leagues back to barnstorming should have mashed me down, but it didn't.

I hadn't wanted to get out of the major leagues and that soft living, but they'd gotten me out—maybe because of my stomach, maybe because they were starting a youth movement in Cleveland, maybe because my salary was too high.

Mr. Veeck wouldn't have let it happen if he'd been around. I know. I talked to him after I got booted by the Indians and he told me not to worry.

"I'll be back in baseball soon, Satch," he said, "and when I am there'll be a job for you."

Knowing that made it easier going back to barnstorming, back to sleeping in my car, back to playing in little parks, back to playing in small towns, back to pitching more innings than any man around.

It was a rough kind of life, but it paid. And I'd been doing it so long I guess it didn't matter. I was used to it.

o o o o o

Chapter Twenty-Eight

EVERYWHERE I WENT I threw with all I had. I didn't loaf any. The more I kept throwing, the more scouts came around looking. Carl Hubbell, the old New York Giant pitcher, saw me in New York and I looked so good he wanted to sign me. His boss, Horace Stoneham, made me an offer. It wasn't anywhere close to what I was making with those barnstorming teams, but I was mighty tempted. I wanted back bad.

I called Mr. Veeck to see what he thought.

"It's not good enough, Satch," he told me. "You just keep on barnstorming and making that good money. I'll have a major league club again soon and then you can move."

"Bill," I said, "I'm waiting for you then."

I wouldn't have done that for nobody else, but Mr. Veeck was special. If you'd have been waiting as long as I had to get in the majors, the guy who got you there'd be something special, too.

I turned down the Giants.

The Boston Braves came looking after that and I turned them down, too. They didn't want to pay me any better than the Giants so I figured I'd better just go ahead and wait for Mr. Veeck.

Some reporters found out I'd gotten those offers and came to see me.

"Satchel, we heard a couple of clubs are trying to sign you," one of them said. "Is that right?"

"Oh, a couple came lookin'," I said. "I had to turn them down. But I'd sure like to go back for another year or so before I quit, if I get the right offer. That is, if the Army don't draft me. You know, they're draftin' us young fellows again."

"You think you have another year or two left before you quit?" that reporter asked.

"Everybody asks me when I'm gonna quit. Well, I'm beginnin' to ask myself now. People say my arm is made of whale-bone and I'm startin' to believe them. But as long as I can fog 'em past those batters, I'll be in there. You see, I love baseball and I love to pitch."

And I kept pitching and hoping that Mr. Veeck'd be getting back into baseball. Then one day I heard from him and I knew I didn't have to do any more hoping. He didn't say he had him a team and he didn't say he was going to give me a job. But he said not to sign any contract with a club in 1951 because if he got himself a team there might be something for me.

That's all I needed to hear. And it wasn't too long before Mr. Veeck announced he'd bought the old St. Louis Browns. Then eight days after I turned forty-five, my old pal told everybody that I was coming back in the majors.

I was like a happy kid. There wasn't anything to worry about this time. I'd been there before. I wasn't a rookie anymore.

Mr. Veeck told me to come up to St. Louis and join the team on July 17.

He said I'd start my first game for Manager Zack Taylor the next day, on July 18, against Washington.

Everybody asked me how long I thought I could go in that first game.

"When I start for the Browns, I expects to go the distance," I said. "All I got to do is change my gait. I'll start out slow and plan to be around late in the game."

The same morning I got to St. Louis I signed my contract. It was like a World Series crowd, there was so many around to watch it.

"They come tougher in the American League than where I've been this year," I told them, "but I think I'm ready for them. I've been here before and I think I can handle 'em. Just remember that first year with Cleveland I won six and lost only one and I was second in the league with an earned-run average of 2.47. And that bad year of mine, in 1949, I was eighth in the league in earned runs with 3.04. That wasn't too bad for a sick man."

"Did you get a bonus from Veeck to sign?" one of those guys around there asked.

"Not that I know of," I told them.

I didn't, either. Fact was, I was going to lose money by leaving the Chicago American Giants. But it wasn't too much and anyway there was a job to do for Mr. Veeck and I came to do it.

But that first game I didn't do too much. We lost to Washington, seven to one.

Zack Taylor didn't seem upset by what happened.

"You had plenty of stuff and pitched better'n I expected you to this soon," he told me.

"I'll do a lot better for you, Mr. Taylor," I told him. "I'll be getting stronger now that I'm up here where I'll have a chance to catch up on my rest. I was pitchin' so much with the American Giants I was about to quit."

"Quit? You?" Zack asked me, real surprised.

"Yeah. Quit. You know, pitch only three times a week instead of six. I'm not iron. And just because I had a little will power and luck, there wasn't any use runnin' it into the ground by pitchin' six days a week."

○　○　○　○　○

I got to know those Browns real quick and I could see some of them needed Ol' Satch to kind of give them advice, like Tommy Byrne.

He was a real strong thrower for the Browns, but the first time I saw him I was real surprised.

"You gonna wear that little thin undershirt when you pitch?" I asked him.

He just grinned.

"That's no way to stay loose and you got to stay loose to get that ball over. Let me tell you my own invention for pitchin'. Get a heavy shirt, cut off the sleeves at the shoulder, then get some rubber and tie down the arms so that no body heat can get away. Man, you stay warm all the time you're out there pitchin'. And when you stay warm you stay loose."

The Browns started taking real quick to what I said after they saw what I could do.

In those two months I pitched for the Browns in 1951, I won three and lost only four with that bad, last-place ball club. And I struck out forty-eight in sixty-two innings and walked only twenty-nine.

What I remember best about those two months was the time when I came up against my old major league manager, Lou Boudreau.

I didn't even win the game but it proved what an old head like Mr. Lou thought of my trouble ball.

Mr. Lou'd gone over to Boston by the time I got to St. Louis and we were playing against them and were tied in the tenth.

Boston had the winning run on third against me and Mr. Lou came in to pinch-hit. The first pitch I threw him was a good fast ball for a strike. I guess that's when he figured his reflexes weren't what they used to be and that he couldn't get around on the kind of stuff I was throwing.

Anyway, on the next pitch Mr. Lou bunted, scoring the winning run against me.

Mr. Lou ran off the field and into his dugout. I ran over after him.

"Hey, Mr. Lou," I yelled.

"Hello, Satch," he said. "What do you want?"

"You know, Mr. Lou, you fooled me buntin' like that. I thought you'd stand up there and slug it out with me."

o   o   o   o   o

Chapter Twenty-Nine

I FOUND OUT ONE THING after I got back into the majors. Old man prejudice hadn't been killed. When I first joined Cleveland, it looked like he had been. But I guess that was because colored boys was so new in the big leagues that everybody treated them pretty good.

But after that newness wore off, those mean folks started acting up again, started letting that meanness run out again.

All those years I'd put in taught me how to handle that kind of trouble real easy, but when it surprised me I could blow up with the best of them.

It surprised me when I got back in the majors because I hadn't expected to run into trouble when I was traveling with big leaguers.

I was barnstorming with some of the boys after that first season with the Browns and we went into some little town in Indiana. It wasn't even down South, but I still couldn't go anywhere. There wasn't any food, any rooms, nothing. They finally got me in the back room of some kitchen and got me some food. But I had to stand to eat.

That really shook me up.

When I got out to the ball park, all these folks who wouldn't let me have a room or some food came up and asked for my autograph.

"Go to hell," I told them.

Ned Garver, who was a top pitcher with the Browns, was standing there by me. He looked kind of surprised when I turned down those autograph-hunters. He didn't know how I was eating up my insides over the way they'd treated me like an animal.

I swung around and faced Ned.

"They won't let me eat here," I snapped, "but they want my autograph. To hell with 'em."

Ned just nodded.

o   o   o   o   o

And I guess it was even before that happened, around about September 1, that I ran into some trouble while we were on our way East for a game and we stopped off in Charleston, West Virginia, to play an exhibition game. I was going to pitch.

They'd told us that they were going to let me stay in the same hotel with the Browns, so I wasn't expecting any trouble.

I just went into the hotel with the other players.

I was busy getting all my luggage together and when I got up to the desk most of the players already'd gotten their keys to their rooms.

I stood there waiting for the clerk, but he wasn't paying any attention. Oh, he looked up at me, but then he just ducked his head down and acted like he was real busy checking some papers.

"I'd like a room, too," I finally said.

He didn't even look up. He turned away and picked up some more papers and started fingering through them.

I could feel that hot blood running through me, but I tried putting a lid on it so it wouldn't boil over.

"I'd like a room," I said again, just a little louder, trying to keep that old anger out of my mouth.

The clerk finally turned around.

He put down those papers he was holding real careful,

like they'd melt. Then he just looked up at me and made a face.

"We don't serve niggers here," he kind of sniffed at me, holding his head back like he was trying to look down his nose.

"I'm with the Browns. They said I could stay here." I was trying to sound quiet and not cause troubles, but I couldn't. I was getting louder. "They said you'd have a room here for me."

That clerk just looked right through me. Something exploded right in my head. I grabbed the edge of the desk and squeezed. I had to squeeze like that to keep my hands down, to keep from hitting that man. I didn't hit him. I just turned around and walked out of that hotel. I went down to the airport. They had a plane leaving for Washington. I bought me a ticket.

Before I got on that plane, some kid at the airport must have recognized me and called my manager. My manager called the airport and they radioed the plane and told me to get off at the next town. I must have cooled off some on that plane because if I hadn't, I don't think I'd have done what my manager said. But what'd happened back in Charleston didn't seem too bad anymore. Things like that'd happened before. You just got to take them.

After I got off the plane, I called my manager and he said the guy who'd run the hotel'd apologized. That clerk just hadn't been told about me staying there and he was letting his own meanness run out. I didn't have enough meanness in me to disappoint those fans just to get even with the meanness in somebody else. I went back.

I had to take a cab to get there in time for the game. That cost a big penny, but I got it back from the club.

○　○　○　○　○

I might have had troubles with other folks, but I always got along with the Browns real good. They were a fine bunch, even if they were last-placers. There were a lot of boys on that club that hadn't been around too much and they sure liked listening to Ol' Satch.

'Course, I confused some of them. I just sort of got in the habit of giving them a different answer to the same old questions every time they asked them.

That's because I had a lot of answers for them. A man who's been all over like I had picks up a lot of news even if he hasn't had a whole lot of schooling.

Those Brownies'd gather around me and just listen and ask and listen.

What most of them was asking about was pitching. I didn't push myself on them with advice, but if they came to me I had some for them.

The best one for coming for advice was Ned Garver.

When I got to the Browns, Ned was on his way to winning twenty games. I could tell he thought I was just one of those overpowering pitchers because in practice I only threw that fast ball.

But it didn't take many games for me to show him different.

After a couple of them, he came up to me and said, "Satch, I was wrong about you. You know more about pitching than most pitchers could ever fathom. Man, you're in a class by yourself when it comes to know-how."

But I didn't know everything and whenever I needed help, Ned was right there. I used to go ask him about Mickey Vernon, the first baseman. Now I've faced the best in the whole world just about, but I never could get Mickey out. He almost killed me every time he hit against me. Before every game I pitched against him, when he was playing for Washington, I used to go up to Ned to see if he'd heard anything new about Mickey.

"What should I throw him?" I asked Ned.

"Maybe you ought to try keeping the ball away from him."

"I did that the last time. It didn't work. You know what, if Washington gets the bases loaded against me and I got a two-run lead, I think I'll just walk that man and save myself a lot of headaches."

o   o   o   o   o

The best thing about being back in the majors was those long, fine trips on the trains, not bumping along on the buses or in a car. What I really liked was that hop on the Wabash from St. Louis to Chicago. They had a dome car on that train and I used to climb up there and all the other boys'd climb up there after me, asking about how it'd been when I was playing on a first-place team. When you're sitting down there in last place, you sure get wet in the mouth thinking and asking about how the uptown folks are living.

On most of those trips I sat with Ned Garver, talking pitching. Ned was a real student.

Next to me, Ned knew more baseball than just about any pitcher in the American League.

Those first few weeks he told me about all the new guys in the league and what they hit and what they didn't. He was right.

"Ned, there's only one thing keepin' you from being the best pitcher in the league," I told him one day after all the stuff he'd told me about pitching to those other teams turned out right.

"What's that?" he asked.

"You don't have that one strikeout pitch, that one thing to get a man when you got him three and two. You need a good fast ball or a real sharp curve."

Ned just sat there a minute, thinking real careful like he always did.

"You're right, Satch," he finally said. "If I had that real good fast ball of yours—the one you got now, not the one you used to have even—I'd be sitting pretty."

And that's all Ned needed. But even with that slow stuff of his, he did right well all along, just using his head.

I didn't joke with Ned too much. He was a real serious boy. But one day I got him to bite good.

We were just talking and Ned asked me what my best relief job was. Now I've had a lot of great ones, but that boy was so serious I just couldn't resist that old temptation.

"That was before I got into pro ball," I told him. "We was in the ninth and was leadin', one to nothin'. The first man up topped the ball and beat the throw. The second man bunted and it looked like it was going foul, but it didn't. Then the third man up walked. Our pitcher had the fourth guy three balls and two strikes and my manager called on me."

"What happened?" Ned asked, real serious.

"Well, I had a ball with me in the dugout and I just dropped it in my pocket. Then I got the game ball from the pitcher I was relieving. When I went back to the resin bag I got that other ball out of my pocket and had me two of them then."

"Yeah? What'd you do then?"

"I just threw those two balls at the same time, one to first and one to third. I picked off both runners and my motion was so good the batter fanned. That was three outs."

Ned wouldn't talk to me for a whole day after that.

o o o o o

That 1951 season was a real picnic for me. When I first got in the majors in 1948, I had to fight all those people who said my being up there was a publicity stunt. But when you win ten and lose only eight in your first two years, that's no publicity stunt.

When I got back with the Browns, people knew I was there because I could pitch. That let me do a little more showboating than I did before. You got to think of the fans if you want to be big in the majors.

'Course, some of that showboating ain't meant just to tickle the fans. Sometimes you use it to win. That's what I did with Larry Doby, my old Cleveland teammate, the second time around that I pitched against him.

The first time he got a couple of hits off me that about cost me a game. I was laying for him the next time. That was in St. Louis and Cleveland came in to play us.

Larry'd been on a real hot streak and before the game he was posing for all kinds of pictures.

I walked over and watched a minute.

"You'd better get all those pictures taken now, Larry," I yelled over at him, "because when the game starts you won't be able to have any taken. You'll be flat on your back."

Now I don't throw at anybody too often. I was always afraid that fast ball'd kill them if it hit them. But with Larry riding that hot hand I knew we had to slow him down.

On the first pitch to him that night, I fired one high and hard and inside, close enough to scare him but not close enough to hit him.

It did what I wanted. He ended up flat on his back, just

249

like I told him he'd be. He was so shook up he didn't cause any trouble that night.

Pitchers have to do things like that. When a batter comes up to the plate, you got to know how you want to get him out and then be able to do it.

If you don't, you don't win any games.

That's why sometimes I'd throw three straight balls to a batter and then act real nervous, like I couldn't get the ball over the plate. That'd get the batter careless. Then I'd fire my trouble ball right by him for three strikes.

But you had to be able to throw the ball as hard as the best in the league to do that. And you'd better have that fine control before you tried something like that.

Whenever I got the chance those days, I'd clown a little. That's what the fans expected.

I remember one game when there were two on and two out and the ball was hit back to me.

I fielded it and started walking toward third base, not even looking at the runner or my first baseman. The crowd went crazy. Then I flipped it backhand to first without even looking at Hank Arft standing over there and got the runner out. I wasn't taking any chances. I'd practiced that for a long time.

That clowning kept a lot of folks happy, but it was mainly my pitching that kept the Browns happy.

It was that pitching that made guys like Ned Garver come up to me and say, "Satch, you deserve being in the Hall of Fame, just from the ability you've shown me here. And if that's not enough of a reason, you ought to get in for the way you promoted baseball all over the country."

o   o   o   o   o

Chapter Thirty

I HADN'T SET any world records pitching in 1951, but I'd done all right and I didn't have any worries about where I was going to be working in 1952.

And with my stomach troubles behind me and with spring training to get ready in, I was hoping for a pretty fair year.

I got a call from Bill Veeck in February and went to St. Louis February 9 to sign my 1952 contract.

They made a big show of it, just like they'd always done before.

"This contract is just as good as the one LeRoy signed in 1948 when we were with the Cleveland Indians," Mr. Veeck told the reporters.

"How old are you now, Satchel?" one of the reporters asked me. "The Browns' record book says you were born in 1892."

"Oh, no. Not that," I said. "I'm only forty-three. I was born in 1908."

That wasn't true, but I figured if my pitching was getting livelier, I ought to be getting younger.

"LeRoy just drops his age two or three years each season," Mr. Veeck said and laughed. "Today's my birthday, too," he said.

"How old are you, Bill?" somebody asked.

"I'm thirty-eight and there's no arguing about it."

While Mr. Veeck was talking, I was thumbing through the Browns' statistic book.

"Hey, they don't have any of my kids listed in here," I said.

"You a father, Satch?" a reporter asked.

"That's right. I got a wife and three kids. One's three, the other's two, and I got a baby three months old. If they weren't listed before, you'd better change it. I want to get some money back from the tax people."

"What are you aiming for in 1952?" another reporter asked.

"I just want to hit .290."

After I signed my fourth contract with Mr. Veeck, the Browns came out with their new record book. I'd told them I was born in 1908, but that didn't make any difference to anybody. They made a big game out of how old I was and in the record book, under my birthday, they wrote:

"September 11, 1892—Z, 1896—Z, 1900—Z, 1904—Z."

At the end of the pitcher's list they had another line: "Z—Take your pick."

o   o   o   o   o

Mr. Veeck'd gotten a new manager for the Browns. He was Rogers Hornsby. I didn't give it much thought until I got to spring training. Then I gave it a lot of thought.

Hornsby and me were from different schools, real different. I guess he'd wanted to be an army general, but never made it. So he just tried running his ball club like an army.

If it hadn't been for Mr. Veeck and the way I felt about him, I wouldn't have stayed.

I'd grown up being used to doing things when and where I wanted and training how I wanted to. But Hornsby didn't think I'd learned enough in all those years to know how to get ready to pitch. If Mr. Hornsby'd known as much about hitting as he thought he knew about pitching, Ty Cobb never would have held all those hitting records. Hornsby would have.

I'll never forget that first day in camp. That's when I found out all about him. He was one of those run-run-run men.

We were all lined up out there on the field and Hornsby came marching past all of us, asking us how old we were.

"I'm sixty-one," I told him, kind of kidding. You don't kid Hornsby.

He asked this kid next to me how old he was and the kid told him seventeen, real truthful-like.

Then Hornsby turned back to me and told me to do the same things that kid of seventeen was doing, running around the field, chasing flies, grabbing grounders, and then running around the field about four more times.

After that workout, I went over to him.

"Mr. Hornsby," I said, "tell me, are you trainin' Ol' Satch for relief pitchin' or for the army?"

I didn't have to do all that running after that, but Hornsby still was a tough man to work for.

But maybe all that work helped. After the season started, I got tangled up in some ball games that'd have about killed me if I hadn't been in the shape I was.

Take that game against Washington on June 3.

I'd gotten off to a real fast start, just like 1948, and I had me four wins and only one loss going into that game. I'd been doing a lot of pitching up to then and I figured they wouldn't use me that night. So before the game, I went into the clubhouse and asked our trainer, Bob Bauman, for a pair of sliding pads.

Buddy Blattner, a sportscaster, was in there.

"You getting those pads because you think you'll get in and have to do some sliding tonight, Satch?" he asked me.

"I ain't thinkin' about slidin' on 'em," I said. "They just

make somethin' soft to sit on out there on that hard bullpen bench."

I got to sit on them for a while, but not the whole night.

Going into the twelfth inning, we were tied up with Washington, two and two. After we got one out in the twelfth, Hornsby signaled for me to come in.

I got out of the twelfth without any trouble, but in the thirteenth and fourteenth, Washington loaded the bases both times. Man, all I could do was wipe that sweat off my forehead and keep pitching. I pitched out of both those innings without any runs scoring. In the thirteenth I struck out Jackie Jensen and Eddie Yost. In the fourteenth I picked up Mel Hoderlein's squeeze bunt and forced a runner at the plate and then I struck out Yost again.

But we weren't scoring either.

I didn't know how much longer I could keep going. Every one of those extra innings seemed like two regular innings.

We went down quick in the top of the sixteenth.

I got through the bottom of the sixteenth without any damage.

It was the seventeenth.

It seemed like the hundredth.

I just fell down on the bench when we went in for our bats in the top of the seventeenth. I didn't hardly move. I just sat there breathing.

But I didn't get to sit long. We got Joe DeMaestri to second base and I was up.

"Let me bat," I said to my manager.

"It's your game. Get up there."

I had two singles in two times up already. Just one more and I might be able to end it.

Just one more.

But I felt that tiredness. The bat weighed a ton.

The crowd was roaring. I looked out at second to Joe

DeMaestri. Just a single'd bring him in. I forgot that tiredness.

All I needed was a hit.

I got it. I singled. Joe DeMaestri went whipping around third and across the plate. We were ahead, three to two. We didn't get any more runs in, but I had that lead. I didn't let it get away. I set down Washington in the last of the seventeenth and we had us a win, a win in the longest game of the season up to then.

I'd given up only four hits in five and two-thirds innings. The win boosted my record to five and one for the year.

That next day Mr. Veeck wired our traveling secretary, Bill Durney, and told him to take me downtown and buy me the best suit of clothes money can buy. I got me a hundred dollar suit.

Mr. Veeck didn't get me that suit just for holding Washington scoreless in that game. No, sir. He bought it because of that good hitting I did.

"Why, that guy slammed out three line singles during his short time in the game and that's more'n he got all last season," Mr. Veeck told a reporter.

He told that same guy that I was the only one on his team he wouldn't trade. For a man they called too old to be in the majors in 1948, that was pretty high stuff in 1952—when I was about forty six.

"I feel reasonably certain that we will make some player deals before the trading deadline June 15," Mr. Veeck said. "But LeRoy won't be among those swapped. He's going to stay with the Browns. And I say this at a time when I know that if any one of the current contenders would land him, LeRoy would pitch them to a pennant.

"Great pitching is nothing unusual for LeRoy. In Washington he knew the best way out of those tight spots was to fan those batters, so he did it. And that simply bears out what I've always said about LeRoy. In a tight spot, on any given pitch, he can throw much harder than any hurler in the game today. No batter is going to have an easy job on his hands when he comes up to the plate against LeRoy with men on base. This isn't my observation alone. I'm simply repeating what some of the best hitters in the league have told me."

He knew what he was talking about. Up into June, I'd given up the only six earned runs all told and I'd even built me up a five-game winning streak. That gave me an over-all earned-run average of 1.92.

o   o   o   o   o

I didn't slow down any in my next big game. That was against Washington, too. It seemed like I was pitching against Washington all the time and Washington was battling for a first-division berth at the time. The Senators were in fifth place. That game went eighteen innings and was the longest in the league that season up to then.

We were tied five and five when I went into the game in the eighth inning. I pitched ten innings of scoreless ball and gave up only five hits, but it didn't do us any good. We weren't scoring either. I went out for a pinch-hitter in the seventeenth and Dave Madison finished up. That game was called after the eighteenth, still all tied up, five and five.

After that game, Bucky Harris, the Washington manager, came over to see me. "Satch," he said, "I swear to God we would be in first place if we had you."

He wasn't the only one talking like that.

Casey Stengel, who did some right fair managing for the New York Yankees, was one of those guys who had something to say.

"If the Yanks don't get ahead in the first six innings," he said, "the Browns bring in that damned old man and then we're sunk."

But the nicest stuff I heard was from my old pal Dizzy Dean.

"Do you know who I'd pitch if I had one game that I had to win this year?" he said. "If he had proper rest, I'd pitch Paige. He's the best pitcher in the league if he has the rest. And if I was managing his club, I'd have made him a startin' pitcher this year. Just think, he'd win fifteen games for you, maybe twenty, just startin' once a week. And think of the drawin' card you'd have with that guy a startin' pitcher."

o o o o o

Going into the first week in August I still had me seven wins against six losses with that second-division Brownie club.

I guess maybe my manager thought a change from that relief pitching'd do me some good.

He scheduled me to start August 6 against the Detroit Tigers. It was only the second time he'd named me to open a game in 1952 and I hadn't pitched me a complete game since 1949 with Cleveland.

I was kind of anxious. I wanted to break out of that slump and I wanted that complete game. I figured that's all I needed to get back on the right track.

From the first pitch, I threw with everything I had. And I kept throwing and throwing and throwing. Detroit couldn't do anything with the old man.

But Virgil Trucks of Detroit was pitching just as tough and when the ninth inning came around nobody had a run yet. It was nothing to nothing.

Even kids wilt in those late innings, but not Ol' Satch. After Virgil went out for a pinch-hitter in the tenth and Hal White took over pitching for Detroit, I still was in there for the Browns.

I got a little worried in the tenth, though. The Tigers loaded the bases on me with nobody out.

They sent in Johnny Pesky to pinch-hit against me and Johnny was one of those .300 hitters.

Clint Courtney, my catcher, came out real fast.

"Be careful here," he told me.

"Ol' Satch knows when to be careful, don't you worry."

I was careful. I wanted this game. I'd pitched too many innings in it to give it away.

I pitched my fast sinker and Johnny Pesky pounded it into the ground and we got a force-out at home plate.

There was one out and no run in yet.

Johnny Groth came up. I fired hard and low to him and he grounded into a force play at home plate, too. Two out and no runs in.

"That's the way," Clint yelled at me. "We're almost home."

I figured we were home. Neil Berry was up and I just fired my trouble ball—three in a row for three called strikes. I was out of the inning without a run scoring.

In the eleventh and twelfth I fired zeros at Detroit again and in the last of the twelfth we won it. We got the bases loaded and Bob Nieman singled home the run that gave us a twelve-inning, one to nothing win.

I'd given up only seven hits, six of them singles, in those twelve innings and'd walked only two and struck out nine.

I didn't even have stomach trouble after that game. Those fans who still thought I just went out there on the mound for laughs knew better now. No man who gets in three extra-inning games like I had is just out for laughs.

o   o   o   o   o

Chapter Thirty-One

THERE'D BEEN YEARS when I'd racked up fifty, sixty, and seventy wins. In 1952, I won only a handful of that many, but they were major league wins and that made up the difference.

That made me the best relief pitcher in baseball.

When the season ended I had a twelve–ten record and I'd saved ten other games with those seventh-place Browns. I'd struck out ninety-one batters and'd given up only fifty-seven walks. My earned-run average was 3.07.

Ol' Satch's name was maybe worth more than it'd ever been, so I just went around living like a king. Why, when my eyes started hurting because of the sun shining off my white Cadillac, I just traded it in on a blue job. I lost money on the deal, but money was something I had to lose.

There was plenty of it around and there'd be more of it in 1953. You could tell that from my contract for that season I signed it on January 10, just four weeks after Lahoma and me'd had our fourth baby—a boy. After three girls, I had me a son.

I couldn't wait to tell all the reporters about him when I got to St. Louis for that contract signing.

"We named him Robert LeRoy," I told the reporters, "and he's just as amazin' as his old man, and you better believe it. He looks six months, no foolin'. Why, man, he was twenty-three inches long when he was born."

But those baseball writers didn't want to just talk about

my first boy. They wanted to talk about me, too. I ain't bashful so I did some talking.

"If we could of had somebody hit the ball out of the infield with a man on third base and one out—shucks, the other clubs do it—we'd have finished higher'n seventh last year," I told them. "They didn't run off from us. They just kept beatin' us by one and two runs. We'll do better in 1953. That kid, Vic Wertz, will make the difference for us himself. But I'll be some help, too. If I can throw overhand early in spring trainin' without arm soreness, I know I'll be all right."

I didn't have any arm soreness, but 1953 turned out to be a pretty bad year for me and the Browns anyway. If I'd known that when I signed, I wouldn't have been talking so big. But all I knew was that I had me a fat contract and Bill Veeck still was my boss and I had a fine guy like Marty Marion to manage me. A man didn't have to worry none when things were going that way.

o   o   o   o   o

After spring training got started, I started hearing how Bill Veeck'd been trying to get the club moved to Baltimore. When the American League turned him down, he said the club was up for sale.

I should have known my luck was starting downhill right then. But I didn't. I didn't think Mr. Veeck'd really get out of St. Louis.

I just put it out of my mind and headed off for the first annual Pacific Coast League Baseball Writers' dinner in the Cocoanut Grove in Los Angeles.

Somebody'd told me I'd have to do some talking at that dinner, but I didn't know they wanted me to give the main speech.

But that's what happened.

I hadn't figured out anything to say, so I just started talking.

"My age kept me tickin' quite awhile," I told them. "No one believes me when I tell 'em how old I am so I'll just keep pitchin'. But lately I've had some troubles with my body. I had troubles gettin' in and out of bed. I told my wife all my grease ran out. She said maybe I'd better give up that game 'cause when anybody had to grease to get in bed and out, the time is close.

"We went out the first day of spring training and I ran some," I went ahead and told them. "I sat down and I couldn't get up. I'm not sayin' that to get some rest, but I believe my manager, Mr. Marion, is in here.

"I never have been much with runnin'. I have long legs, all right, but that don't make it. But I guess the time is gettin' mighty close when I'll have to quit. Gettin' harder and harder for Ol' Satch to limber up. Probably my joints is gettin' stiff from the lack of grease.

"And I'm gettin' stiff from standin' up, so I'd better sit down."

That's just what I did and Phil Harris, the movie star, stood up. He was supposed to talk after me.

"After that," Phil said, "I wouldn't give this spot to the cleaners."

o　　o　　o　　o　　o

I went back to spring training after that dinner and I got there just in time to go to San Francisco for an exhibition game. Man, was it cold there. Before the game, Marty Marion told me to warm up.

"It's too cold for that," I told him.

"But I got you scheduled to pitch here, Satch, and you got to pitch. You'd better warm up."

That's what I did. I went into the clubhouse and got warm. Then I came out.

"I'll take three throws now and we can start," I told Marty.

I tried it a few innings and it was so cold I couldn't get my hand in my glove.

"I guess I'll have to take you out," Marty told me.

"You'd better 'cause I don't think I can go back."

Marty pulled me.

"Maybe since you're out of the game you'd like to go over and give that young kid some pointers?" Marty asked me, pointing to a rookie we had on our club.

"I like to help those young men," I said, "but I've been carryin' youngsters like them so long I think I'll have to put 'em down."

"Why do you keep pitchin' then?" Marty asked me.

" 'Cause of money and women," I said.

"Money and women?"

"That's right. They're the two strongest things in the world. The things you do for a woman you wouldn't do for anything else. Same with money."

Marty didn't ask me any more questions that night.

o   o   o   o   o

By the time the 1953 season opened, most of us'd forgotten all about Mr. Veeck trying to sell the club. All we were thinking about was getting off to a fast start.

The way we got started we'd have made one of those turtles look fast.

But we were drawing some fans anyway. Nobody'll argue when I say a lot of those fans showed up because of me. Everybody was saying how I was one of the few big draws left in the game. Why, the fans even came out when I wasn't pitching.

They wanted to see me in that special chair Mr. Veeck'd bought for me to sit in out in the bullpen.

It was one of those contour chairs and it had an awning over it to keep the sun off me.

I'd just sit there and doze a little until Marty Marion signaled for me to come in. Then I'd just loaf out to the pitching mound.

But when I got there, I wasn't loafing any.

I threw as hard as I always did, but luck just wasn't with me at all.

I remember one game when I was pitching against Boston and there were two men on base and I had two strikes on Tom Umphlett.

Marty Marion came out and told me to throw Umphlett a high fast ball.

"Not that, Marty," I said.

But Marty said to throw it.

I did and Umphlett tripled home what turned out to be the winning runs. After the game, Marty called all us players together and told us he was taking full responsibility for what'd happened.

"Are you gonna take the loss, too?" I asked.

He didn't.

I don't guess it would have made any difference if he did. I lost enough games in 1953 so one more didn't matter. No matter how much I looked around that season, I just couldn't find those wins. I finished up with a three and nine record.

That was the worst year I'd ever had.

It upset me. But I guess it upset Lahoma even worse.

"Don't you worry," I told her, trying to ease her mind. "They ain't gonna drop me just for one bad year. I still can throw and I'll have me my job back. Just don't you worry."

Lahoma didn't quit worrying. We had those kids to take care of. She'd snuck off a little of that money I'd made and put it aside just to take care of the kids if something bad happened, but there wasn't enough to last too long if I ran out of work.

"I'll have me some work," I kept telling her. "The Browns still need me."

But before the 1954 season even started, there weren't any Browns any more. They were sold and the American League let the new owners move the club to Baltimore.

I got a letter after that. The new bosses told me they were starting a youth movement and didn't have room for an old man like me.

Man, if I hadn't needed a job so bad, that letter'd have seemed almost funny to me. They used to say, "If you were only white you could be in the major leagues." Now it was, "If you weren't so old you could be in the major leagues."

After I read that letter I tore all over that house of mine. Maybe I thought I'd find a major league job hiding in one of the rooms. It got so bad I couldn't even stay in the house. I got in my car and drove crazy-like all over. I had to do that to let off steam. When a man gets older, that steam builds up faster.

My stomach got all tightened up and my head about split. I was up there in age and getting booted out could mean I'd never get back in the big time. That made things bad enough, but not having a job made them worse. I couldn't just sit down and retire. I had to get some work. But I didn't even know where to start looking. I wasn't sure of anything. Everything looked mighty black.

Then the sun came out again for Ol' Satch.

I started getting barnstorming offers from all over the country. Those promoters'd read where the Baltimore Orioles'd let me go and knowing I was free they came running. They figured my name still was big enough to fill a lot of ball parks. And they must have thought I still could pitch good enough to keep filling those parks after the folks once saw me.

With them on my side, I started getting that confidence back again.

o   o   o   o   o

Lahoma and me went over all those offers real careful and I finally took one with a barnstorming club being run by Abe Saperstein, the man who'd recommended me for my first major league job.

But before I could go join his club, I had to settle a little trouble with the law in Kansas City.

I'd gotten arrested just a little after midnight back on January 1, 1954, after I had an accident. They charged me with driving while intoxicated and careless driving and set the trial for March 4.

I made sure I showed up for that trial. That arrest was about my thirtieth for speeding and careless driving in Kansas City, and they said if I didn't show up they'd put me away forever.

The arresting officer was the only one who testified against me. He said when he got to the accident scene I was in my new Cadillac, just sitting.

"Paige told me he had two bottles of beer," the officer said.

Then I got on the stand.

"I was in the Blue Room at the Street Hotel," I told the judge. "I was sittin' there talkin' to the bartender, Kingfish. I had me one bottle of beer and was just sittin' there and talkin'."

Jesse Fisher, the Kingfish, also testified for me.

"Satch was normal when he came in and he had only one beer," he said.

After all the talking was done, the judge called me up in front of him.

"Satch," the judge said, "I'll drop the charge of driving while intoxicated because there is reasonable doubt. But you were going too fast. Your license shows you have been in other accidents and that is not good. I find you guilty of careless driving and fine you twenty-five dollars."

Looking back on that fine, I just figure it cost me twenty-five dollars to get me a "first" in speeding tickets, just like all those "firsts" I had in baseball. That's because the judge told me I'd been the first traffic violator in Kansas City in 1954.

o   o   o   o   o

After I paid that fine, I left town and joined Abe Saperstein's barnstorming club. I pitched in 148 games that season.

I was making money, but I was just a wandering man again, going from one town to another, one game to another.

I did the same thing in 1955, but with my old team, the Kansas City Monarchs. Mr. Wilkinson wasn't around any more, but Tom Baird was still there.

Playing for the Monarchs in 1955 wouldn't make any man rich. There just wasn't enough fans watching Negro league baseball any more so the players could make big money.

On top of all this, the Monarchs started running into even more trouble. The Philadelphia Athletics'd been sold and they were moved to Kansas City for the 1955 season. Old Blues' Stadium, the minor league park in Kansas City where the Monarchs used to play, was turned into Municipal Stadium for the major league team and the Monarchs were told they couldn't rent it any more.

The Monarchs had to become a road team and I heard noises that they'd fold after the season was over because of that.

It seemed like everywhere I was going now I was hitting one of those slides downhill.

Then I got taken off that sliding board. And it was Bill Veeck who took me off, like he'd done in 1948 and 1951.

Mr. Veeck'd gotten himself the vice-president's job on the Miami Marlins in the International League, one of the top minor leagues, and he gave me that old call.

I had me a steady job again, a good salary, and a place to light my family when school in Kansas City was over.

Joining up with Miami was a real picnic for me. It was Miami's first year in the International League and that gave Mr. Veeck a real audience to put on a show for.

He did, too.

That opening night game, Mr. Veeck decided to fly me into the ball park in a helicopter. They got me out to the airfield where that helicopter was and it looked to me like nothin' but a big lawn mower.

The man that ran it showed me how it worked, but it still didn't look safe to Ol' Satch. But they got me in it, and up in the air I was so scared that pilot and me was like husband and wife until we landed in the ball park. I hopped out of that plane and those Miami fans went crazy. And they wanted to see me pitch, too. But I didn't get in that first game. I just took me a rocking chair ride. Mr. Veeck'd given me a big rocking chair to sit in out in the bullpen and I made good use of it.

After about three or four games'd gone by and I still hadn't pitched, people began talking about how I was just there to get laughs. Man, people always seemed to be talking that way about Ol' Satch. But I showed them different when I pitched my first game. I shut out the defending champions from Montreal with only four singles and won, three to nothing. I was the first Miami pitcher to go the route in our first fourteen games that season.

And I was a man going on fifty while those other pitchers hadn't even started shaving yet.

After that game, I couldn't help playing high-hat.

"I can go nine just as easy as I can go three—maybe easier 'cause I can use all my pitches like I did today," I told some reporter. "I can use that screwball, fast ball, slider, curver, knuckler, everything. And I can pace myself. You might not know that 'cause I just don't talk about what I can do too much. I let them other guys talk and wonder about how far I can go."

o   o   o   o   o

Chapter Thirty-Two

LAHOMA AND THE KIDS liked Miami just as good as me. They went swimming about every day and lived real high.

"I love it here," Lahoma told me. "Everybody is so wonderful to us I almost feel like as big a celebrity as you. And we can be together the whole summer this way. I wish it could be this way always."

I felt almost the same way about it that Lahoma did. A man can't run all his life. But as tired as I'd gotten over all that moving all those years, I still was hoping maybe I'd have to move once more. The way I was throwing for Miami, I figured I should be back in the majors for a spell in no time. And I'd have just about put off that settling down forever for one more crack at the majors.

I was going so good with Miami that it even surprised me. Maybe it was because of all that relaxing I was getting there, just laying around in the sun and fishing and all between games.

Whatever it was, I wasn't about to fuss with it.

In no time, I'd gotten me five wins against only two losses and I was leading the league with a 1.50 earned-run average.

My pitching was keeping us right around first place.

"I don't know where we'd be without you," Don Osborn, my manager, told me.

"Don't you worry about it. You get me some help and I'll have us right up there in first place."

Don Osborn wasn't always that happy with me in 1956. He got pretty mad once.

We had us a charter plane to fly up to some games in Rochester and I kind of got my times all mixed up and missed that bird.

When the bosses found out about that, they came howling.

"You get a commercial flight and catch up with the team in Rochester," they told me, and they weren't kidding. "And you'll just have to foot the bill yourself."

That took about every penny I had. When I got to Rochester, I got up to Don Osborn's room fast.

"Man, I ain't got no money," I told him.

"That's too bad," he said. He was burning good.

"It sure does take a piece of change to get up here," I said. I was hoping he'd give me a couple of dollars. "Why, I got here with a dollar and a half and that wasn't even cab fare to the hotel. I ain't even got eatin' money, Don, and I suspect I'll have to speak to somebody about that."

"What'd you do with that dollar and a half?" Don asked me. He still was mad.

"I got me a little coffee and rolls when I got in."

Don just looked at me for a minute. Then he started grinning. He wasn't hot at me anymore, that was for sure. I felt a lot better.

"You gonna get me some eatin' money?" I asked.

"We'll get you some."

"By the way, Don, you seen that trainer around the hotel? Fetch him for me. I needs him."

o   o   o   o   o

When you got Mr. Veeck around a place, things happen. If they don't, he makes them happen. That's the way it was in Miami that first season.

And one of the big things Mr. Veeck wanted to have happen was a new attendance record. And when they wanted attendance records anywhere, they wanted Ol' Satch to pitch.

Along about August Mr. Veeck began talking about trying to beat the major league attendance record for a night game. That was 78,382 folks.

That was set in Cleveland's Municipal Stadium in 1948 when the Indians were playing the Chicago White Sox.

And Ol' Satch pitched that game for Cleveland.

Mr. Veeck figured if he couldn't top that record, he'd shoot at the minor league record of 56,391.

They set that in Jersey City in 1941, but Mr. Veeck thought if he could get better than fifty thousand out to a game, it'd be a new record. The Jersey City park held only about thirty thousand and those fifty-six thousand were the number of tickets sold.

Mr. Veeck decided to go for that record in our game August 7 against the Columbus Jets. He scheduled the game in the Orange Bowl in Miami. That's a football field and they never'd played a minor league game there before, but it was the only place around that'd hold enough people to get the record.

Mr. Veeck got ahold of a lot of show folks to put on some entertainment before the game and he turned the whole thing into a charity game to get more folks out.

They called it "The Baseball Party to End All Baseball Parties."

That's sure what it looked like with all those singers and entertainers they were going to have there—folks like Ginny Simms, Margaret Whiting, Cab Calloway, and a bunch of others.

When time for that game got close, I started getting worried. I figured Mr. Veeck might try flying me into the Orange Bowl in a helicopter or something worse.

I ran over to Mr. Veeck a couple of days before the game.

"There ain't gonna be any parachutin' or anythin' like that for me," I told him.

He promised there wouldn't be.

That let me just concentrate on the game. There was more than just an attendance record riding on that game. We were only a half game out of second place and only two games behind Toronto in first, even though we'd been on a five-game losing streak. We needed every win we could get to stay in the race.

And I had me the league-leading earned-run average to protect. I'd allowed only 1.58 runs every nine innings up to then while winning eight and losing only three.

Nobody was going to take that away from me, not with maybe a record crowd watching.

I knew I wasn't going to have an easy time in that Orange Bowl. The fences was real close there. A man'd have to pitch careful.

That's just what I was planning on doing.

When I got ready to go to the ball park that night, I wasn't thinking too much about the game, though. There were so many big show folks there I got all excited about getting some pictures of them.

I got me a great big satchel and put all my camera equipment in it and lugged it out to the Orange Bowl. I had to get me some help. I wasn't real sure how to load up that new camera I'd bought just to take those pictures.

But I finally got it fixed and went over to get Cab Calloway's picture. He was an old buddy of mine. I can remember times when I used to do a little singing when he was around. It was just for fun, but he got a kick out of it.

When I was about halfway over to where Cab was standing, he saw me and came rushing over.

"It's been a long time, Satch," he told me and shook my hand. "Here you are still pitching, too. From what I hear you're still a young cat."

"I'm young enough to do a soft shuffle."

"Maybe you ought to be dancing with us instead of pitching for Miami, then."

"Man, there's only one thing I can do better'n shuffling. That's pitchin' and that's what I'm here for. You just watch." I wandered back to the bullpen and started loosening up while they put on the show.

Folks kept coming into the stadium all during the show and by the time we were ready to start the game the place was really jumping. There were 51,713 there and that was close enough to being some kind of record to suit me.

"See all them folks out there," I said to my manager, Don Osborn. "Well, they're really gonna see a show now. Don't you worry about this game."

He didn't either.

We got a run in the last half of the first inning to go ahead, one to nothing. In the last half of the second we got the bases loaded and I was up.

Bob Kuzava'd walked the batter in front of me to fill the bases with one out so he could pitch to me. I didn't like him thinking so little of my hitting so I just cracked one of his pitches into left center. By the time they got the ball, I was on second base and we had three more runs. I was ahead, four to nothing.

I was pitching just as good as I was hitting. For the first six innings I didn't give up a run and Columbus got only two hits off me.

I'd always figured when you got those record crowds out you had to try a little harder and really show them something. That's what I was doing.

But all that running on that double in the second must have kind of tired me. In the seventh, Russ Sullivan doubled off me and then Butch McCord singled him home. I stopped Columbus then, but in the eighth it started all over again.

Dick Getter and Bill Kern hit back-to-back singles.

I just clamped down hard with my teeth. They weren't getting me out of there that easy.

I beared down and got Johnny Lipon to hit into a double play. There were two out and I thought I might get out of the inning.

But I was dead tired.

I just couldn't fog that ball by Curt Roberts. He didn't hit me hard, but he blooped a single out to center and scored Getter.

Don Osborn came out to the mound to talk to me then.

"You're looking tired, Satch," he said.

"I guess I am."

"Don't worry. You've shown them plenty. Go on in and take a rest. Jack Spring's all warmed up. We'll let him finish it."

I didn't argue any. I'd saved so many games for those young pitchers I figured it was time one of them saved one for me.

Anyway, I'd given up only seven hits in seven and two-thirds innings and I'd struck me out five. That was a good night's work for anybody, even for a record crowd.

Jack came in there and threw that fast ball by the next four hitters without letting them hardly touch the ball. We scored two more in the last of the eighth and that wrapped it up for us, six to two.

I'd gotten me my ninth win in twelve decisions and that win moved us past Rochester into second place in the league.

They tried talking to me about my pitching after that game, but I was talking about my double in the second inning.

I talked about that double for four days.

It'd busted up the game, hadn't it?

○ ○ ○ ○ ○

Just to show that game wasn't luck, a week later I came back and started against Rochester in one of those seven-inning first games of a double-header. My club got me three runs in the first inning and I had me enough to win. For the first three innings I didn't give up a hit. In the fourth inning Tommy Burgess singled off me. That was the only hit I gave up. Only three other batters got on base against me. One got on when my third baseman fumbled the ball for an error, and I walked two guys.

When it was all done I had me ten wins against only three losses and a one-hit, four to nothing shutout.

"Too bad you didn't get that no-hitter," somebody told me.

"Don't you feel too bad, boy," I said. "I already pitched about one hundred in my time."

That put my earned-run average at 1.50, and that still was tops in the league.

"What'd you throw out there, Satch?" somebody asked me after the game.

"I used bloopers, loopers, and even some of those drops," I told them. "And I tossed up my jump ball, bee ball, screwball, hurry-up ball, and bat-dodger. Rochester saw 'em all."

I finished up the season with eleven wins and only four losses and an earned-run average of 1.86. I was the top pitcher in the league.

That ain't bad when a man's pushed past fifty.

○ ○ ○ ○ ○

Chapter Thirty-Three

I HEADED BACK to Miami for the 1957 season. Mr. Veeck'd pulled out of there after the 1956 season and I was mighty sorry that he was gone. But being sorry didn't keep me from winning ten and losing only eight with a ball club that won only about half its games. And my earned-run average still was one of the best in the league. They got to me for only 2.42 earned runs a game.

Just to show that Ol' Satch's control was still there, I walked only eleven batters in the forty games I pitched in.

That next year I played at Miami again, and I still was pitching strong, but I just couldn't get along with those boys who'd taken over as bosses after Mr. Veeck'd gone. I started having bookkeeping troubles with the front office. It kept getting worse and worse, too. Maybe if they'd been paying me real big money, I wouldn't have cared. But they'd slipped my salary down after Mr. Veeck'd left and I was making only about nine thousand a year with them.

As old as I was getting, I knew I could beat that barnstorming. But I didn't want to go back to all that traveling, not with a family like I had. I was tired of running.

You don't get to sit when you're barnstorming. That's okay for a young man, but when you're my age you got to count the years you got left and plan on sitting still some while they pass.

Even though I felt that way, it still got harder and harder

to stay with Miami. But there wasn't anything else I'd heard about that I could do if I didn't go barnstorming.

There wasn't anything until I started hearing those rumors about some people out in Hollywood talking to Mr. Veeck and some other folks about getting me in a movie.

"That might be the break I'm lookin' for," I told Lahoma. "I don't know how it'll work out, but my arm don't have a whole lot of years left and I got to find me somethin' else. And I want to get out of here."

Lahoma was feeling the same way as me. We both still loved Miami, but when things go sour at work you got to head someplace else or you get sour. Anyway, she had those big stars in her eyes whenever we talked about movies. It sure is funny. A man can be big stuff in baseball and his wife knows it, but because it's something he's doing every day it don't seem like anything. But being in the movies seemed mighty glamorous to her. She went walking around like she was on clouds.

Only nothing much else came up about the movie through the rest of the summer, but lots of things happened with me and the Miami ball club.

About the end of July we went on a thirteen-game road trip and they didn't give me any meal money. And they weren't giving me my salary. I took it about as long as I could but about August 1 I got so fed up I walked out on the club in Rochester.

All I wanted them to do was just pay me what they thought they owed me and let me go free.

Joe Ryan, our general manager, got ahold of me.

"You've had advances on your salary and that's why you didn't get a paycheck," he told me. "And you didn't get your meal money because you weren't present when it was passed out."

Now I didn't remember anything about those advances on my salary, but with Lahoma back in Kansas City for a visit,

I didn't have anybody who could do any checking for me so there wasn't much I could do.

I wasn't much on that bookkeeping. So I just took his word for it and joined the club again. I didn't want to, but there wasn't anything else except barnstorming and I still didn't want to do that. I put on my uniform again. I only was retired about an hour, I guess. Things quieted down a little then, but a little later, on August 4, my manager, Kerby Farrell, who'd taken Don Osborn's place, put me on the inactive list.

"It's not for disciplinary purposes because of that walkout," he told me. "You just don't figure to pitch much when we're up in this cold climate around Rochester and Montreal."

I still was burned up good.

Being on the inactive list meant I had to stay out at least ten days and that meant ten days without any pay.

I asked for my release, but Miami wouldn't give it to me. That made me even madder.

"I'm retired from them, but they ain't retired from me," I told a reporter.

They'd finally pushed me so far I was ready to go back to barnstorming. All I needed was that release. But when they didn't give it to me, I had to go back and pitch for them for the rest of the season. They had a contract.

"I won't go back there next year, that's for sure," I told Lahoma when she got back. "I'll finish out this year and that's it. I'm through with Miami."

"But, Satch," she cried, "the kids. What'll we do?"

"We'll do somethin'. There're still plenty that want to see Ol' Satch. I'll have to do some travelin', but it's better'n goin' back to Miami. There're some things you just gotta do and when they treat you bad like they've done here, you just got to take care of your pride, no matter what."

Lahoma knew me. She knew how I felt about my pride.

She didn't push me and I guess her sticking by me like that must have been all I needed to change my luck. Things started breaking my way right after that. Those rumors about a movie job came true and I was offered a part.

On September 30 I signed for a role in *The Wonderful Country*. It was going to be a cowboy picture with Robert Mitchum and Julie London in it.

I finished out the season with Miami. But I could hardly wait to get to that movie-making business and get away from that Miami club. I figured somebody didn't like Ol' Satch.

I wasn't running out on baseball. It just looked like that maybe baseball was running out on Ol' Satch, the way nobody seemed to be wanting me. But I didn't do any worrying about that, not yet. I had me a picture to think about. It was just a one-picture deal, but I was hoping it might open up something big for me.

o   o   o   o   o

I headed for Kansas City just as soon as the season was over. I had to get me a passport. They was going to film that movie in Durango, Mexico.

Everybody was excited when I got home, but I guess Lahoma and Shirley, her daughter from her first marriage, were the most excited. Shirley, who'd lived with us after Lahoma and me'd gotten married, was about eighteen then and I guess a movie star was really something to her.

They pushed me out of the house and down to see the passport man almost as soon as I got in the house.

I didn't have any troubles getting that passport, but the man filling it out for me seemed a little worried about my age.

"How old are you?" he asked me.

"I'm forty-nine," I said, fibbing him a little.

"Well, you're the only one who knows so I'll put forty-nine down. By the way, how long have you been pitching?"

"Forty years," I said.

He just looked and looked and then gave me that passport real quick.

"I got my passport," I told Lahoma when I got home. "It didn't take any old time."

"Then I'll go right down and get me one," she said. "And Shirley will too."

"We can't all go. Who'll watch little Lula? She's only eight months old. You can't go off and leave her."

"I'll take her with us."

"But . . ."

"Now you listen to me, Satchel. I'm going and so is Shirley and the baby. When you're playing baseball we never get a chance to go with you because you're always on the move. But down in Mexico you'll be in one place."

They all went with me.

I guess a man don't have to be off by himself all the time, anyway.

o   o   o   o   o

I got baseball clear off my mind after I got down to Durango to make that movie. There was too much else to think about. I'd never been an actor before. I was all worried about learning my lines and acting right and even riding a horse.

But those stars like Julie London and Robert Mitchum erased those worries real quick. They were real helpful, telling me how I should play the part of a cavalry sergeant in that western.

I started studying up on my script like I used to study up on baseball—eating and sleeping it.

After a few days, I was all for that movie business. I liked the idea of the money. I wasn't making no ten thousand like a lot said, but what I was making was pretty good and it sure was easy earning.

For the first time in my life I really gave some deep thinking to getting out of baseball. I'd toyed around with the idea some for a couple or three years, but this was the first time I'd had something else to take its place.

"If I can make the grade," I told Lahoma, "me and baseball is through."

"Are you sure you like the movies?"

"Like it? I love it. You get to sit down a lot and the money's good. But before I decide for sure, I got to see how this picture turns out and what kind of actor I am."

I figured maybe I'd be pretty good. Right after we first started shooting, my director, Bob Parrish, came up and told me, "Satch, you're batting .750 in those rushes we've got so far."

"Well, then maybe I won't be tossin' my high hard one for anybody next season," I said. "Anyhow, it's time I started thinkin' about a permanent job."

"Satch," Bob told me, "when the word gets around Hollywood I think you're going to be very much in demand. It wouldn't surprise me if you never played baseball again."

It turned out he was wrong, just like a lot of other people before him were wrong when they said I never was going to play anymore.

After I finished up that movie, I went back to Kansas City. People came from all over trying to find out about Ol' Satch in the movies.

They were saying to me, "What! Ol' Satch on a horse?" And they couldn't believe it. They remembered me on the baseball diamond.

But I was on a horse. I didn't know anything about riding one, but after Chuck Robertson, a stunt man, took me under his wing and taught me about riding, I made the grade. Some of those people who heard about me riding on a horse told me, "We've been thinking you're too old even to walk any more, too old to be hurrying around, much less ride on a horse."

But there I was in the saddle. Holding those reins was all new to me. I'd had nothing but a baseball in my hand for the last thirty-five years, about.

You never saw brakes like a horse has. Every time that horse put on its brakes, I'd start to sail over his head. I never fell off and hit the ground, but I sure dropped low a few times.

The hardest part of that movie was learning to cry. In one part, after burying three of my buddies, I had to cry. It wasn't easy. It'd been a long time since anyone saw me cry.

But picture-making was fascinating, especially when you see how they make the wind blow and the rain fall and then put the whole thing together.

The more I talked about that movie-making, the more I got to like the idea better and better.

But I just didn't know if there'd be any more of it, ever. Nobody out in Hollywood was offering me any jobs after I got back from Mexico, even if my director'd thought they would.

"If nobody comes looking for me, maybe in three or four years I'll go out to Hollywood looking for them," I told Lahoma.

"But what are you going to do now?"

"Play baseball, just like always. There ain't anything else."

"Are you going back to Miami then?"

"I ain't goin' back there. They'd have to get some new boys runnin' the place before I'd do that."

o   o   o   o   o

Chapter Thirty-Four

I'D MADE UP MY MIND about not going back to Miami and I stuck by it. I kept after those Miami bosses the rest of the winter and they finally gave me my release.

I was a free man. I could do what I wanted to, just like I'd almost always done.

I started looking around for a job just as soon as they let me go.

Some folks in Kansas City came up with big talk about putting me in a restaurant or a night club or something like that and I started thinking maybe I'd get out of baseball. That way I could settle down with my family and I wouldn't have to worry about how long I could keep pitching.

But that big talk turned out to be nothing but talk.

I never saw any restaurant or anything else.

Right then I knew whatever I got going I'd have to start myself.

And a man my age don't usually think of starting something he don't know anything about. He does what he knows best.

Pitching was what I knew.

When I started getting some offers to pitch in 1959 and that old baseball bug started to bite again, I knew for sure I couldn't give up baseball yet, even if somebody offered me a whole bunch of restaurants.

Baseball was going to have to give me up.

I didn't think that'd happen, not for a few more years

anyway. Ol' Satch just wasn't the kind of guy who wore out. I'd have to wear away.

And I made sure that wasn't going to happen too fast by taking care of old number one. I got my rest, I ate light, I kept busy, and I didn't agitate myself, so I could stay actified.

That way I knew I still was ready to play any time, even if I was going on fifty-three. It might be barnstorming, but it still was playing.

And I kept hoping that as long as I could keep throwing, there was always a chance I'd get back in the majors.

If I could make the majors just one last time, maybe that'd be enough to push me closer to the Hall of Fame.

I didn't know many that should have been closer than me.

I wasn't the only one thinking that way. David Condon of the Chicago *Tribune* wrote in his paper, "If voting for the Hall of Fame was started all over again, Satchel Paige would be No. 5 on our ballot—behind Babe Ruth, Ty Cobb, Rogers Hornsby and Stan Musial . . ."

Babe, Ty, and Rogers played a long time back. Stan was still playing. But Ol' Satch played when Babe and Ty and Rogers was playing. And I still was playing when Stan was.

One thing I knew. I'd been around too long to just up and quit.

I didn't.

After that movie I hooked up with a barnstorming club.

It seemed funny that after better than thirty years of professional pitching, I was back to barnstorming.

Only there was a difference. I wasn't a nigger kid in Mobile anymore, playing for a jug of lemonade or maybe fifty dollars a month and almost starving. Now I was a big name and I was getting big money.

Nobody seemed to care about Satch being an old man. He could still throw that bee ball for a couple or three innings and folks still wanted to see him throw. There were plenty of barnstorming jobs in 1959 and 1960 and 1961. And even those minor leagues still wanted some of me. Why, after I finished up barnstorming just before the end of the regular 1961 season the Portland, Oregon team in the Pacific Coast League offered me a job.

I took it.

That's just about the top minor league, but those boys weren't too tough for Ol' Satch. It was the other way around. I only got to pitch twenty-five innings before the season ended, but in those twenty-five innings I got me nineteen strikeouts. I had me a 2.88 earned-run average, too.

And the old arm still had more pitches in it. I could tell. So after I was finished up with Portland, I headed back to Kansas City to start job-hunting again. But the only job I was after was a pitching job.

Someday it'll end, maybe before I even figure it will. Then I'll have to look for something new. I won't be able to just retire when that happens. Me and that money parted so fast all along that I'll have to keep looking for more of it— enough to take care of my family.

But Ol' Satch ain't worried about finding something new.

There's bound to be people who'll want a man who's done what I've done, who's got that big name like Ol' Satch.

And until they want me, I'll just keep pitching—maybe forever.

Some folks say I already have.

o   o   o   o   o

Afterword

by David Lipman

LeRoy (Satchel) Paige did not pitch forever.

He died Tuesday, June 8, 1982—just three days after the city of Kansas City named a youth baseball park after him. He was a month short of his seventy-sixth birthday.

He had, however, attained an immortality of another sort by then. Eleven years before his death he had become only the third African-American player and the first black pitcher to be voted into baseball's Hall of Fame in Cooperstown, New York.

But the road to Cooperstown was as full of twists and turns as his extraordinary career had been. Hall of Fame rules decreed that a baseball player must have ten years in the major leagues to qualify for inclusion and, of course, Satchel did not have that many.

He did have a legendary career that had spanned the greatest days in the old Negro leagues and had not ended until he pitched three amazing innings for the Kansas City Athletics in 1965, when he was an unbelievable fifty-nine years old. Charles O. Finley, the eccentric millionaire who owned the Kansas City team, had called Satchel up for what became his final hurrah in the major leagues.

More than a decade had passed since Satchel had made his last major league appearance. That was September 25, 1965, when the ageless wonder placed his size 14 shoe on the rubber of the pitching mound in Kansas City. His opponents: the slugging Boston Red Sox, led by Carl Yastrzemski and Tony Conigliaro. Satchel had been a major leaguer before most of those Red Sox were big enough to swing a bat.

The United Press International report on the game was brief and to the point: "Ageless LeRoy (Satchel) Paige pitched scoreless baseball for three innings for Kansas City, but the Boston Red Sox used late-inning home runs by Lee Thomas and Tony Conigliaro to defeat the Athletics tonight, 5–2." Satchel gave up just one hit in pitching the first three innings. Carl Yastrzemski got the only hit off Satchel. He doubled off a 3–0 pitch, proving that he had learned his ancient baseball history well: Whoever heard of Satchel walking a batter?

Finley indicated after the game that he was considering putting Satchel on the A's coaching list so that the pitcher could take another step toward qualifying for a major league pension under the five-year minimum rule. Satchel confided that he would have liked to join the Athletics as a coach, but he could not violate his contract with Abe Saperstein and the Harlem Globetrotters.

When Satchel, who had been released as a major leaguer after the 1953 season, was let go as a minor league pitcher in 1961, Saperstein stepped forward to rescue financially the near-penniless hurler. Satchel not only was under contract to Saperstein but also felt deeply obligated to remain with the man who had rescued him from near oblivion.

So Satchel resumed his nomadic ways, making personal appearances, as well as barnstorming. And he still pulled the fans. He had come full circle, it seemed. From early June until late August the old man still would climb up to the top of the mound every day to outsmart the batters who had been his friendly enemies for more than half a lifetime.

"They wouldn't let me sit," he said half-complainingly, half-pleased after one such game. "They've got to have me pitch. I've got this team during the summer at Spy Hill resort in Saskatchewan and we play a lot of Canadian teams. But they don't want to play my team unless I pitch. They don't stop and think that here's a man maybe fifty-five, maybe sixty years old. Maybe they've got fathers who're fifty years old and can't bend over and tie their shoe laces, but they don't think that maybe Ol' Satch is that old, that it's hard on him." With a pause, he quickly added, "It's not the arm; it's the wind."

Short of wind or not, Satchel had spent much of a lifetime dazzling fans of the barnstormers, the semiprofessional players who performed more for love than money.

His barnstorming contributions had not officially gone unnoted. In 1964, he had been named as the outstanding player in the history of the National Baseball Congress, the country's premier semiprofessional baseball organization. He beat out 15,359 other players who had participated for more than three decades in the semipro tournament held by the NBG in Wichita, Kansas.

In 1968, however, he had been unable to resume barnstorming as the baseball season got underway. He had been ill, possibly with emphysema and, it was whispered, the onset of heart trouble. He stayed at home in Kansas City. During recuperation complications of the spirit had set in.

At that time a white political broker in Kansas City, Louis Wagner, urged Satchel to run in the August Missouri primary against the incumbent state representative, Leon M. Jordan. Jordan's political accomplishments, in what until 1954 had been a segregated state, made him as much a black folk hero as was Satchel. Wagner was bent on breaking Jordan's tight political hold in the eleventh district, and he apparently believed Satchel had a chance of doing it. It did not take long for Satchel to realize he had made a mistake. He remained in the race, but he acknowledged to one reporter, "Politics—I got as much business here as a mule in a garage." He did not win.

But at this low time, the major leagues beckoned Satchel once again. On Aug. 12, 1968, William C. Bartholomay, president of the Atlanta Braves of the National League, signed Satchel to a contract as an adviser and possible part-time pitcher.

Bartholomay was considered a cold fish for his baseball machinations, but he gave the lie to that description with his actions. He indicated that Satchel would be on the active roster through the remainder of the 1968 season and would be retained in one capacity or another through 1969 so that he could log the 158 additional days on a major league roster that he needed to qualify for baseball's minimum pension.

Satchel was his usual blunt self: "I don't know if I can pitch now. I'll have to go out and try to unfold first." He was not called upon to pitch or even do much coaching. Bartholomay was merely repaying Satchel for what major league baseball had done to him and for what baseball owed him. Most of those connected with the game accepted the situation with approval. As the *Memphis Commercial Appeal* put it, "Thus it is that Satch, the first Negro pitcher in the American League, will receive a reward he has richly earned."

But Satchel was not content with that. He grumbled about not having a chance to play. Finally, he was allowed to pitch two exhibition innings before the last game of the season. It was a hot Sunday afternoon in September, Marshall Frady, who wrote for *True Magazine,* recalled: "Then, working with his casual self-absorbed and deliberate unhaste, Paige . . . systematically snuffed out a lineup of Atlanta and Los Angeles batsmen." In his two innings, Satchel, now a mature sixty-two, put down Junior Gilliam, Wayne Causey, Clete Boyer, Gil Garrido, Don Drysdale, and Hank Aaron. Even in his sixties, with the ailments of age beginning to dog his footsteps, Satchel could still put the ball over the plate.

As the 1969 season drew to an end, Satchel was given his unconditional release. But his time on the stage of major league baseball was not over yet. Inside and outside of organized baseball, more and more voices were being heard calling for the great heroes of the Negro leagues to be honored by election to baseball's Hall of Fame in Cooperstown, New York.

There was James (Cool Papa) Bell, the slick, fleet center fielder . . . George (Mule) Suttles, the big first baseman who used to pummel the car barn behind the short left field fence at the black ball park in St. Louis . . . Josh Gibson, the black Babe Ruth. And, of course, there was LeRoy (Satchel) Paige.

No one ever will know how many of those men and others might have made the majors if professional baseball had not drawn an invisible color line from 1898 to 1946. That cruel mistake could not be reversed now, but one thing could be done: those great African-American stars could be made eligible for the Hall of Fame.

The outcry grew so loud that, finally, in 1971, the Hall of Fame, under heavy pressure from major league baseball, announced that players who had starred in the old Negro leagues would be eligible for special inclusion at Cooperstown. But just one player would be selected each year. A special ten-man committee was appointed to make the first of the annual selections, based on exceptional achievements on the diamond and overall contributions to baseball.

Satchel Paige was the unanimous choice.

On Feb. 9, 1971, the office of the commissioner of major league baseball issued the following formal statement: "Bowie Kuhn, with the cooperation of Paul S. Kerr, president of the National Baseball Hall of Fame and Museum, is pleased to announce that LeRoy (Satchel) Paige, ageless patriarch of the pitching mound, was selected Tuesday by a special committee to be honored in the National Baseball Museum." Kuhn added that a bronze plaque listing Satchel's achievements would be hung in the Hall of Fame as part of a new exhibit commemorating the contributions of the Negro leagues to baseball. The exhibits, however, would be housed in a special section and not intermingled with the major league honorees picked by members of the Baseball Writers Association of America.

Bowie Kuhn delivered his formal statement announcing Satchel's selection at a press conference at Toots Shor's restaurant in New York City. The day, which should have been the first of many days of bittersweet celebration, turned "mean and sour," wrote famed columnist Jimmy Cannon. "Baseball was apologizing to Satchel Paige for what it had done to him, but the bickering questions didn't make the press conference in Toots Shor's seem that way," he continued. "They were valid but seemed degrading when uttered in Paige's presence. "No one could answer truly if Paige was still segregated in the Hall of Fame as he was when he played in the Negro leagues. It seemed wrong to tell a man he is involved in another hype when he believes he is being honored as a special guy."

"Did Satchel mind being housed in the Hall of Fame's instant black ghetto?" he was asked. "I don't feel segregated," he replied.

But, as the *New York Times* columnist Robert Lipsyte recalled, the questions had continued: How did he feel about those years of exclusion, didn't he think baseball could do better now, did he think real progress had been made? Lipsyte wrote:

Paige, for a little while, seemed confused. His sunny day was turning chilly. Bowie Kuhn and others stepped in to deflect the talk, and those who were asking questions relented as the lips of Paige and his wife, who was wearing a corsage, tightened.

Almost 65, very dark, very tall, stick-thin, Paige that day held an easy dignity and brightened again as the discussion turned to his next birthday, the three big league innings he pitched six years ago at 59, his so-called philosophies: "Don't look back. Something might be gaining on you." White men in the room that day laughed much harder than they had to and looked at each other and slapped their knees.

But the black men there were not so impressed by the event.

Satchel Paige, after all, was the Negro leagues' greatest gate attraction. He was able to make his living playing baseball for more than 40 years and he made more than $40,000 a year for a number of years in his peak.

The so-called "immortalization" of Satchel Paige was an ideal whose time had passed . . . The special niche at Cooperstown satisfied no one.

But Satchel, when asked about his dismal wait for his big league chance and for his selection to the Hall of Fame, shrugged off bitterness, if it was there, and said simply, "I had my nose to the window a long time."

As Cannon recalled it, "The great pitcher played it for laughs as the television lamps turned their glare on him . . . He has style and he didn't get heavy when the baseball journalists did. He understands how to keep a good day going because he has been cheated out of a lot of them. He stood there as the journalists defaced what had happened to him with their crabbed questions. Some made it appear that he shouldn't have been there. But he is the one who was hurt, and most of the committee that selected him is black and played with him or against him in the same leagues."

"Is he in the Hall of Fame?" repeated Bowie Kuhn, sitting alongside Satchel. "Technically, no. Realistically, yes."

Satchel, somehow, put any destructive bitterness aside. "I was satisfied with my world out there," he said.

However, the "separate-but-equal" plan for the Hall did not stand. Not long after the press conference, Commissioner Kuhn, who had never favored the divided Hall, and Paul Kirk, the museum's president, announced that Satchel and all future inductees from the Negro leagues would be given full memberships in the main Hall of Fame. Said a joyous Satchel Paige: "I was just going along with the program and I didn't have no kick or no say when they put me in that separate wing. But getting into the real Hall of Fame is the greatest thing that ever happened to me in baseball."

Six years, minus about a month, after he had thrown his last pitch in a major league game, Satchel Paige was in green and gentle Cooperstown, remote in time and place. It was as if he had never been anyplace else. Before the ceremonies, the boys of baseball and Satchel were sitting around, spinning tales, and somebody said it certainly had taken Satchel a long time to get to this quaint hamlet nestled in the Catskill Mountains, where baseball's immortals held forth. Satchel, now surely about to become an immortal, agreed. He said he had been in some big towns and some small towns, but never any with the meaning of Cooperstown. Robert Lipsyte described it as the place "where the ghosts of Babe Ruth and Ty Cobb and Walter Johnson ride the winds in the mountains on cold winter nights," and surely Satchel Paige would join them, whistling his bee ball down the chilly valleys.

If Satchel was in awe, he was his usual loquacious self at the ceremonies. He was not the only giant of baseball there that day. Sharing the platform with him were former St. Louis Cardinal outfielder Chick Hafey, Boston Red Sox outfielder Harry Hooper, and New York Giants pitcher Rube Marquard. Missing were Dave Bancroft, former Philadelphia Phillies shortstop, and former New York Yankee and New York Mets baseball executive George Weiss, who were too ill to make the trip to Cooperstown. Two other honorees—Jake Beckley, a pre-1900 National League first baseman, and Joe Kelley, an outfielder for Baltimore in the 1890s, were being honored posthumously. They had been singled out by the Hall of Fame's Committee on Veterans.

It was Satchel Paige who captured the spotlight. He received the largest hand from the crowd when he was introduced by Commissioner Kuhn. The tall, gaunt, slightly stooped Satchel moved slowly, deliberately, toward the microphone with that patented gait that had brought uncountable crowds to their feet over almost a half-century. He wore horn-rimmed glasses and sported a neatly trimmed mustache. As he turned his worn, leathery face toward the crowd, a second spine-tingling, spontaneous round of applause swept over him.

"Thank you, Commissioner and my fans and baseball players from all around—as far as Honolulu, Mexico, and I don't know where the rest of 'em come from. I know they're my friends, I know that. I got some of the best names called to me since I've been here," he said, speaking to the several hundred onlookers seated in front of the Library Building. "And when I was pitching against half of them in there," he continued, nodding toward the building behind him, "I can remember when some of the men in there called me some ba-a-a-d names, when I used to pitch against them."

The crowd laughed in appreciation as Satchel recalled his success

against many of baseball's greatest sluggers of the 1920s, '30s, and
'40s—men who had faced Satchel in exhibition games and had freely
admitted his excellence.

"They found out I was really for real," he said. "We played up in
Canada and if I didn't pitch every day they didn't want the ball club. I
pitched 165 ball games in a row because if I didn't pitch they didn't want
the club in town. So I began to learn how to pitch by the hour, or by the
week, or whatever you may call it. And so I guess all that got me up here
to Cooperstown. And this fellow here today," Satchel continued with a
smile, as he referred to former Cleveland Indians owner Bill Veeck, the
man who had brought him into major league baseball. "They wanted to
run both of us out of town in 1948 when he got me to the Cleveland Indians. They said to him, you can have anyone but Satchel; he's too old to
vote. Well, Mr. Veeck, I got you off the hook today . . . I am the
proudest man on earth today, and my wife and sister and sister-in-law
and my son all feel the same way. It's a wonderful day and one man who
appreciates it is LeRoy Satchel Paige."

So he finally occupied his true place in professional baseball—after a
near lifetime of exclusion and separation. But his playing days, even his
barnstorming days, were now behind him. That left him with only his
major league pension to keep him going financially—and that was
barely sufficient.

Then a lifelong admirer of Satchel's, A. Ray Smith, who also was a
successful businessman and a minor league team owner, stepped in.
Smith employed Satchel as vice-president of "sales and promotion" for
Smith's minor league team, the Tulsa Oilers. Later, Smith moved his
Triple A minor league club to Springfield, Illinois, and then Louisville,
Kentucky. Satchel traveled with him each move. Wherever he was, his
base of operation was a red and white table, frequently tucked in between a beer stand and a popcorn machine in the stands of Smith's
American Association team. Young fans who were not even born when
Satchel finished pitching and oldsters who swore their fathers had told
them about Satchel when they were just kids flocked around him wherever he went. And the aging Satchel, growing more and more drained
by emphysema and a heart ailment, would smilingly oblige, scrawling
his name for each on one of his little white business cards. It never mat-
tered how many.

Honors continued to fall his way. Among them was election to the Missouri Sports Hall of Fame, which honored him in 1979 when he was seventy-three. Almost three years later, he received what he called an honor approaching that of his induction into the Hall of Fame: the designation of the LeRoy (Satchel) Paige Stadium, a baseball park for youths in Kansas City.

"Nobody on earth could feel as good as I do now," he said during the dedication ceremonies, which he attended in a wheelchair on Saturday, June 5, 1982.

Three days later, on June 8, LeRoy (Satchel) Paige was dead. At the age of seventy-five, Satchel suffered a fatal heart attack at his home, where he had been confined in poor health.

"One of Satch's golden rules was, 'Don't look back . . . something might be gaining on you,'" said A. Ray Smith. "Last Tuesday he looked back and something was gaining on him—God—and the Almighty took this great legend with him."

Upon learning of Satchel's death, Commissioner Kuhn said, "It's too bad major league fans never had a chance to see him in his prime, for he was one of the greatest pitchers of all time. Some fine athletes are forgotten when they're gone. Satch will never be."

"Do you think they'll remember me?" Satchel had asked at his induction into the Hall of Fame.

Maybe forever.

NOTE: Special thanks to my wife, Marilyn Vittert Lipman, for her critical work in organizing and editing this afterword. My thanks also to two wonderful colleagues at the *St. Louis Post-Dispatch*, Linda Sucich and Mary Welsh, for their assistance.